GETTING INTO MEDICAL SCHOOL

Ninth Edition

The Premedical Student's Guidebook

By Sanford J. Brown, M.D.

Director, Mendocino Foundation for Health Education
Family Practice and Preventive Medicine, Fort Bragg, California
Member, National Association of Advisors for the Health Professions
Premedical Adviser, College of the Redwoods, Fort Bragg, California

BARRON'S

All inquiries should be addressed to:
Barron's Educational Series, Inc.
250 Wireless Boulevard
Hauppauge, New York 11788
http://www.barronseduc.com

Library of Congress Catalog Card No. 00-107770

International Standard Book No. 0-7641-1344-5

PRINTED IN THE UNITED STATES OF AMERICA
9 8 7 6 5

Dedication

This book is dedicated to Sue, Gabe, Margot, Cee-Cee, Ginger, Bruiser, Lily, Amy, Sunny Boy, and Tommy T.

Acknowledgments

When an author is fortunate enough to have his book remain in print for twenty-six years through nine revisions, there are numerous people to thank. In the beginning, I received invaluable assistance from two of my professors at the Medical College of Wisconsin: Dr. Sidney Shindell and Dr. Walter Zeit. Dr. Shindell, now retired, allowed me to begin work on the book as my senior project and gave freely of his time, encouragement, and counsel. Dr. Zeit, now deceased, shared with me his knowledge of pre- and post-Flexnerian medicine.

Karen Levine provided the marvelous illustrations and updated them for this edition, and Dr. David Nash, who was a medical student at the time, rewrote much of an earlier edition.

For this edition, I have to thank Marilyn Hoffman, coordinator for pre-professional advising at the University of Utah, for her invaluable contribution of updating the textual data, and Carolyn Lex, a premedical student at the University of California at Davis, for her contribution to the section on summer programs.

A debt of gratitude to my editors at Barron's: Max Reed and Anna Damaskos, for assuming responsibility for updating the information on individual medical schools and giving me total freedom while working with me in the revising process.

Thanks to the American Association of Medical Colleges, the National Association of Advisors for the Health Professions, and The American Academy of Family Physicians for much of the hard data included in this edition.

Finally, a loving appreciation to my family for minimal grumbling for the times when I had to put them on the back burner in order to write. I hope it will be a long time before the tenth edition needs to be written.

Oh…and a thank-you to all of you people and organizations on the World Wide Web who put enough information out there so that I was able to do most of my research at home.

Contents

PREFACE   vii
INTRODUCTION   xi

1 Choosing a College, Choosing a Major   1

It's Not Where You Go to School or What You Study, 1 The
Myth of the Premedical Major, 3 Getting A's in the Sciences, 4
The Physician As a Scientist, 5 Abraham Flexner and His Flexner
Report, 6 Emphasis on the Sciences, 7 What Kind of Doctor Do
You Want to Become? 8 Avoid the Extra Science Courses, 10

2 The Premed Syndrome   13

The Premedical Mind, 13 The Premedical Society and the
Premedical Adviser, 14 Not Always an Expert, 15 Does Your
Adviser Attend the Meetings? 16 Get Acquainted...See What
They Write About You, 18 The Premedical Student, 20 The
Premedical Syndrome, 22 A Maniac in Pursuit of Medicine, 23
Failure Is Always a Possibility, 25

3 The Medical College Admission Test (MCAT)   27

The Most Important Criterion, 27 MCAT—a Means for
Comparison, 28 The Test, 30 How Is It Scored? 31 Preparing
for the MCAT, 31 Preparatory Courses, 33

4 Applying to a Medical School—When, Where, and How   37

How Many Applications? 37 Early Decision, 39 Combined
MD/PhD Programs, 40 Cost of Applying, 41 Meeting the
Costs, 42 Minority Students, 46 From Quotas to Affirmative
Action, 48 Staying In Can Be Harder Than Getting In, 53
Women, 56 Special Interest Groups, 57 Making Application—
the AMCAS, 58 Writing the Personal Statement, 59 What Makes
You Different? 61 Recommendations, 63 The Interview, 67

5 How Medical School Admissions Committees Evaluate Applicants 73

Can the Applicant Make It? 73 Determining the Motivation, 75

6 Rejection and Your Alternatives 79

Rejection and Reapplication, 79 Consider Reapplying, 81 Attending a Foreign Medical School, 88

7 Amazing Success Stories 95

8 The Future of Medicine? 117

Appendixes

Appendix I: Summer Programs for the Premed   125
Appendix II: Directory of American Medical
                   Schools   137
Appendix III: Survival Bibliography   265

Index to U.S. Medical Schools 275

Preface

It's hard for me to believe that *Getting into Medical School* was first published twenty-six years ago. When I wrote it, as a senior medical student in 1972–73, I had the motivation of wanting to tell my story—that of an atypical premed who had somehow made it into medical school—to other unusual applicants and aspirants. I remember writing the original manuscript almost nonstop in three weeks—in longhand! (This was before the era of word processing.) It was purely anecdotal. During the next year I added meat to the bones in the form of statistics, quotations, and other relevant data. In 1974, the first edition of *GIMS* was published. Now, I'm delighted to be writing yet another preface—this time for the ninth edition. Remaining in print for all these years makes me hope that not a few discouraged premeds have taken heart from my writing, persevered, and succeeded in their quests. I know that many have.

Traditionally, I have used the preface to bring my readers up to date on my professional activities and my attitudes and thoughts about medicine, and have usually ended with a heartening statement about what makes a good physician. To some extent, I still like what I have said. To quote the first edition: "A professor of mine once said, 'What this country needs is fewer MDs and more physicians.' I believe what he meant was that we need more people to take care of the *whole* patient and not just his or her pathology. By that criterion, you don't have to be a great scientist to be a good physician. All you have to be is a good human being." And to quote the sixth: "Let each of you recognize the limits of health, the limits of your skill, and use creativity to find satisfaction in your healing art." Those sentiments still ring true for me; I find no need to change them.

What has changed, however, is the medical profession, and in some ways the change has been dramatic. In 1989, in the preface to the seventh edition, I had this to say: "In the past fifteen years, from when I first began to practice, we have seen a doctor shortage turn into, in some areas, a doctor glut. Malpractice premiums have risen precipitously and forced some practitioners either out of practice or into a different type of practice. There is much less physician autonomy as the solo practitioner is replaced by HMOs, PPOs, and IPAs, as well as forms of group practice. And, on the other side of the equation, the applicant pool to medical schools has been declining for the past seven years. This has a lot of medical school deans and premedical advisers worried, as they fear that the caliber of the entering medical student may be declining. I, for one, do not share this concern.

"Medicine has always attracted people with varied interests. Primarily, there is the desire to serve, to be useful, to make people better through our ministrations. But there is also the need for autonomy, for financial security, for continual busyness, and for mobility. For some people these needs are primary, and these are the people, I believe, who are now making alternative career choices, thereby reducing the applicant pool. What's left is still the stuff fine physicians are made of. Letters I've been receiving from discouraged premeds over the years convince me of it.

"Since *GIMS* was first published, I've received hundreds of letters from my readers. Several years ago, I chose the best of them for a new book, *You Can Get into Medical School: Letters from Premeds.* Some represent fresh inquiries; others are follow-ups from earlier correspondences in which the aspirant either did or did not matriculate into a medical school. The successes and failures, as well as the personal and intimate premedical concerns expressed by readers of *GIMS,* formed a natural sequel to this book. *You Can Get into Medical School* is available from the Mendocino Foundation for $9.95 postpaid.

"Since writing the preface for the sixth edition, my work focus has changed. Always giving lip service to preventive medicine, 1 was finally able to actualize my concept of it through a program called *HealthTrends.* In it, we computer track the changes in our patients' health over time and alert them when they become at risk for a disease. The idea is to suggest lifestyle changes to reverse abnormal trends, thus obviating a future need for medicine. The patient receives a full physical as well as multiple computer printouts on his or her health. All of this information is incorporated into a chart that is the patient's to keep and bring back yearly for updating. In time we hope to accumulate enough of a database on each patient to show him or her graphic depictions of changing health patterns. *HealthTrends* gives substance to the ritual of the yearly physical and has been personally satisfying to me as well. Patients become more than a series of episodic diagnoses; they are seen as total individuals, and a clear picture of how their lifestyles influence their health emerges.

"The computer will become, I predict, as important to the practice of medicine as the automobile and telephone. Not just an instrument for billing and sending timely reminders, the computer will revolutionize the way we practice. Artificial intelligence, databasing, and interactive video are already making inroads into physicians' consciousness. Premeds need to become computer literate. Fluency in Spanish won't hurt either. (Besides not learning how to play the piano, taking six years of high school and college French is the only other thing I rue.)

"Despite the vagaries of economics, there will always be patients and there will always be physicians and other health-care workers to care for them. And no matter how much medicine changes, it will always offer its practitioners challenge, reward, and a sense of purposefulness. I continue to encourage altruistic and inquisitive spirits to choose a medical career. It remains a great profession."

I look at these words, eleven years later, and marvel at my prescience while I remain somewhat embarrassed by my optimism. The corporatization of American medicine is now nearly complete. The MBAs are now riding herd over the MDs, and we live in a world of managed care and capitated lives. Physicians no longer work for themselves; indeed, it is virtually impossible to hang out a shingle in many places in America and earn a living. We work in large groups, are paid a salary, and our performance is monitored in myriad ways, with careful attention to the bottom line of costs and profits. Allegiances are now to stockholders, not to doctors or patients. Many of the motivating factors that stimulated bright young men and women to choose medicine in the past—autonomy, high pay commensurate with hard work, and specialty and living area choice—are no longer operant. And yet, astoundingly, there are more applicants to medical school than ever before. Since the tough years of the mid-to-late 1980s, when there were fewer than two applicants for every place in medical schools, there are now nearly three. These numbers are still rising, whereas first-year places in medical schools are declining. I remain confounded by these phenomena.

It has never been my intent to convince my readers to opt for medicine. That's a personal choice. Once committed, it has been my intent to provide you with the best possible advice. That is what this book is all about. It has been my custom to bring you up to date about my own medical practice and offer some predictions for the future. This year I am not so sanguine.

I continue to be a solo practitioner providing fee-for-service medicine in a rural area. But now I feel like a dinosaur rather than a maverick. I am a preferred provider for many insurers, which simply means that I have agreed to accept their fee schedules to retain my patients. I still consider myself self-employed, as I have to pay my own overhead, but have organizations willing to purchase my practice and render me an employee. It's tempting, but it's not why I went into medicine.

I have now been in practice for twenty-six years, time enough to see several generations of patients. *Continuity of care* is not just a phrase; it's real and it's rewarding. My patients consider me not only their doctor but their friend, and it's given me great pleasure to age along with them while being afforded the privilege of knowing them and their families so well. I fear for the doctor-patient relationship in the way medicine is now being practiced.

My wellness program, *HealthTrends,* has entered its thirteenth year and continues to delight. I have watched many of my patients make positive changes in their health because of the information they have been fed back, both in their charts and on screen, year after year. They have stopped smoking, started exercising, and lost weight. They have reduced their stressors. Many drive less, drink less, and consume less salt, cholesterol, and fat. Seeing graphic depictions of their changing health patterns has been a great motivator. As a result, I have fewer inpatients and more time to do the things that I enjoy, like dirt-bike riding, bicycling, playing racquetball, and making firewood. Preventive medicine is good for the doctor as well as for the patient.

I have stopped practicing emergency medicine, and am working a bit more in my office. I guess I'm slowing down. It's always been gratifying for me to have the variety of practice that rural medicine affords. I became a generalist because I was unwilling to waste any of my medical education; living in a small town has let me use most of it.

I again encourage comments and questions from my readers. I am now offering a comprehensive premedical advisory service. Inquiries may be made during workday hours via phone (707-964-3500), by letter (POB 1377, Mendocino, CA 95460), through e-mail (sbrown@mcn.org), or at my Web site (www.mcn.org/b/mfhe). I am primarily interested in you nontraditional, atypical, not-straight-arrow students, but will also consider advising 4.0 science majors with 15 MCAT scores who wind up rejected by medical schools. As the Ann Landers of the premedical world, I welcome all queries. Go ahead and drop me a line!

Introduction

Again this year, almost three times as many premed students will apply to medical school as will be accepted. Even though the number of places in U.S. medical schools has risen steadily from 8,298 in 1960–61 to 13,697 in 1972–73 to 16,686 in 1987–88 where it leveled off (in 1999 there were 16,221 new first-year entrants), there has been an increase in applicants of more than 500 percent for the same time period. This year it is anticipated that more than 38,000 students will apply for fewer than 17,000 places. In 1967–68, 52 percent of applicants were admitted; in 1981–82, 47 percent were admitted; in 1987–88, 59 percent were admitted. This year, fewer than 42 percent will be admitted. These figures show that there simply are not enough places in the medical schools for all who have completed the premedical curriculum and are eager to become MDs.

In the main, I'm not going to use this book to discuss the unfolding transformation of American medicine, although I do feel that I owe my readers a projection for the future. Premedical and medical education is a long tunnel, sometimes lasting over fifteen years, and I would be remiss in not offering some thoughts about what awaits you. I have added a final chapter with that in mind. Primarily, though, I am going to use this book to get you, the premedical student, *out* of the conventional and often erroneous ways of thinking about how to get into a medical school and *into* a more informed and advantageous position. After all, we haven't all had the same advantages, so this book will attempt to be an equalizer.

I am talking also to the premed dropout and the unsuccessful applicant: students from minority groups, borderline nonminority students, those with financial problems, women, students from colleges where there is no premedical adviser, and, generally, students who, for one reason or another, have been discouraged from continuing in the premed curriculum. This book is a survival kit, if you like, for the committed. It is a step-by-step guide that anyone who wants to become a physician can put to use anywhere along the course of his or her premedical education. It will cover, from high school onward, the gamut of decision-making, traumatic events that every premed must face, ranging from choosing a college and a major to accepting a medical school, and to what to do—short of suicide—if you are rejected by them all. Included are chapters on what it means to be a premed, the Medical College Admission Test, how to apply to medical schools, the way in which actual medical school admissions committees evaluate applicants, summer programs and preceptorships for premeds, amazing success stories, acceptance or rejection and your alternatives, and the future of medicine.

Since medical schools cannot absorb even 50 percent of qualified applicants, it may seem paradoxical to take an interest in the students who either drop out of premed or are unsuccessful applicants. My feeling, simply, is that surviving the rigors of the premedical curriculum is not the most important prerequisite for becoming a good physician. Although a medical school's first concern in admitting applicants has traditionally been "Will they get through?" and not "What kind of physicians will they make?" I prefer to reverse this order of importance. I do not believe, for instance, that organic chemistry should be the most highly regarded academic experience of the premed. The reason that it is so regarded is that memorizing an organic chemistry textbook may simulate the most rigorous tasks of first- and second-year medical school, and medical school admissions committees feel that anyone who can handle it satisfactorily can pass basic medical sciences. Memorization may well be the last refuge of the unimaginative mind; nevertheless, the person with a capacity to absorb a lot of data will be favored by admissions committees over an individual who thinks more abstractly.

Encouragingly, the times have brought change. More and more applicants to medical schools are showing a variety of backgrounds that may include not only a nonscience major but an interim period in their education as well. Some have worked; others have traveled. Many are older applicants. Once having taken the required courses, nearly anyone who is otherwise qualified can go to medical school today.

There is room in medicine for all types of interests. Contrary to popular myth, every doctor is not a scientist who sees patients one minute and makes great scientific discoveries the next. Although most physicians do direct patient care, not every doctor sees patients. Some work for the Public Health Service tracking down sources of contagious disease; others are employed by state and local health departments to run immunization and multiphasic screening programs. Many doctors prefer teaching and academic medicine to private practice, and a few find satisfaction in editing medical journals and in medical illustration. There are currently fifty-odd specialties and subspecialties in the area of medicine, and this number will certainly increase. In the future, more doctors will be involved in planning health care delivery systems on city, state, and federal levels. More young physicians will realize that preventing disease is easier than curing it and will come to consider health education, epidemiology, and community medicine as specialty fields. And with concern for our ecology increasing exponentially with time, environmental and industrial medicine and nutrition can be expected to attract more and more attention. Many doctors now combine their MDs with degrees in law and business.

Memorization may be the last refuge of the unimaginative mind.

Medicine today can find a place for artists, photographers, educators, and historians. It needs biomedical engineers and computer programmers, administrators and basic research scientists. Medicine is the meeting ground of the arts and sciences. Its potential is limitless. It welcomes all kinds of people because diversity works against stagnation and aids growth. I mean to encourage all students to consider medicine as a career, not just the biologist, chemist, and physicist but also the psychologist, sociologist, and economist, the anthropologist, journalist, and philosopher—and, of course, the poet.

CHAPTER 1

Choosing a College, Choosing a Major

Many people know early that they want to be physicians. Some have never wanted to be anything else. Others make their career choices in high school and in college. And there are the few who, like myself, decide on medicine after completing their college education. A sufficiently large number of students settle on medicine in high school to justify treating as the first order of business the choice of a college.

It's Not Where You Go to School or What You Study

It may come as news to some that the undergraduate institution attended carries little weight with many medical schools. You can be accepted into medical school from virtually any accredited college or university, and your own academic credentials are vastly more important than the reputation of your school. It *is* true, however, that some undergraduate institutions are more successful than others at placing their graduates in medical schools. The student working the percentages in applying to college should ask to know the relative rather than the absolute number of graduates admitted to medical school from that institution during the preceding five years.

I suggest that it is foolish to see college merely as a stepping-stone to medical school. College can be a unique experience and a great deal more fun than graduate education. So choose your college for reasons other than

Many people know early that they want to be physicians.

its premedical program, which you can get anywhere. Attend a small school if you would prefer or a large school if you want anonymity or an active campus life. Accept a school with an outstanding English or theater arts and drama department. Go to a region of the country where you have never been before. Take your junior year abroad. Experiment.

> Remember that once you become a doctor, your patients won't care where you went to college.

People won't even care where you attended medical school or ask about the grades you earned or if you graduated with honors. They will only be concerned that you understand them and their medical problems. So if you use your college years to broaden your base of experience, in the long run you'll be doing your patients a service.

The Myth of the Premedical Major

Wherever you go there are, of course, the exigencies of the premedical program, and I do mean to talk about them. First, however, let us explode once and for all the myth of the premedical major. You cannot go to college and major in premed. Following a premed curriculum means nothing more than taking the basic science courses required by most medical schools. Minimum requirements are usually one year of general biology, one year of physics, one year each of inorganic and organic chemistry—all with lab. Other required subjects vary with the medical school and may include English, mathematics, calculus, and other more specialized science courses.

Medical schools always look at an applicant's science and nonscience cumulative grade point average, with emphasis on the science GPA (into which math grades are averaged). This has numerous implications, for if you are a nonscience major, each science course you take will have a considerable effect on your science average, whereas those majoring in science can do poorly in one course without any devastating effect. On the other hand, it is true that science is a tougher major than either the humanities or social sciences, and science majors applying to medical schools have lower overall cumulative averages than their nonscience major counterparts. What follows from all of this?

> Majoring in a nonscience will probably raise
> your overall GPA and put you in a more
> advantageous position when seeking
> admission to a medical college.

Medical school admission committees today welcome the applicant who did not major in science. However, they must be sufficiently impressed with your premedical course grades to admit you.

Getting A's in the Sciences

How, then, can you do well in the required sciences? In the first place, do not make the mistake that many premeds make. I hear students say that a grade of C from school X is the equivalent of a B from school Y or of an A from school Z. This is pure myth. An A goes down as an A and a B as a B. There are no hard conversion factors in evaluating applicants' grades from different schools although, informally, some schools are viewed more selectively than others. So if a required premed course is ridiculously hard, or the competition is especially rough, and science is not your strong suit, then do yourself a favor and take the course somewhere else. This is extremely important, because many medical schools will not even look at your application unless you have a B+ (3.3–3.5) average or better in science, as well as overall.

The extremes to which some universities may go to "keep students competitive" is astounding. My own undergraduate school is a case in point. It had early achieved a reputation as a science school, although it had excellent liberal arts departments. Naturally, it attracted many science students—far more, in fact, than it had the faculty or facilities to train. Most of the influx wanted to concentrate in biology, although physics and chemistry also received more people than they could comfortably handle. The situation was somewhat tolerable at the lower course levels but would have become cataclysmic if all students had been permitted to advance to their junior and senior years with normal attrition rates. To ease matters, all students intending to major in biology and physics as well as in engineering were routed first through freshman inorganic chemistry along with all the budding chemists. "Into the valley of death rode the six hundred," including the premeds. I was so intimidated by my school's science department that I waited for the

Department of Earth and Space Sciences to open its doors before I dared fulfill my university's science requirements. When I finally did take premed inorganic chemistry, it was in night school at a local community college.

I do not mean to suggest that your professors are out to fail you, but some departments do believe in making things purposely difficult, for reasons of either pride or practicality. My advice is simply not to bother with them. Take that inorganic or organic chemistry course in summer school or community college. Many of my premedical adviser colleagues feel strongly that premedical requirements should not be taken at a two-year school. I believe that it is appropriate for community college students to be premeds and that biology and inorganic chemistry may be taken there. Naturally, medical schools will want to make sure that students who get A's in community colleges also get A's at four-year schools when completing their premedical courses. I can also emphatically state that a grade of D from Harvard in inorganic chemistry will keep you out of medical school, whereas an A from a community college will not.

The Physician As a Scientist

The emphasis that has been placed on the basic sciences in recent years has given many people the erroneous impression that all doctors are scientists. This is simply untrue, but the evolution of the idea is an interesting bit of medical history. At this point, it might be helpful to examine it and see how the idea of physician as scientist has evolved and influenced medical school admission policies during recent years.

The first medical schools in this country were those associated with established universities such as Harvard, the University of Pennsylvania, and the University of Maryland. These schools were, for their day, reasonably substantial medical schools with high academic standards.

During the years of the great immigration to this country, many of the newcomers already had a European medical degree, whereas others wished to study medicine in the European tradition after they arrived. In Europe, a physician who had attained any degree of eminence was called *professor*. A European who became sick did not go to a practitioner, specialist, or consultant but to a professor at some medical center. When an immigrant became sick, he or she, too, wanted to go to a professor. It was part of the European heritage. However, in most states there were no medical schools and consequently no professors.

It wasn't long before groups of physicians began to band together and start medical schools of their own. Probably one of the motives behind this was that these doctors could then hold professorships in their own medical schools, thereby acquiring the title of professor. This type of school, known as the proprietary medical school, was organized for prestige and profit and flourished until 1906, when there were about 160 medical schools in the country. With the exception of those affiliated with the older universities, all the rest were proprietary schools.

In most cases, the proprietary schools had low academic standards and sometimes admitted students without a high school education. Virtually anyone was admitted who could pay the tuition, and when enrollment dropped, the professors went out to solicit students. There were no state agencies to regulate the practice of medicine. Persons attending proprietary schools, as well as those attending some major universities, spent two years after high school studying medicine and two summers of preceptorship with local practitioners. With this meager background students went out to practice. Licensure requirement was that the student merely have graduated from any of the medical schools then existent.

Abraham Flexner and His Flexner Report

By the turn of the century, the Carnegie Foundation for the Advancement of Teaching, which had been engaged in activities to improve the quality of teaching in general, employed Abraham Flexner, who was not a physician, to make a survey of medical education in the United States. In 1909, Flexner personally visited every medical school in the country and evaluated the schools on the basis of their requirements for admission, the caliber of their faculty, and the quality of their laboratories and physical facilities. When he finished, he formulated the now famous *Flexner Report,* which was published by the Carnegie Foundation in 1910.

In this report, medical schools were classified as A, B, or C type schools. Many of the medical schools then operating received a C rating. All of those rated C were proprietary type schools. Following the *Flexner Report,* the states established boards of medical examiners and passed medical practice acts. These boards instituted examinations for medical licensure and said, in effect, that a person was not eligible to take the exam unless that person had graduated from a Class A school. This immediately put the

Class B and Class C schools out of business, so that by 1920 there were only 72 medical schools left in the United States.

It was recommended in the *Flexner Report* that medical schools, in order to qualify for Class A rating, become affiliated with universities that could provide the student with a reasonable academic background and good laboratory facilities. Requirements for admission to medical school quickly included a year of liberal arts education after high school. As time went on it was recognized that, as knowledge in all fields increased, more preparation was necessary.

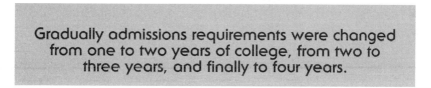

Gradually admissions requirements were changed from one to two years of college, from two to three years, and finally to four years.

Today almost all medical schools require that applicants have a bachelor's degree.

Emphasis on the Sciences

Another change occurred. As emphasis for admission to medical school was placed more and more heavily on the scientific disciplines, premedical programs in the liberal arts colleges came to center around comparative vertebrate anatomy, general biology, physics, and chemistry. By the 1930s, the broad liberal arts education fostered by the old premedical programs was subdued almost totally by scientific training. This attitude lasted until after World War II. Then, in the late 1940s and early 1950s, medical schools began to encourage applicants to take a fourth year and use it to study the humanities. For a short while, students began choosing non-science majors. Few who wanted to go to medical school intended careers in full-time scientific research or academic medicine.

In the late 1950s, the wheel again came full circle. There was an explosion in scientific and technical information beginning with Russia's *Sputnik* in 1957. Suddenly vast amounts of money became available for research. Medical schools, supported by government grants, hired more faculty for full-time research positions. Aided by government money, medical schools expanded their laboratories in the basic sciences. Less attention was paid to community medical care and medical schools began to favor students who had majored in biology or chemistry, with preference given to those who had taken higher-level courses. Premeds responded by studying the more advanced and more difficult sciences, resulting in an upgrading of the preparation of the matriculating medical student. The model for this generation of students became the academic physician who spent 70 percent of his or her time in research and 30 percent in patient care.

The situation remained unchanged until the mid-1960s, when a large number of students in the physical sciences began to apply to medical school with the intent of becoming biomedical engineers. It was the era of the pacemaker and other spectacular technical solutions to medical problems. Then, in 1968, the picture changed again. The majority of young people had turned against the Vietnam War, the poor were becoming increasingly visible, and the inequities in the American way of life stood out glaringly. Premedical students responded by becoming family physicians rather than specialists. Many of the graduates of the 1970s and 1980s were attracted to the subspecialties that have burgeoned from the technological advances of the last two decades—angiography and angioplasty, CT scanning, nuclear MRI, organ transplantation, and the medical laser, as well as computer applications to the medical sciences. Today's graduates are more responsive to market demands and are choosing primary care specialties.

What Kind of Doctor Do You Want to Become?

With myriad alternatives in a medical career, the issue of what to major in is more a question of what type of physician you wish eventually to become and what you might want to do should you *not* get into medical school. If you want a life of medical research, by all means enter medical school with a strong background in the basic sciences. If your interests in medicine are more social, however, then ten years hence an undergraduate major in sociology or economics will probably be more advantageous to you than one in biology or chemistry. And if, like most entering college students, you are undecided, then major in whatever turns you on.

Choose a major according to your strengths, interests, and alternate career objectives. Do you think you'd like a major in music or drama? Does the study of anthropology intrigue you? Would you mind four years of reading great literature or sculpting, drawing, or painting? Do these things! As long as you take the required premedical courses, no college major will handicap you or make you less prepared to perform adequately in medical school. And where except in college will you ever again have the chance to study Chaucer, Egyptian hieroglyphics, or pre-Socratic philosophy? College is your opportunity to develop your full potential; use it for just that. Medical school will give you all the science you will ever need to be a competent physician, I assure you. You should enjoy and have ability in science, but that doesn't mean you have to major in it. It is true that nonscience majors usually find the first two years of med school, which is mostly basic science, to be more overwhelming than it is for science majors. However, once into the clinical experiences, which require more problem-solving and communication skills, everyone seems to be on equal footing.

Here's a letter I received several years ago from a premed who took my advice:

> Dear Dr. Brown,
> Since I last wrote to you I've had a diverse and interesting undergraduate experience. Due to various requirements, being an English major and a premed at Harvard has been very challenging because, unlike biology majors whose premed courses count toward their major, I've had few electives. However, I do not at all regret pursuing a liberal arts education before going to medical school. I had the chance to go straight into a six-year medical program but felt my life would be poorer for passing up a four-year undergraduate education and I now know the decision to be an English major was a very good one.
> I thank you for not being pragmatic and advising premeds to major in the sciences but instead to try to have the best and most fulfilling undergraduate experience possible. Many of my friends have regretted majoring in the sciences. I don't see how undergraduates can be happy with constantly sacrificing the present for some vague future situation. Medical school should be a priority but not the only one. Undergraduates should keep the big picture in clear view and study what they find truly interesting. They'll probably end up with a more successful college career, grade-wise, to boot!
>
> Ed Spillane

According to AAMC's 2000–01 *Medical School Admissions Requirements,* for the 1998–99 entering class, students who majored in one of the physical sciences had the highest overall acceptance rate to medical school. However, nonscience majors—in fields such as economics and philosophy—had an acceptance rate higher than those who majored in the biological sciences (45.5 vs. 39.9 percent). Anthropology majors had a 53.5 percent acceptance rate; foreign language majors, a 52.7 percent rate; and English majors, a 50.5 percent rate! Interestingly, those who majored in other health professions, such as pharmacy or nursing had the lowest acceptance rate—26.9 percent. Thus, it is obvious that a non-science major is not a handicap but more likely an asset when applying to medical schools.

In summary, major in whatever you would like and do well in the pre-medical science courses. Use your college years for personal growth and don't burden yourself with a major that's not intellectually satisfying. Not only will college become a more pleasurable experience but you're bound to do well in courses that you enjoy and boost your GPA besides!

Avoid the Extra Science Courses

I often hear undergraduates talk about taking science courses that will "help" them in medical school, by which I suppose they mean courses in biochemistry, physiology, comparative anatomy, and the like. It is true that those courses may make the first year of medical school somewhat easier. However, the degree of simplicity of the course must also be seen as directly proportional to the amount of boredom it generates. Coming to med school with an English major, I found my first year truly difficult but quite fascinating, because everything I learned was new to me.

> Unless you have a genuine interest in scientific material, you are not necessarily doing yourself a favor by taking extra science courses.

This is only logical. In the first place, you always do one thing at the expense of another. That course in statistics may mean passing up the one in creative writing offered by the novelist in residence at your university. Second, the way a course is taught at one school may be totally unrelated to the way it is handled at another. For example, the freshman biochemistry course at my medical school was so atypical that former biochemistry majors had difficulty passing it. Third, medical schools may not care how many science courses you have taken as long as you meet their requirements and they are convinced you can do medical school work. In addition, some medical schools may not accept credit earned in these courses.

Also keep in mind those skills that will be essential once you become a physician—communications, logic, business, computers, language, and knowing how to work in a multicultural society—when you are searching for electives to take during your junior and senior years.

A survey that appeared in the Winter 1996 issue of *The Advisor* polled fourth-year medical students at nine medical schools and found that 42 percent cited philosophy and 18 percent bioethics as good to exceptional courses for premedical preparation. Science courses came in third with 14 percent. Students were unanimous in advising premeds to get a broad background beyond science courses, take courses for pleasure, and learn how to learn and to solve problems.

What undergraduates fail to understand about medical school is that with diligence and perseverance anyone with average intelligence can pass through it successfully.

> **The hardest obstacle to overcome in becoming a physician is getting admitted to a medical school.**

About 60 percent of those applicants considered fully qualified are rejected, whereas fewer than 5 percent of any entering class fails to graduate, and most of these failures are for nonacademic reasons. A friend of mine is fond of asking, "What do they call the person who graduates last in his medical school class?" The answer, of course, is "doctor."

I believe that performance in premedical courses, on the Medical College Admissions Test, or even during the first two years of medical school is no indication of the kind of physician you will become. Your success as a practitioner is more a function of your personality, character, and native intelligence than of your grades. Medicine has always been more of an art than a science. Science is but one of the tools the doctor uses to deliver total care to the patient. It is not the only tool.

Science is but one of the tools the doctor uses to
deliver total care to the patient.

CHAPTER 2

The Premed Syndrome

Once you have decided to opt for medicine, you become a premed. It's that simple. It has nothing to do with joining a premedical club or acquiring a premedical adviser. Nor is it required that you be attending a college or university. It all has to do with consciousness.

The Premedical Mind

Being premed is a state of mind. Some people know when they're five years old, with their first chemistry set or doctor's bag. A friend of mine became a definite premed at age twelve, when his father gave him a copy of *Gray's Anatomy*—unabridged. When I was in college, the last thing I thought to become was a doctor, so I wasn't a premed until after I graduated.

According to AAMC's *2000–01 Medical School Admissions Requirements*, 49 percent of the applicants for the 1998 entering class were less than 24 years old. These students also had the highest acceptance rate—72 percent for applicants age 20 and under and 52 percent for applicants ages 21–23. Although there is a generally declining acceptance rate for applicants over age 24, it is notable that in 1998 the mean age for all accepted applicants was 25 and that applicants 38 years old and over had an acceptance rate of 20 percent. For those ages 35–37, the acceptance rate was 25 percent. Thus, even among applicants in their late thirties, one out of four to one out of five get in. Because only one out of three get in overall, these statistics do not augur badly for the older applicant.

Most medical schools require completion of at least three years of college, and prefer four, before they will admit you. Many require or prefer that a bachelor's degree be completed prior to entrance. There are special six-year programs for high school seniors leading to the combined BA or BS and MD degrees. For those who wish to pursue them, the American Association of Medical Colleges' *AAMC Admissions Requirements* book offers an entire chapter of information on medical schools offering a combined college/MD program. These are highly competitive. If you're not in any hurry to become a doctor, I would advise spending four years in college and using your senior year for electives to take something other than premedical science courses. Many doctors who spent only three years in college often mourn the loss of that fourth year.

The Premedical Society and the Premedical Adviser

Once you are a matriculated college student, your school may offer facilities and services to assist you. Notably, there will be a premedical club and a premedical adviser. Regarding the former, I can offer the words of Marx (Groucho, not Karl), who said that he would not belong to any club that would accept him as a member. Apart from their annual pilgrimage to medical schools, the value of such clubs is debatable. Joining the club may even make you uneasy, because you will be seeing the same people you regularly compete with in your premedical courses.

> Medical schools couldn't care less if you were a member of the premedical society.

It makes no sense for you to join because you think it will look impressive on your record. Also, it is important to remember that these societies are clubs sponsored by the students and are not considered a service of the university. Events they sponsor are open to all premeds and may include speakers on health-care reform, MCAT prep, different areas of medical practice, and even an admissions dean or two from a nearby medical school. On the other hand, the premedical adviser is a service of the university, and ignoring the adviser would be foolhardy, as he or she can be critical to your case.

I took it on blind faith that the premedical adviser knew his business.

My own premedical adviser, after hearing my story, asked me what I was going to do when I didn't get into medical school. Fortunately I was obsessed with the idea of becoming a doctor, and since he didn't give me the encouraging counsel I wished to hear, I simply did not hear him. The question of whether or not his advice was good advice never entered my mind. However, when I first realized that his position had no job description, I began to wonder about the premedical adviser's credentials and experience and about what exactly he could do for me that I couldn't do for myself. What follows is a profile of the premedical adviser that answers these questions and may also answer some others that you perhaps have.

Not Always an Expert

First off, premedical advisers are rarely, if ever, physicians themselves. They are almost always faculty members at the university who have taken an interest in the plight of the premedical student. Although premedical advisers can be members of any department, they are most frequently from the science faculty. At many places, the job is part time and the adviser puts in a few mornings or afternoons a week without extra pay, although at some of the larger universities, health professions advising has become a full-time job.

The majority of schools have one premedical adviser; some have more than one, and others have none at all. In the latter case, the faculty itself assumes the role of adviser to the premed students. In many places, serving as the premedical adviser may take the place of having to serve on other faculty committees or on the faculty senate. As with most academic committee work, the term of a premedical adviser may be surprisingly short. Or, one adviser may serve for quite a long time and then (possibly in the middle of your own college career) relinquish the post to a fresh recruit. It is important for the student to know how long the adviser has held that post so that it will be possible to evaluate accordingly the advice rendered. Experience at this job is of key importance.

> Some advisers, like some teachers, keep only
> one step ahead of their students.

There is no required formal educational process for advisers to go through before they assume their position. The premedical adviser holds no degree or certification for the job, is not licensed, and is not subject to peer review. The adviser is only as good as personal interest and involvement allow. However, a National Association of Advisors for the Health Professions has existed for over twenty-five years and holds yearly meetings for the Northeast, Southeast, Western, and Central regions as well as a biannual national meeting. Although many premedical advisers belong to this organization, not all attend the yearly meeting in their region. The meetings offer a sort of refresher course on the state of education in the health professions and gives the advisers a chance to have their questions answered by the medical school admissions people who attend as well as to make personal contacts. Matters taken up at the meetings may include how to write an evaluation for a student applying to medical school, current trends in admissions, and up-to-date information on the MCAT, as well as commentary on the way medicine is currently being practiced.

Does Your Adviser Attend the Meetings?

This organization offers its members a quarterly journal, called *The Advisor*, and a between-the-issues supplement. It also has a premedical advisers' reference manual available exclusively to active pre-health professional advisers that supplements the AAMC's *Official Guide to Medical School Admissions Requirements* with information not generally available to premeds. These publications, together with the yearly regional meetings and one national meeting of the association, constitute the prime opportunities for premed advisers to keep up in the field. In 1987, and again in 1995, I attended the Western Regional Meeting at Asilomar, California. I was impressed with the agenda and also with the dedication and sincerity of the premedical advisers whom I met.

My advice to you is to find out if your premed adviser belongs to this association. If he or she does not, then look for someone who does. This, in addition to experience, is the best way to judge your adviser's reliability. Most premedical advisers will talk to you even if you're not a student at their college, so don't be shy about calling up and asking for an appointment.

It is noteworthy that the NAAHP has several publications for sale to premeds. They are *Medical Professions Admissions Guide: Strategy for Success; Write for Success: Preparing a Successful Professional School Application;* and *The Medical School Interview.* Cassette tapes from the national meetings are also available. NAAHP offers a travel program with discounted airfares for students going to health professions school interviews and the organization has information for students on its Web site www.naahp.org. You can also contact the NAAHP at POB 1518, Champaign, IL 61824-1518, or by phone at (217) 355-0063, or by fax at (217) 355-1287.

The question arises, "What can my premedical adviser tell me that I can't find out for myself?" In truth, it may not be very much. The core of the premedical adviser's knowledge comes from publications that are readily available to the public. The core book is *Medical School Admissions Requirements,* put out by the AAMC. Included are chapters on selection factors for each school, specific admissions requirements, tuition figures, financial aid information and sources, minority admissions information, combined degree programs, MCAT and AMCAS data, and much more. This book is updated yearly and is truly the official guide. In addition, the adviser receives a newsletter, published by the AAMC, which may have occasional nuggets of information. A very helpful publication is the *Journal of the American Medical Association,* which can be found in most libraries. Each year this journal gives a complete profile of the entering freshman class to medical school. Included are the number of applications and applicants, their GPAs, average MCAT scores, the number accepted and rejected, and pertinent analyses of factors affecting medical school admissions. As far as printed matter is concerned, you can probably lay your hands on as much stuff as your adviser. If you don't feel like digging up your own information, you should feel free to ask your adviser if you can peruse the office files. As far as I know, there are no secret documents there, so I see no reason for objection.

Certainly your adviser can provide valuable help, and if yours is conscientious you may not even have need of this book. Most of the things I talk about—i.e., choosing a major, taking the MCAT, applying to medical school, and facing alternatives—should be covered adequately by your adviser during your four years as an undergraduate. One of the functions of this book is to serve as a primary adviser for students who have none at their school and to offer a second opinion for those dissatisfied with what they have already been told.

Get Acquainted . . . See What They Write About You

Now, it is most important to get acquainted with your premed adviser—whether or not you take any advice—because most medical schools require a letter of recommendation from the premedical committee, which may be made up wholly or in part by the premedical adviser, and the majority of colleges and universities nationwide offer committee or composite adviser letters of some kind.

Later we will talk about the kinds of recommendations faculty members may write. It is important for students to remember, however, that in most cases these recommendations are not sent directly to the medical schools to which you apply. The premedical committee drafts and sends a composite letter. Though your professors may describe you in the most glowing terms, the *tone* of the committee's letter will clearly depend on how well you are known to the person drafting it—usually the premedical adviser.

The following are two actual letters from premedical committees. They appeared in an issue of *The Advisor* that reported on a symposium of letters of evaluation sponsored by the Western Association of Advisors for the Health Professions. The presentation from which these two letters are excerpted was made by Dr. John P. Steward of the Stanford University School of Medicine. The comments following the letters are Dr. Steward's.

FIRST LETTER:

Premedical Adviser:

Not much need to add to underscore the fact that _____ is a gem. I enjoyed my first encounter with this very bright lad three years ago when, as a freshman who had already traveled abroad as far as _____ and _____, he was then plowing through all kinds of advanced courses, displaying the energy and enormous enthusiasm which were to mark every step of his journey through _____. He had come to college imbued with the drive to become a doctor from the earliest age and with the simplest of explanations: "I just want to be able to help people." His next greatest ambition was to get back to Europe, to get to know people; and he has done every kind of menial labor, even jerking sodas, to earn the money. Sure enough, the next summer found him working for _____ in _____, and now he has only just returned from the greatly enriching experience of a junior year abroad where he was registered in school exactly the same as _____ students, not as a foreigner, in an experimental center in _____, a development of the University of _____, but the cosmopolitan life has in no way diminished his single-minded con-centration on becoming a physician. Furthermore, it is perfectly clear that here is a young man who has pursued the epitome of the lib-eral arts program not in the least with any idea of minimizing the sciences, as his very high standing in all the required courses testify— he is only saving them up for medical school! It is not possible that we will be presenting a stronger or more engaging candidate this year—a star.

COMMENTS ON LETTER:

The helpful parts of the letter were . . . the way the premedical adviser summarized his candidate. This excellent letter is typical of letters coming from this academically excellent institution.

SECOND LETTER:

Premedical Adviser:

_____ is enrolled in the premedical curriculum of this University and is applying for admission to your School of Medicine. He is expected to graduate with a Bachelor's Degree in June 1971.

At the present time, _____'s cumulative grade point average is 3.64.

The premedical faculty of the College of Science acts as a committee to pass on applicants for recommendation to medical school. After due consideration of his case, the five members of _____ committee were unanimous in recommending him as an excellent candidate.

One committee member commented that he had a pleasant personality—on the quiet side—and would expect him to be in the upper half of his class.

The possible ratings given to applicants who receive the recom-mendations of the Committee are not recommended, fair candidate, good candidate, excellent candidate.

COMMENTS ON LETTER:

This is an instance where we have no choice but to say here is a student that, as far as we are concerned, we don't care what his GPA is, and we don't want to know anything else about him if this is all the premedical adviser could say.

Again, we will interpret what you write in light of the fact that we assume you have done your best.

Once you have developed a personal relationship with your adviser, you can be sure that the letter of evaluation will show the admissions committees that you're more than just another premed.

The Premedical Student

Having discussed the premedical adviser, the next order of business is the premedical student. What do other people see in him or her? What is the student's self-image?

Peer group evaluations usually label premed students "grade-grubbers," "gunners," or "greasers," depending on the part of the country they come from. Other disparaging adjectives used for the premed are ruthless, antisocial, narrow-minded, insincere, cutthroat, dull, and brownnosing. On the other hand, students who see the premeds more as a benign than as a malignant force have described them as idealistic, dedicated, and brilliant.

Among faculty members the premedical student is usually highly regarded. Unfavorable comments from this group are that premeds are more concerned with grades than subject matter and are not fully interested in participation in the whole college experience. On the favorable side, professors often remark that premeds are desirable students who make many contributions to the extracurricular program of their colleges.

What of the premed's own self-image? Certainly many students exhibit elitist tendencies—all the more so the longer they remain premeds. Others, for whom the curriculum is an ordeal, see what they are sacrificing in time and may actually feel relatively deprived when comparing themselves with their classmates. Still others may have no self-image at all connected with being premed. In the true democratic spirit, they do not see themselves as fundamentally different from their peers. At the core, though, if the premed is motivated by a desire to aid others, by a need for self-gratification, for financial security, or for power, prestige, knowledge, or a challenging and varied career, that student is likely to feel good about what he or she is doing and to have a positive self-image. If, however, the student has an unsatisfied, subliminal yearning to be a physical education teacher but a parent in the medical profession is calling all the shots, then that student is not going to be very happy as a premed or in medical school.

Consider this letter that I received several years ago from the anxious father of a premed:

> Dear Dr. Brown,
>   Sorry to bother you, but I need the favor or your advice. My daughter is a premed in her junior year at Cornell University. She made the very mistakes in her first two undergraduate years that you have advised to avoid in your book.
>   She was brilliant in her high school studies even though she began school in this country in the eighth grade (we immigrated from India about eight years ago). She got accepted at Cornell University as an Early Decision student in 1977.
>   At Cornell she took a chemistry major. She thought this would help her get admitted to medical school. This involved taking higher chemistry, math, and physics courses. She got C in chemistry, C+ in physics, and B in math. Her grades in nonscience subjects are B+. Her grades in biology average B.
>   In her junior year she changed her major from chemistry to microbiology and she did better academically last semester. She wants to repeat some courses to raise her GPA but she is being advised that, after completing higher science courses, she should not retake lower courses (although the lower courses meet the requirements of medical college and her new major).
>   We shall appreciate your advice and guidance in the matter as we are totally ignorant of the system in this country. We do not mind if she spends an extra year repeating her courses.
>   Raj Mulati

Although I can appreciate this father's concern, I somehow wonder why this letter didn't come from his daughter. I am always suspicious of queries that come not from the premedical student themselves but from family members or friends. I ask myself, what is the source of this person's desire to study medicine? Is she self-directed or other-directed? Is she pursuing a premedical program because she wants to be a physician or just to please her parents? Admissions committees ask the same questions. Studies show that attrition among medical students has more to do with motivation than any other single factor. If a person genuinely wants to become a physician, the medical school curriculum is a minor obstacle. The major obstacle is getting into medical school in the first place. Academically, medical students are sound. But if a physician parent is pressuring a son or daughter to follow in their footsteps, or a parent wants a physician in the family and that student would rather be sailing, then flunking out is a real possibility. My medical school classmates were not geniuses; they were hard workers. Medical school involves long hours, tedious work, and requires a high degree of personal sacrifice. With proper motivation, it can also be highly rewarding and a lot of fun.

The Premedical Syndrome

For those who don't genuinely want to become doctors, the premed curriculum, not to mention medical school, will be sheer hell. To those at peace with themselves, it can be a joy. Yet some students who genuinely want to study medicine are not at all at peace with themselves, and they let the rigors of the premed curriculum interfere with their self-development. They suffer from what I call the premedical syndrome.

The affliction is readily diagnosed. On any college campus, those suffering from the premed syndrome are the students who look as if they've been in a pressure cooker. Worn and haggard, but very determined, they are the last to leave the library at night and the first to arrive in the morning. They don't go out much, unless there's a lecture on diabetes or heart disease. Their extracurricular activities consist of membership in the premedical society and flipping a Frisbee for physical fitness. Artistically, all of their drawing is done with a number two lead pencil on IBM sheets. Musically, they are satisfied with AM radio. Ask them to demonstrate or sign a petition, and they say, "What, and blow med school?!" Psychologically, they are anal-retentive types who make up daily schedules so they won't forget anything.

> **Their lab notebooks are impeccably neat. Major headings are underlined in red, minor ones in blue.**

They never miss a class without getting the notes. All homework assignments are handed in on time. Before examinations they study incessantly, develop a tachycardia, and become diaphoretic. This anxiety is theoretically linked with an impending sense of doom, but the symptoms promptly abate after they "ace," "gun," or are "all over" the exam. If they do poorly, they are miserable and hard to live with.

The syndrome is marked by exacerbations (failures) and remissions (successes) culminating in a crisis (acceptance or rejection). The individual may recover completely (is accepted), be left with permanent residual damage (is rejected), or may pass into a carrier state (reapplies again the next year).

A Maniac in Pursuit of Medicine

This was written in gross caricature, of course. All the same it is not hard to see why the premed is maniacal in the pursuit of medicine. In our society the premedical student runs a particular risk and has far more to lose than any other preprofessional. Of all the professions, none turns away qualified applicants as frequently as does medicine. In addition, one quarter of your college career will be spent taking courses that, should you complete them

Worn and haggard, they are the last to leave
the library at night and the first to arrive in the morning.

successfully, will serve only to qualify you for admission into a medical school. Contrast this situation to law, for which no specific academic preparation is required of aspiring students.

The premedical student may have majored in science with no intention of becoming a scientist or studied literature without any desire to teach. The primary goal is medicine, and unless prepared for the possibility of not gaining admission to professional school, the student may have nothing at all on which to fall back.

Failure Is Always a Possibility

The sad fact is that the students who are not admitted have most probably lost out not because they are at fault but because the system cannot absorb them, even though they may be competent, sincere, and dedicated. There are alternatives for the rejected applicants, and I will be talking about them later; however, *the ambitious pursuit of medical school acceptance is not a guarantee of success.* If you are prepared to make the commitment and to cope with possible failure and uncertainty about the future practice of medicine then read on. Otherwise, if you haven't already marked up the pages, see if you can't get some money back at the bookstore.

CHAPTER 3

The Medical College Admission Test (MCAT)

The Most Important Criterion

Besides your GPA, there is, probably, no single more important criterion for admission to medical school today than your performance on the Medical College Admission Test. Because it is hard for admissions committees to rate one college against another, the MCAT provides a standard by which all candidates may be compared. The MCAT is one path in the admissions process that everyone must follow. Virtually all schools require you to report MCAT scores.

Now, if you have been anything other than a superior undergraduate student, the MCAT is especially for your benefit. It is your chance to show off and show up all those compulsive premeds who study incessantly and give you a guilty conscience for going out and having a good time. Even if you have a borderline GPA, high scores on this exam will indicate to medical schools that you have the potential to do work that will be up to their standards. On the other hand, low MCAT scores from a student with a high GPA might indicate someone who has reached his or her limits in college and may not be able to handle the more difficult work load of medical school.

After all, don't you spend countless hours studying to boost your grade point average? How much time have you spent to assure yourself high scores on this all-important test? It is a fact that your performance on this six-hour exam will help or hurt you as much as that GPA you sweated for during your entire college career.

MCAT—a Means for Comparison

By now, I hope you are wondering why the MCAT is of such great consequence and what you can do to be ready for it. To begin with, you must realize that in selecting applicants, medical schools are eternally looking for the single most consistent predictor of medical school success. In the past, success has correlated most reliably with GPA, but using grade points has caused two major problems. One is that grades are not always comparable from college to college. The attempt to evaluate institutional rigor and grade inflation is informal at best. Admissions committees may err at the extremes either by assuming more differences between schools than actually exist or by not accepting the fact that colleges actually do differ in their academic standards.

The second difficulty with grade points has emerged more recently: a modification of the grading system at many universities, with evaluations replacing letter grades as a more meaningful way to assess a student's ability. Indeed, this pass-fail trend has been adopted by medical schools, with the result that many have done away with class rankings and today operate exclusively on a satisfactory-unsatisfactory grading system. At this point, however, medical schools feel justified in using nonletter grades because, by the process of selection, they have prejudged the student to be capable of becoming a physician and see little advantage in continuing to foster a competitive atmosphere. However, many medical schools are trying to incorporate a high pass and a low pass in their grading system. The reason is that greater distinction is needed in monitoring medical student performance in response to competition for residency programs. On the undergraduate level, these changes may be beneficial to the students seeking self-improvement, but they have made the task of selecting among applicants to medical school increasingly difficult.

To briefly recap, medical school admissions committees must consider whether the grade itself is a valid measure of the applicant's performance. If the applicant presents a "pass" instead of a letter grade, the task of evaluation is that much harder, since what constitutes satisfactory completion of the course is usually not described on the transcript.

When admissions committees finally do lose faith in the GPA as a means of selecting students who are bright enough to graduate from a school of medicine, there will be only one objective criterion left—the MCAT. It will be the last bastion of objectivity left to the medical school, the only means by which applicants may be differentiated in an impartial manner.

Although it is unfair, the initial selection of medical students by factors other than grade point averages and MCAT scores poses other logistic difficulties. Picture the dilemma in the modern medical school's registrar's office. Every year four- to six-thousand applications arrive for one- to two-hundred freshman class places. How to sort them out? Clearly, there are two alternatives. Either you can have an admissions committee of seventy-five to one-hundred people so that each applicant will get personal attention, or you can feed GPAs, MCAT scores, and lesser factors into the computer and review only those applicants who make a cutoff. The former approach happens at a minority of medical schools. The latter method is more universal, for obvious reasons. Large admissions committees are unwieldy; smaller ones function more easily. Consensus is easier to reach, and decisions among applicants can be made more quickly. But small committees do not have the time to read through thousands of applicants. Hence, initial, nonpersonalized screening.

Now, if students are going to be judged initially by a computer, there must be a way to turn their academic achievements into a score. A formula is devised, which varies from school to school. Essentially, grades are weighed along with MCAT scores. Some college years may be weighed slightly more than others (junior over freshman) and perhaps some majors over others or some colleges over others, but this is minor compared with GPAs and MCATs. Standardized test scores give medical schools an impartial way to rate students from different schools, with different majors, of different races and sexes. For all their differences, these premeds arrived at a testing center at the same time to sit through an all-day marathon exam that is designed ultimately to lend an air of fairness to the decision of who does and who does not get into medical school.

I am no fan of the MCAT. I think it is basically unfair because it favors students who are good at taking tests (although it also gives the applicant from Podunk U. a better chance). It does not differentiate between good and excellent medical students and sheds no light on an applicant's suitability to be a physician. The only purpose it serves is to make the admission committee's job easier. And it is also in the proprietary interest of the AAMC, which owns and writes the MCAT and keeps the fees.

Rather than rant about MCAT's imperfections, it would be simpler to accept the reality that taking the MCAT, like death and taxes, is inevitable for anyone wanting to attend a U.S. medical school. The exam has changed and will continue to change as more people demand that it become more relevant to the kinds of physicians we would like to produce. But for now it is important to do well enough on it to be invited to a personal interview, where an admissions committee member can see more of who you really are.

The Test

Although the test is scheduled for all day, the actual test-taking time is 5¾ hours. The rest of the time is for lunch and two breaks. The exam has four components: verbal reasoning, physical sciences, a writing sample, and biological sciences. One-hundred minutes are allotted for each seventy-seven-question science section, eighty-five minutes for sixty-five verbal reasoning questions, and sixty minutes for the two writing samples. The verbal reasoning section does not test for subject matter knowledge; all the information needed to answer the questions is provided in the passages. The science sections, on the other hand, do assume knowledge of the premedical science requirements, even though data may be presented in graphs, tables, or charts. The essay section is meant to evaluate applicants' writing skills. Two written essays are required; neither is about why you want to be a physician or on the technical aspects of the sciences. Rather, they are on social, cultural, or emotionally charged issues and are not meant as much to elicit a right answer as to see how you think and organize your thoughts. On a past MCAT, for example, test takers were asked to consider these two statements—*Price is not necessarily a reflection of value* and *In politics, good intentions cannot justify bad actions*—and write two essays explaining what these statements mean. Another statement I wish the AAMC would consider using is *The best test takers do not necessarily make the best doctors!*

How Is It Scored?

According to the *MCAT Student Manual,* "your total score is a reflection of your right answers only. This means that a wrong answer will be scored exactly the same as a no answer." In other words, do not leave any space blank; answer every single question, even if you have to guess. You will not be penalized, so the best policy is to fill in every answer space. This is crucial to remember.

The scores are reported on a scale ranging from 1 (lowest) to 15 (highest). Raw scores are converted to a score on the 15-point scale. Let's say you get 42 out of 60 questions correct on one section; this would probably convert to an 11 or 12 on the scale. In this manner, even though there might be a slight difference in the raw scores among several students, their interval score (1 to 15) will be the same.

The essay sample is scored on an alphabetic continuum of J through T, with T representing the clearest, most coherent, and best organized writing. Although scores among accepted applicants vary with race/ethnicity and sex, most students will have to score 9s or better and P or better to remain competitive for medical school.

Preparing for the MCAT

To the question "Can I prepare for the MCAT?" the answer is an emphatic YES. Some of the ways to prepare are obvious, and you probably already know them. If you are at all conscientious, you may already have purchased

Answer every single question, even if you have to guess.

one of the books that have questions simulating the MCAT. Those I have seen pattern their questions after the actual MCAT and should give you a good idea of what to expect. A few tips—start using these books early (not a week before the exam) and look up the things you do not know. Get into a routine of doing a number of pages or questions each day and stick to it. This kind of discipline, incidentally, will also get you through medical school.

It is a very good idea to take this exam as seriously as you took organic chemistry. If need be, pretend that the MCAT is simply another premed course in which you must do well in order to get into medical school. It would be wise to start your systematic review procedure about six months before you plan to take the real thing. Get psyched early and build up your confidence so that you can perform really well on the test.

Preparatory Courses

There is currently much controversy surrounding the merits of taking a special prep or cram course for the MCAT exam. Inasmuch as these types of commercial courses are expensive and time consuming, you really have to be seriously committed to doing well on the exam.

However, the MCAT preparation centers can help you prepare for the exam in one very important way—building confidence. If you've paid good money for a course (money that you would have used for new CDs!), then you will force yourself to study and review your notes. In this manner you will increase your confidence because of a sense of preparation and knowing that you are not facing the test cold. If you are confident in your own performance, this will decrease the anxiety level that accompanies the MCAT, and your scores are bound to be higher. Remember, it is a two-way street. The prep courses won't help you if you don't give the necessary hours to review and to do practice problems.

Lastly, save all your notes and tests from all the important science courses—biology, general chemistry, organic chemistry, and physics. In this way you will be able to review your own material and look over your review sheets from previous study binges. Why waste all of that work that you had to do anyway? Good students keep their notes in binders or folders so that they are still legible a year or two later. It wouldn't hurt to retake some of your class tests as practice to help point out to yourself areas in which you may need some extra work.

The major preparatory courses are offered in most cities. The local offices of these commercial centers can be found in the yellow pages, or just ask around at your college and you will be surprised at how many people have taken the course themselves. In other words, you also should keep your eyes and ears open about what is going on at your school and what the going rates are for such courses.

I posed the question of preparatory courses to Dr. Thomas L. Pearce, premedical adviser at the University of Virginia. This was his response:

"Students must not expect that 'review' MCAT courses are really *science review* courses. Usually they are simple courses in examology; they try to teach students how to take a specific test on a specific date, namely the MCAT. This entails teaching test-taking techniques as much as, or more than, reviewing the required premedical sciences. Obviously topics covered in these 'review' courses include premedical subjects, but the emphasis is on taking the test, not reviewing comprehensively the material to be tested.

"I believe that students are just as well off, if not better off, by reviewing *extensively* and *independently* the subject matter on which they will be tested. All undergraduates I have taught these past thirteen years have been experienced test takers, for they have been taking standardized tests for many years. I advise my students to take any 'review' courses they wish; I *never* advise them to rely completely on such courses. I urge them strongly to review all their class notes, every page of their introductory texts in biology, inorganic and organic chemistry and physics, and to buy the science review book written by James Flowers, available in paperback for $18. In addition I urge all of them to buy the *MCAT Student Manual* (2nd edition), which contains useful information about parameters of subjects on which they are to be tested, as well as *Barron's How to Prepare for the Medical College Admissions Test,* which contains reviews of subject matter as well as full-length practice exams. There are several books available which contain *only* practice MCATs; generally these are good to use as well, but only after the review studying has been done."

Before leaving the subject of the MCAT, I must take up two frequently asked questions: "When should I take the MCAT?" and "When is it necessary to take it more than once?" There is no doubt in my mind that the MCAT should first be taken in the spring of your junior year. Unless you plan to pick up a summer course, the additional time afforded by taking the exam in the fall will not be a distinct advantage. In fact, you will lose a great deal of momentum. By taking the MCAT in the spring, you will have your scores by summer, and you can begin to apply to medical schools June 15 for AMCAS schools and often earlier for non-AMCAS schools. However, if you wait until the fall of your senior year to take it, your scores won't be posted until October (it takes seven to nine weeks for you and the medical schools to receive your scores). By the time the schools receive the scores, add them to your file, and move your application on for processing, it could be November or December. By that time, many of your friends will have already had interviews, and some may even have been accepted by a medical school. This will do little to lessen your anxiety. So unless there are unusual circumstances (e.g., you decide in your senior year to become a premed), take the MCAT in the spring. Of course, candidates for early admission to medical school (after three years of college) should take the exam in the fall of their junior year.

There is only one situation in which the MCAT should be repeated. This is if you have scored poorly in science and are positive your score was a fluke or know that you can do better. If you were sick on the day of the exam, misunderstood directions, or simply had other things on your mind and were distracted, then by all means repeat the MCAT. But if you have no good excuse for your performance and do not intend to do intensive remedial work, remember that two mediocre scores look worse than one.

The MCAT is a tough exam by anybody's standards. You must do well on the test or your chances of acceptance are very slim. It is better to take the exam very seriously and to prepare for it than be angry with yourself after having done poorly. Everyone must take the MCAT. The more confident you are, the better you will do. That confidence comes from good study habits and a well-planned review procedure prior to the test.

What follows is a list of academic resources to prepare you for the MCAT. All are available from the AAMC.

1- *The MCAT Student Manual.* An absolute must-have book.

2- *AAMC MCAT Practice* Tests 1, 2, 3, 4. Actual MCATs from the 1990s.

3- *Scoring the MCAT Writing Sample.*

4- *Preparing for the MCAT.* An AAMC videotape.

5- *The MCAT Annual Announcement.* Comes out during February of each year. Includes introductory test information and 19 pages of Writing Sample prompts.

Do not forget to review your old textbooks in biology, chemistry, and physics.

To conclude this chapter, I append a table that shows the average MCAT scores and GPAs for candidates accepted to medical school in a recent year. Comparing these scores with your own will give you some idea of your competitiveness.

MCAT AND GPA BY RACE/ETHNICITY AND SEX FOR ACCEPTED APPLICANTS

ACCEPTED APPLICANTS	BLACK	AMERICAN INDIAN	MEXICAN AMERICAN	MAINLAND PUERTO RICAN	WHITE	ASIAN/ PACIFIC ISLANDER	OTHER HISPANIC	C'WEALTH PUERTO RICAN
FEMALES								
MCAT								
Verbal Reasoning	7.7	8.9	8.3	7.7	9.9	9.5	9.2	6.0
Physical Sciences	7.0	7.6	7.8	7.7	9.4	10.0	8.9	6.5
Biological Sciences	7.4	8.2	8.4	7.9	9.8	10.1	9.4	7.2
Writing Sample (median)	O	O	O	O	P	P	P	L
GPA								
Science	3.03	3.17	3.13	3.16	3.55	3.52	3.35	3.21
Other	3.42	3.45	3.38	3.53	3.65	3.69	3.56	3.64
Total	3.19	3.29	3.23	3.34	3.59	3.59	3.45	3.40
MALES								
MCAT								
Verbal Reasoning	7.6	8.9	8.3	8.2	9.8	9.6	9.0	6.3
Physical Sciences	7.7	8.7	8.6	8.3	10.3	11.0	9.7	7.2
Biological Sciences	7.9	8.8	9.1	8.7	10.3	10.7	9.7	7.5
Writing Sample (median)	N	N	O	N	P	P	P	L
GPA								
Science	3.00	3.17	3.14	3.13	3.53	3.56	3.38	3.09
Other	3.31	3.34	3.34	3.37	3.57	3.62	3.49	3.43
Total	3.13	3.25	3.22	3.22	3.54	3.58	3.43	3.23

Source: AAMC Section for Student Services, Final National Admission Action Summary Report 1995— Writing samples: higher alphabet letter indicates higher score.

CHAPTER 4

Applying to a Medical School—When, Where, and How

We have finally arrived at the really big step. So far all your energies have gone into fulfilling the requirements for medical school acceptance. You have completed most, if not all, of your premedical courses, taken the MCAT, and amassed a portfolio of recommendations from professors. Now it is time to put those grades, test scores, and plaudits to use and to couple them with some hard-core facts. Getting into a medical school is often a matter of having information other people do not have because they never bothered to find out and were never told. In this game, a little knowledge is an essential asset.

How Many Applications?

Let us begin our discussion with the surprising statistic that every year some medical school applicants apply to only one school. Can anyone afford to do that? Absolutely not! Not even if your father and mother sit on the admissions committee and you are a *summa cum* from Harvard. If you are rejected by your one school, you are out of luck, whereas other students—with lesser credentials—who applied to numerous schools may have been accepted by one of them. One acceptance is really all it takes. Going to your last-choice school is infinitely preferable to going to none at all!

Applicant numbers fluctuate every year. According to the AAMC "Applicants, Matriculants, Graduates Facts" annual reports, during the years 1989–95 applicant numbers increased by a whopping 73 percent—breaking all

records in the history of medical education. There are a number of specula-
tions on the reasons for this increase, including the economy and the perceived
stability of a health professions career, TV shows, and an increase in interest in
humanitarian careers—for whatever reasons, medicine was, and still is, a very
popular career choice. Since 1995, however, applicant numbers have been
decreasing slowly each year by a total of about 17 percent. Even though this is
good news for current applicants, it does not mean that getting in has become
easy. Because it is still very competitive, it is important to apply to a variety of
medical schools to maximize your chances for acceptance.

For the 1998–99 entering class, the AAMC's *2000–01 Medical School
Admissions Requirements* reported 481,336 appplications filed by 41,004
individuals—an average of twelve applications per applicant. Before the large
increase, students averaged only nine applications. Applicants have been rec-
ognizing the importance of applying to an adequate number of schools. Of
the 41,004 applicants for 1998, 42.4 percent were offered admission. Those
AMCAS applicants who applied to twenty or more AMCAS-participating
schools averaged 44.3 percent acceptance rate. The number of schools you
choose may depend on a variety of factors, such as your competitiveness for
the individual schools you are considering and the number of schools in your
state or region that give some kind of priority to residents of that area. You
also want to take a look at the programs and opportunities available to you—
do these schools fit with your learning style, interests, and goals?

> **The first law of survival is to apply to as many
> schools as is feasible.**

By feasible I do not mean that the number of applications you send out
should be limited by your finances or by your boredom with filling out
forms. You should apply to all schools to which your acceptance is a realistic
possibility. No matter who you are, where you live, or what undergraduate
college you attended, the number of such schools approaches twelve to fifteen or more.

There are a few rules of thumb to observe when choosing the schools to
which to apply. First, it is always advisable to apply to schools in your part of
the country, especially to schools in your home state, or if there is no medical school in your state, to those that have contract agreements for residents

of your state. State-supported medical schools are required to give priority to qualified in-state residents and usually consider only exemplary out-of-state students. At many state schools, those few nonresidents who are admitted may be only or primarily MD/PhD candidates, underrepresented minority students, or students with ties to that state (former residents or nonresidents who are currently attending school in the state). A number of private institutions are also heavily state supported and lean toward taking in-state residents. Very few schools, in fact, are truly representative of the entire country. Few accept more applicants from any state other than their own, and fewer still accept more out-of-region than in-region enrollees. According to the *Medical School Admissions Requirements (MSAR)*, in 1998, only thirty-nine schools accepted 50 percent or more of their entering class from outside their state, and most of these were private schools. [1]

Consider the schools in your geographic area as primary targets. Always include a number of private schools, particularly those that profess to be geographically egalitarian. However, if you are an underrepresented minority student or a qualified MD/PhD candidate, you may have more of a chance in the nonresident pool. Also be aware that there are a few medical schools whose main mission is to educate underrepresented minorities and educationally or economically disadvantaged students. Check individual school Web sites, and read carefully the information in the annual publication by the AAMC, *Medical School Admissions Requirements for the U.S. and Canada,* which profiles every med school and indicates numbers of nonresidents admitted and other admissions criteria. Also contact the schools if you have questions regarding the admission of nonresidents.

Above all, APPLY EARLY!!

Early Decision

With reference to early application, some students may wish to participate in the Early Decision Plan (EDP). With this program, highly qualified students with a strong preference for one particular school may apply to that single medical school by the August 1 EDP deadline and await, hopefully, an acceptance by early fall. This is a binding agreement—if you are accepted, you must attend that school and cannot apply anywhere else. Because of the early deadline, it is also necessary to have taken the MCAT prior to August.

The EDP has several advantages. For the successful student, it means the heat will be off by the beginning of the senior year. It is also a tremendous havings of dollars that would have been spent applying to other med schools, and you are in a small (although very competitive) applicant pool. At some schools, candidates who are not accepted EDP are automatically deferred to the regular decision pool and even given a second set of interviews; thus, you are looked at twice. To the medical schools, it represents savings of both time and paperwork, because EDP students would otherwise have applied to an average of thirteen schools each and, as most EDP candidates are highly qualified, their applications would have been processed in detail. It also gives the med schools a chance to select some top candidates who might otherwise get away from them if those candidates applied to other schools.

On the other hand, there are several limitations to the EDP program. The first is that, if accepted by the school applied to, the student is obliged to go there and may not apply elsewhere. The big disadvantage, however, is that the applicant is not certain of admission until October 1 of the senior year and may not apply to any other schools before that date. Thus, the rejected EDP applicant will be applying late to other schools. There are ninety-four medical schools that offer EDP. In 1998 there were 2,301 EDP candidates and 1,269 (55.1 percent) were accepted under the EDP program (as reported in *MSAR 2000–01*).

It is important to weigh your choice of applying EDP carefully. If you feel you are competitive for EDP at the school you have chosen and that school is truly your first choice, then go for it. But have your back-up list of schools ready to go in case you are not accepted EDP. If you do not get accepted EDP, you will need to quickly get out your applications to the other schools, and even then you will be initiating your application quite late for some. With the current large number of applicants, this can truly be a disadvantage. Some private schools (where your chances might be the best after your state/regional institutions) are currently receiving 10,000 or more applications. Applying late in those pools can be a problem. You may wish to check with some of the other schools you are considering to see how much of a disadvantage this would be. Note: Some state schools require nonresidents to apply through the EDP.

Combined MD/PhD Programs

Combined MD/PhD programs are intended for students who are seriously committed to a career in research. A competitive applicant should have excellent MCATs and GPA, usually have majored in science, have participated extensively in research prior to application, and have strong letters of recommendation from faculty singing praises as to your research abilities. These programs are very small and most are highly competitive.

The combined MD/PhD allows you to complete both degrees in a shorter period of time than if you did them separately. The programs usually take seven years to complete, not including residency training. Because the student is pursuing a long training in research and planning on a less lucrative career in academic medicine, programs usually offer annual stipends, cover the cost of PhD tuition, and sometimes pay for part or all of medical school tuition. In addition to the standard medical school application, the student is usually required to file separate materials to the PhD program. It also requires that you research the medical schools that offer the PhD in the area of your interest.

Most medical schools offer an MD/PhD in one form or another. These programs are listed in the AAMC's *Medical School Admissions Requirements* book. The most highly regarded programs are Medical Scientist Training Programs (MSTPs) funded by the National Institutes of Health (NIH). For more information on MSTPs, contact: Medical Scientist Training Program, National Institute of General Medical Sciences, National Institutes of Health, 45 Center Drive, MSC 6200, Bethesda, MD 20892-6200, or phone (302) 594-5560.

Cost of Applying

Beg or borrow the money you will need to apply to medical schools. There will be two fees to pay for those schools that are members of the standardized application service AMCAS (American Medical College Application Service): the AMCAS processing fee and the individual school fees. For 1999, the AMCAS fee was $55 for one school and a sliding scale after that (fifteen schools cost $525). Individual school fees range from nothing to $100, with the majority in the $40–65 range. Approximately forty-five schools have fees of $60 or higher. It is possible to spend upward of $1,200 filing applications, but if you have picked your schools carefully enough, it is worth the coin. Let's face it—should you be admitted, compared to what you will spend on your medical education, $50,000–$140,000—exclusive of costs of living— application fees are just a drop in the bucket. Consider this an investment in your career goal and the potential return on your investment.

For those students with extreme financial limitations whose inability to pay the fee would inhibit application to medical school, AMCAS does offer a fee waiver for up to ten member schools. The waiver form is included in the AMCAS packet.

I do not mean to suggest that you should apply to one-hundred medical schools or even fifty of them. Medical schools like to know that you want them as much as they want you. It is expected that you apply to a healthy number of schools, but if you have made arbitrary application to too many schools, your contention that you really want to go to one of them will seem hollow. However, if you have applied to a reasonable number of carefully selected schools, you can safely expound at your personal interview your reasons for wishing to attend each of them without your word being doubted. It will not appear that you want to go to any medical school that will accept you.

At your personal interviews, you may be asked to how many other schools you have applied. Being less than truthful will get you into a great deal of trouble, because all your applications are known to the AAMC. This is another reason to choose carefully.

Meeting the Costs

The rising cost of medical education and the amount of debt you are likely to incur is a concern for almost every applicant. It should not deter you from your career goal, however. Financial aid is available to cover the cost of education and living expenses, but it is mostly in the form of loans. The average indebtedness for students who graduated in 1998 was $85,180. Students who come from upper-class families may not give the cost of medical education a second thought, but it must be kept in mind that most students do have to borrow to attend medical school. Financial aid remains a major problem for most minority students. In 1996, 18 percent of African-American applicants and 22 percent of Native-American applicants came from families whose parental annual income was below $20,000.

Many organizations do offer financial assistance, some specifically for minority students, such as the Indian Health Services or the National Hispanic Scholarship Funds. Do research in the financial aid office or library at your school and inquire at the minority affairs offices at the medical schools to which you are applying.

The following is just a partial list of loans and fellowships available to students entering medical school. Once you are in medical school there are also some scholarships for second-, third-, and fourth-year students. (All federal programs require that you be a U.S. citizen, U.S. national, or U.S. permanent resident.)

Make application to a reasonable number
of carefully selected schools.

1- American Medical Women's Association, Inc., 801 North Fairfax Street, Suite 400, Alexandria, VA 22314 (www.amwa-doc.org). Scholarships and minimal loan programs for active AMWA members. Minimum renewable loan programs are available. Applicants must be women students enrolled in their second, third, or fourth year at an accredited U.S. medical or osteopathic school. Repayment of loans begins six months after graduation.

2- Armed Forces Health Professions Scholarship Program. U.S. Air Force, Army, and Navy. Scholarship recipients, who must agree to serve on active duty, are awarded tuition, associated educational costs, a stipend, and annual pay allowances. Air Force: Medical Recruiting, Division HQ, USAFRS/RSOHM, 550 D Street West, Suite 1, Randolph AFB, TX 78150-4527 (www.airforce.gov); Army: U.S. Army Recruiting Command, Attn. RCRO-HS-MC, 1307 Third Avenue, Fort Knox, KY 40121-2716, 1-800-USA-ARMY (www.goarmy.gov); and Navy: Commander, Navy Recruiting Command (Code 32), 801 North Randolph Street, Arlington, VA 22203-1991, 1-800-USA-NAVY (www.navyjobs.gov).

3- National Medical Fellowships, Inc., 110 West 32nd Street, New York, NY 10001 (www.nmf-online.org). Fellowships, based primarily on financial need, are given on a competitive basis to minority students already accepted into medical school. They are renewable and cover tuition and living expenses. Their helpful publication *Informed Decision Making Part 1: Sources of Financial Assistance for Medical Students*, available for $15, lists many different scholarships and loans for minority and nonminority students.

4- Indian Health Service (IHS) Scholarship Program. IHS, a bureau of the U.S. Public Health Service, provides scholarships that include tuition and fees. Loan repayment program also available. Contact IHS at 12300 Twinbrood Parkway, Suite 100, Rockville, MD 20852 or (301) 443-6197.

5- National Health Service Corps Scholarship Program, 2070 Chain Bridge Road, Suite 450, Vienna, VA 22182-2536, 1-800-221-9393 (www.bphc.hrsa.gov/nhsc). Scholarship recipients, who must agree to serve in federally designated health manpower shortage areas, are awarded tuition, associated educational costs, and a monthly stipend. To be eligible you must be going into an approved primary care specialty. Loan repayment program also offered.

6- State-sponsored scholarships or loan repayment programs for individuals committed to choosing a primary care specialty and are willing to practice in an underserved area of the state. Check with the individual state's department of health or a school of medicine in that state. Listings for state programs can also be found at www.aamc.org/stuapps.

In addition to the sources just listed, financial assistance is usually made available to medical students in the form of a mix of direct scholarships and loans. The amount of a scholarship award is determined by most schools primarily on the basis of economic need and not on academic performance. Thus, the student with a greater need and adequate to above-average academic record usually receives more scholarship assistance than loan money. Funds for either of these two types of assistance come from a variety of sources. Some are:

1- Directly from the medical school itself, usually from endowments made to the school for use in the support of students.

2- The federally supported Primary Care Loan provides funding to students who demonstrate need and are committed to a career as a generalist physician (i.e., family practice, general internal medicine, general pediatrics, or preventive medicine/public health). Regardless of tax status, the expected contribution of parents or spouse is considered. Currently, a student may borrow up to the cost of attendance, payable over a period of ten to twenty-five years at an interest rate of 5 percent, subject to change.

3- The Federal Perkins Loan is a federally supported loan program that awards based on need and available funds at each school. The maximum yearly amount is $5,000, with up to a ceiling of $30,000 and an interest rate of 5 percent during repayment.

4- The Federal Subsidized Stafford Student Loan works this way: the student borrows money from a private lender and the federal government subsidizes the interest on the loan while the student is enrolled. The student may borrow up to $8,500 per academic year with maximum cap of $65,500; repayment begins six months after graduation with an 8.25 percent interest cap.

5- Under the Federal Unsubsidized Stafford Loan, students may borrow from a private lender regardless of need at the same interest rate as the subsidized, but the borrower is responsible for accrued interest.

Maximum annual amount is $38,500 less Subsidized Stafford, and total borrowed is capped at $138,500 less Subsidized Stafford.

6- Other loans and scholarships targeted at students in primary care: Scholarships for Disadvantaged Students (SDS), Loans for Disadvantaged Students (LDS), Financial Aid for Disadvantaged Health Professions Students (FADHPS).

7- Private comprehensive loan programs such as Medloans, MedCap, and the Access Group are private lenders through which medical students may obtain some federally sponsored loans as well as private loan funds. Through these loans, qualified students may borrow private funds beyond what is covered with federal funds up to the cost of education. Interest rates vary.

8- Check Web sites www.fastweb.com and www.finaid.org for a large general listing of scholarships nationwide.

Minority Students

Increasing the numbers of underrepresented minority physicians has been a priority of medical schools for many years. Underrepresented minorities are defined by the AAMC as African-Americans, Native-Americans, Mexican-Americans, and mainland Puerto Ricans. These four groups are underrepresented in medical schools and in the profession and have also had a history of discrimination and exclusion in the United States. According to 1990 U.S. Census figures, our population was comprised of 19.4 percent underrepresented minorities, although according to current AAMC data, only 11.6 percent of 1998 medical school entrants are underrepresented minorities.[2] As our population becomes increasingly more diverse, the medical community is striving to provide our country with a more equitable representation. African-Americans account for 12 percent of our population, but only 8 percent of all medical students and about 3.5 percent of all physicians. Hispanics constitute 9 percent of the population and only 4 percent of the nation's physicians, whereas Native-Americans are 0.8 percent of the population and 0.1 percent of all doctors. [5]

According to AAMC's 2000–01 *Medical School Admissions Requirements,* in 1998 the nation's medical schools enrolled 1,872 new underrepresented minority students, only 11.6 percent of all new entrants. Although minority student enrollments have made great strides since the 1960s, a disparity still exists. The number of minorities entering medical school peaked in 1994 at 2,014, but as the total number of applicants has declined nationally, so has the number of minority applicants. Only 7.4 percent of first-year students in 1998 were African-American. Of these 1,201 students, 146 (12 percent) were attending Howard University, Meharry Medical College, and Morehouse College, predominantly African-American institutions. This is a dramatic change since 1969, when 75 percent of African-American medical students were enrolled at Howard and Meharry. However, historically African-American schools still provide African-American students with attractive features including more faculty role models, lower cost, fewer socialization problems, and extensive mentoring and support programs.

To address the issue of disparity, the AAMC initiated a program in 1991 called *Project 3000 by 2000* to increase the number of underrepresented minorities entering medical school each year to 3,000 by the year 2000. Under the program, medical schools work with high schools and colleges to provide early encouragement and support programs to prospective applicants. Many minority students do not have physician/scientist role models, receive little encouragement to achieve academically, and are often not prepared educationally to enter medical school. A goal of this program is to establish early communication with young minority students to provide them with more opportunity.

Every medical school in the United States has now appointed an administrator to coordinate Project 3000 by 2000 efforts in their communities. After the project's inception, the AAMC reported that the number of new underrepresented minority applicants increased by 40 percent and new matriculants increased by 27 percent during 1991–94, with a peak enrollment of 2,014 in 1994. However, during 1995 minority applicant numbers slowed, and in 1996 went into decline—some of this decline is likely due to recent legal challenges to affirmative action in many states. Consequently, the goals of this project have not yet been met, but the project continues to strive toward the goal of increasing the number of underrepresented minorities in medicine. Most medical schools also have resources to recruit and offer support programs to minority students once they enter, and many premedical advisers and minority affairs offices at undergraduate institutions provide assistance programs. If you are a minority student, you are encouraged to take advantage of these resources.

The Medical Minority Applicant Registry (Med-MAR), a service offered by the AAMC, provides the opportunity for underrepresented minority

Medical schools are bending over backward to solicit
qualified minority group students.

students to have their biographical information and MCAT scores sent to
admissions offices of all U.S. medical schools at no cost. This gives qualified students a chance to be looked at by schools across the country. The
medical schools can then contact the students they are interested in for
more information. At the time you take the MCAT, just indicate your
interest in this program.

From Quotas to Affirmative Action

For many years, there have been questions whether the special efforts to
recruit minority group students are appropriate, moral, and legal. Medical
school administrators are beset from two sides. On the one hand, the angry
white, middle-class applicant who has been rejected threatens to sue
because an academically less qualified minority group student was accepted
in his or her stead. On the other hand, there is an urgent national need for
a more representative pool of physicians, and medical schools are well aware
of that fact.

Perhaps it is important to gain a historical perspective. The expert opinion of five New York State Supreme Court justices was solicited by the AAMC in the 1970s. The consensus was that medical schools should be encouraged to increase minority enrollment and should undertake to ensure appropriate support mechanisms. The following items were put forth by the judges for consideration:

1- The United States Supreme Court, through various interpretations of the Constitution, has not forbidden programs designed to increase access of minority groups to higher education. Measures instituted to correct racial imbalance have been upheld as constitutional.

2- Remedial and tutorial support programs in graduate and professional education are justified, necessary, and compelling.

3- Admissions committees should consider many factors in making a decision, and factors that go beyond statistical and mathematical determinants are allowable and important. A committee that goes beyond consideration of scores, grades, and rank order in aptitude tests seems eminently rational because it seeks to "humanize" the process of selecting prospective members of the profession.

4- Experimentation in selecting a class is both desirable and permitted. The tendency to get away from rigid categories is also healthy as long as experimental and special programs are published and clearly defined as different from the normal or traditional practices.

5- Admissions committees clearly have the obligation and right to expand or restrict admissions criteria—although expansion of criteria is preferable and desirable. New and reasonable criteria may be included when considering applicants: that is, the nature of societal and community needs viewed from a national as well as a local perspective, the school's surrounding neighborhood and its special requirements a clear preference on the part of the candidate to pursue a specific community-oriented experience upon completion of the course of study, and the applicant's extracurricular activities when examined against the immediate societal need and his or her long-range plan. No commitments by the student are necessary—just as an expression of future interest and an honest belief that the applicant will most probably fulfill the commitment which made that candidate's selection so compelling.

All of these factors and others provide a rational basis for making a judgment other than on a score or grade comparison. Grades alone cannot accurately predict performance.

6- Establishing given percentages or quotas of minority students to be accepted in a class poses predictable problems. This should be avoided at all costs.

7- Medical schools may stimulate interest by creating mechanisms for recruitment, tutorial support, and special preparatory courses in order to qualify and ultimately enroll minority students. [3]

During the decade following this recommendation, medical school enrollment of underrepresented minorities surged from 3.12 percent in 1969 to 8 percent in 1979. Since then, enrollment increases have continued at a much slower pace and stand today at a total enrollment of 12 percent. [2]

It should be pointed out, however, that when predominantly white schools began to admit minority students, they did so not by taking away admissions opportunities from white applicants but by increasing the class size. For several years after the affirmative action push began, the absolute number of white students attending medical school increased. This is no longer true. From 1985 to 1995, the number of first-year underrepresented minority medical students increased from 8.8 percent of entrants to 12.4 percent. The number of white first-year students decreased from 81.1 percent to 64.9 percent of entrants. The largest increase has been for Asian/Pacific Islanders, from 6.7 percent to 18.2 percent of first-year entrants. [2]

In 1978, the Supreme Court handed down a landmark ruling in the famous Allan Bakke case. In both 1973 and 1974, Allan Bakke was an unsuccessful applicant to the University of California at Davis School of Medicine. At that time, Davis had a special admissions program: 16 places out of 100 in the freshman class were reserved for disadvantaged, minority applicants. Mr. Bakke felt that these outright racial quotas, by which minority students with "lesser credentials" (lower GPAs and MCAT scores) were admitted preferentially over him, were a form of reverse discrimination, that they violated his constitutional rights, and ought not to be allowed. The University felt that this preference was an acceptable form of affirmative action. The case went to the United States Supreme Court for a final decision.

What that court decided, by only a one-justice majority, was that institutional preference solely because of race was in violation of the principle of equal protection, and therefore unconstitutional. It was an unlawful interpretation of the meaning of affirmative action. Thus, UC—Davis's quota system was disallowed and Allan Bakke was ordered admitted to that medical school.

In writing the decision, Justice Powell defined the conditions under which race could be used as a basis for institutional admissions. Race may be a factor when it contributes to "the attainment of a diverse student body" and to "the robust exchange of ideas." It may not be used "to assure . . . some specified percentage of a particular group merely because of its race or ethnic origin." Nor may race be used to help certain groups perceived as victims of societal discrimination. Nor may it be used to alleviate a perceived shortage of medical manpower in underserved areas. The uses of race as a justifiable criterion for admission to medical school are, therefore, very narrow.

If ethnically based admission is unconstitutional, how do minority group members now fare in the admissions process? Actually, quite well. Admissions programs may still place a lawful emphasis on race; it may be deemed a plus in a particular applicant's file and weighed heavily. I do not believe that the Bakke decision has slowed the admission of minorities to medical schools. It has merely required that those schools establish guidelines and proceed on an individual, case-by-case basis. Racial "quotas" have been replaced by racial "awareness," and the effort to bring underrepresented minorities to medical school is called "affirmative action."

Very recently, affirmative action practices have once again come to the forefront and are being examined by many states. In 1995, the California Board of Regents ruled to abandon the use of race alone in college and university admissions in that state. The *Salt Lake Tribune,* in July 1995, reported that the Fifth U.S. Circuit Court of Appeals in New Orleans ruled in favor of four white, non-Hispanic students who were denied admission to the University of Texas law school even though they had higher grades than minority applicants who were admitted. The school had set lower test score standards and had established a separate review board for minority applicants and minimum target enrollments. This circuit court ruling, which applies only in Texas, Louisiana, and Mississippi, seems to contradict the 1978 Bakke decision, which did uphold the use of race as a factor in admission. In 1998, the state of Washington approved a proposition similar to the California proposition. In addition to these recent decisions, numerous other states have introduced bills to revise affirmative action laws.

Medical schools are very concerned about the impact of diminished affirmative action programs. According to an AAMC press release in December 1998, since 1996 the number of underrepresented minorities applying to medical schools dropped in California by 19 percent and in Texas, Louisiana, and Mississippi by 22 percent. The current AAMC Position on Equal

Opportunity reaffirms the principle of equal opportunity and affirmative action programs aimed at increasing the proportion of underrepresented minorities in the health professions.

Opponents of affirmative action in this theater, however, say that the AAMC is playing a numbers game that can lead to reverse discrimination against white males. After the tremendous increase in applicant numbers from 1988–96, applicant numbers have been decreasing slowly since then— from the all-time high of 46,968 in 1996 to 41,003 in 1998. During the years of large increases, the gains in acceptance were not with whites and less with white males. According to the AAMC's "FACTS" data, since 1991 the number of white males graduating from medical school has declined by 15 percent, whereas the number of graduating underrepresented minorities has increased by 27 percent. At the same time, there was an increase of only 209 new seats in all medical schools. Statistically, the gains in acceptance were not with whites and less with white males. In fact, since 1988, the rate of white males graduating from medical school has been declining at 2 percent per year.

Looking at test scores it is obvious that underrepresented minorities (URMs) have been held to a different standard. In 1996, the average verbal reasoning score on the MCAT for accepted white males was 9.9, and the average cum GPA was 3.58. For accepted black males, it was 8.1 and 3.23. For rejected white males, it was 8.0. For accepted black males, it was 8.1. This is not to say that grades should be the be-all and end-all of admission criteria, but critics contend that assuming that noncognitive skills such as kindness, dedication, and altruism are possessed at greater rates by URMs is improbable and being used as a pretext to admit them over whites in lieu of favoritism based on race and ethnicity. Countering this, affirmative action proponents state that diversity is desirable, and we need to level the playing field.

What follows from all of this? The bottom line is that, I believe, there are incredible opportunities today for minority applicants, from financial aid to enrichment programs, many of which occur during the summer. Most of the U.S. medical schools offer them and they target high school students, college students interested in entering the health professions who need to enhance their basic study skills or gain exposure to a particular field of interest, and graduate students. They run, on the average, six to ten weeks. Many are stipended and most include room and board and a travel allowance. The AAMC's *Minority Opportunities in U.S. Medical Schools* includes a comprehensive list of summer enrichment programs and AAMC also runs its own excellent summer program, the Minority Medical Education Program (MMEP) at various med school sites around the country. You can access information about MMEP at http://www.aamc.org/meded/minority/mmep/start.htm.

As for financial aid, URMs have all the resources available to any applicant with financial need, including loans made directly from the medical school, federal funds, and low-interest bank loans. Additionally, National Medical Fellowships provide grants-in-aid to minority group students to reduce the amount of their loan indebtedness. Every medical school has a contact person or office for minority affairs to assist applicants with financial hardship. The AAMC guidebook provides a comprehensive listing of these.

An engaging chart I came across lists undergraduate programs during 1997–98 with the most underrepresented minority students accepted to medical schools. Although the relative percentages of premeds admitted was not given, it did make for interesting reading:

Xavier	70	Michigan	33
UCLA	42	Morehouse	30
Duke	42	Texas Austin	30
Howard	39	Berkeley	29
Spelman	35	Illinois-Urbana	28
Harvard	33	San Diego	28
Stanford	33		

Staying In Can Be Harder Than Getting In

It would be unfair to minority group members who read this book not to present a complete picture of the situation. Although it may now be relatively easier than in the past for minority students to get into medical school, graduating is more difficult than for white students. An article in a 1993 issue of *The New Physician* reported that, according to AMA figures, in 1985 the retention rate of first-year underrepresented minority medical students was 91 percent compared to the 97 percent rate for all other students. African-Americans and Native-Americans dropped out at a rate of 11 percent, Mexican-Americans at a rate of 5 percent and mainland Puerto Ricans at 8 percent. The overall attrition rate for all medical school students was under 3 percent. [5] According to a 1998 AAMC report "Questions and

Answers on Affirmative Action in Medical Education," by the end of 1997, 87 percent of 1990 underrepresented minority matriculants had graduated from medical school compared to 95 percent of whites and 94 percent of Asians.

The New Physician article states that "medical schools are learning that it takes far more than brains to become a doctor, and this is doubly true for minorities. Students of color must hurdle dozens of obstacles in medical school—many of which are common to all students, but others of which are unique to minorities." Minority students often must deal with a variety of cultural conflicts that white students rarely encounter. Values and beliefs may be contrary to what is expected in medical training, particularly for Native-Americans. For example, Navajos believe that touching a dead body is taboo. Also, the extremely competitive atmosphere runs counter to the idea of collectivism inherent in many Native-American tribes. For Native-American medical students who grew up in isolated reservations, living far away from family and familiar cultural surroundings can be a difficult challenge on top of an already stressful medical curriculum. Many minority students are also the first in their families to finish high school and attend college, let alone professional school. There is the added pressure of meeting the expectations of their families, succeeding, and overcoming stereotypes.

Unlike many of their white counterparts, many underrepresented students have never known a physician of color. Few receive encouragement to pursue their dreams of becoming a doctor. In fact, many receive just the opposite—the message that they should not consider higher education. Once in medical school, there are few faculty role models. According to the AAMC *Minority Student Opportunities* handbook, in 1997 only 19 percent of medical school faculty members were nonwhite, and only 4 percent were underrepresented minorities. (This includes the faculties of historically black medical schools.) In 1997–98, the AMA reported that only 2,325 of first-year residents were black or hispanic, compared to 12,109 white residents. *The New Physician* article also states that "the dearth of role models among faculty and residents is one of the most frequently cited causes of attrition of minority medical students . . . so critical, in fact, that the U.S. Public Health Service has awarded the National Medical Association a contract to establish a national minority mentor network to match physicians of color with students in need of support and encouragement." Mentoring can also help with important career decisions. This same article also cited a recent Robert Wood Johnson Foundation study that suggested that minority medical students do not receive as much encouragement as white students to pursue careers in academic medicine and research. They are more often steered toward primary care and enter those specialties at a higher rate than nonminorities.

Academic preparation is another major factor in minority drop-out rates. According to *The New Physician* article, in 1991 22 percent of minority students who interrupted their education did so for academic reasons, compared to 3 percent of nonminorities. Some minority students need to strengthen academic skills. To address this issue, many schools offer prematriculation programs to help students improve necessary skills before the first year begins. Some offer flexible curricula and five-year plans for underrepresented minorities and other disadvantaged students who may be experiencing difficulties. Because retention is also tied to performance on board exams, many schools also provide programs to prepare students for boards. Part I of the national boards, covering basic sciences, is regarded as the tougher of the two parts and is required by some schools before students can move on to the third year. This exam can be especially challenging for students who speak English as their second language.

Another major factor for minority students is the rising cost of attending medical school. The average debt level of minority medical students is higher than for nonminorities. However, according to AAMC figures reported in *The New Physician,* few minority students indicate financial problems as a reason for leaving medical school. Some educators believe that it is more of a problem than students report and that minority students experience financial burdens more often than nonminorities. They may more often be single parents, older students with more extensive obligations, or caretakers in the family.

To briefly recapitulate: As long as their representation in medical schools is disproportionate to their percentage of the total population, qualified URMs should consider themselves prime applicants. As their premedical preparation improves, so does their medical school performance, and fewer are failing to complete the curriculum and become MDs. Financial aid remains available for all, in the form of loans and scholarships, and as more African-Americans, Native-Americans, Mexican-Americans, and Puerto Ricans matriculate, their feelings of isolation and alienation are reduced. Medical schools are leaning over backward not only to accept them but also to see to it that they graduate. The attitude no longer seems to be "We accepted you, now show us how good you are," but "We accepted you because we want you to become physicians. We will help you because we have an investment in your future."

Women

Women are applying to and entering medical school in greater numbers than ever before. At some medical schools, half or more of the entering classes are women. However, in the practice of medicine, women are still underrepresented—in some specialties more than others. (About 20 percent of U.S. physicians are women, up from only 8 percent in 1970.) [2] Thus, admissions committees continue to seek a gender balance in their entering classes. As more and more women have entered medicine, medical schools and the profession have learned to work with them on issues specific to gender, such as family planning. In the past, women medical students had a higher attrition rate than men, and there was some concern about how a woman would use her medical education. Would she soon leave the profession to have and raise children? Today, most women physicians take a short leave of absence from their practice for childbirth and new infant care as any working woman would do. There is also some indication that current health care reform trends, i.e., more physicians in salaried positions in group or HMO settings, allow women even more flexibility. However, a few admissions committee members seem to be still living in the past, and women may still encounter some interview questions about their plans and how they fit with medical education and practice.

"Woman has so apparent a function in certain medical specialties and seemingly so assured a place in general medicine under some obvious limitations that the struggle for wider educational opportunities for the sex was predestined to an early success in medicine." That was written by Abraham Flexner in the famous *Flexner Report* of 1910. However, although women were freely admitted to medical college in those days, only a small percentage of those who matriculated eventually graduated.

Flexner's conclusion was that "as the opportunities of women have increased, not decreased . . . their enrollment should have augmented if there is any strong demand for women physicians or any strong ungratified desire on the part of women to enter the profession, one or the other of these conditions is lacking—perhaps both."

Had Mr. Flexner interviewed some of those women, he might have discovered other reasons why only 15 percent to 20 percent of the matriculants graduated from medical school in 1909–10. Family commitments, social pressures, and economics were doubtless on the list of reasons a woman had for leaving medical school before graduation. These pressures are still effective, but today most women who enter medical school not only graduate but also outperform the men.

Some (or a few) women called to a medical school for an interview are still asked how they plan to mix a marriage and a career (see The Interview, page 66). The committee members will make the tacit assumption that if the woman is not now married, she eventually will be. However, they do not hold firmly to the idea that marriage and a career are incompatible for a woman, so there's no reason to say you're going to be a missionary doctor when you really do hope to marry and raise a family.

AAMC statistics reported in the *2000–01 Medical School Admissions Requirements* show that the percentage of women enrolled in medical school is increasing every year. In competition for the available places, the 1998–99 applicant pool included 17,787 women, 43.2 percent of whom were accepted. Women accounted for 43.4 percent of the applicant pool for that year and 44.3 percent of new first-year entrants. Much of this increase in women enrollees has been among minority group students. [2]

The number and the percentage of women in residency programs have also been increasing steadily. As recently as 1977, one third of all specialties had no female residents. Today, women are represented in all specialty and subspecialty areas. Most women physicians are concentrated in three specialties: internal medicine, pediatrics, and family practice. Many are also in OB/GYN and psychiatry. Very few women go into the surgical fields, and discrimination still seems to exist in some of those areas. [6]

Special Interest Groups

Many people still believe that there are special interest groups influential in getting students into a medical school. Thus alumni associations take on an undue importance, as does the private individual who makes a substantial contribution to the medical school library. Rarely does it happen any more that anyone gets into a medical school simply because a close relative went there and, contrary to the mythology, nobody buys his or her way into a medical school today. It just isn't done. There is that occasional student who, by directive of the dean, must be admitted, but this is by no means a common occurrence. Indeed, sons and daughters of faculty members gain admission no more easily than anyone else. Given personal idiosyncrasies and individual preferences, it may safely be said that medical school admissions committees are about as democratic a group as you will find anywhere.

Making Application—the AMCAS

Filling out application forms can be tedious work, not to mention complex, costly, and likely to produce considerable anxiety. To make things somewhat easier the AAMC devised the American Medical College Application Service (AMCAS), a centralized process by which the student fills out only one application for admission, furnishes only one set of transcripts, and applies to as many of the participating medical schools as desired. The medical school then notifies the applicant of further steps necessary to complete the application at each particular school. The service's big advantage to the applicant is that it saves time and paperwork. It serves the medical schools by transmitting only completed application forms standardized by computer and by providing statistical analyses. The student must still pay each school's application fee, plus an AMCAS service fee, which is determined by the number of applications sent out. One-hundred-thirteen medical schools participate in AMCAS. For those that are not members, you must request their individual application materials directly from the school's admissions office.

You may obtain the AMCAS application packet or disk from the AAMC or from the premed adviser at your institution. You must use the form designated for the specific year of your projected medical school entrance. Each year the application form is updated, so make sure you have the correct one. In 1996, the AAMC went electronic, and you can now complete the entire application form on disk and mail it in to the AMCAS office. The new AMCAS-E application (available only for IBM Windows) is downloadable from the AAMC Web site (www.aamc.org), or you can obtain diskettes from your premed advisor or directly from AMCAS. The paper version is still available, but it is much easier and more efficient to complete the electronic application. For the entering class of 2002, the application will be a Web-based application that will allow you to submit it electronically.

AMCAS begins receiving completed applications on June 1. It is important to file your application early. Most admissions committees function on a rolling basis, which means they do not wait for their deadlines to begin considering applicants and inviting them for interviews. Even if you are taking the August MCAT, it is still wise to file your AMCAS application early in the summer. It takes at least two to three weeks for AMCAS to process your application and distribute it to the schools and more time for the schools to respond to you with their request for secondary material. Many schools will invite you to complete your application even before they see your MCAT scores. Do everything as early as possible to expedite the completion of your application materials. Take the time, however, to complete the application as carefully and professionally as possible. You are presenting yourself as a candidate for professional school. Attention to detail is important. Make sure that you proofread everything for accuracy, correct all typographical errors, and keep a copy of the disk for your records. Then, submit your application with the appropriate service fees directly to AMCAS.

AMCAS also requires you to have official transcripts sent directly to them from all the colleges you've attended. Acknowledgment of the receipt of your application will be sent to you by e-mail if you have provided an address. Otherwise you need to call the AMCAS Voice Response System to verify receipt. You will receive regular Transcript Status reports indicating transcripts received, but it is wise not to wait for these. Check the status of your application using your AMCAS ID number and PIN on the AMCAS Applicant Status Web site (www.aamc.org/stuapps). After your application has been processed, you will receive a Transmittal Notification, which is a copy of the statistical summary of your academic record and a confirmation of the list of schools that will receive the application. Carefully review this summary and make sure everything is correct.

Writing the Personal Statement

The AMCAS form requires much objective information. Needless to say, you should fill out these parts accurately, because a mistake here will delay the processing and forwarding of your application for at least several weeks. If you omit information or make a major mistake, your form will be returned to you for correction. The form asks for a complete listing of all of your coursework in chronological order and biographical information including a list of academic honors, extracurricular activities, volunteer experience, community service, and employment during college years. Be thorough here and as descriptive as possible given the limited space provided—this is your resume.

The form also has a page for personal comments to provide personal information that is not included in the other part of the application. Most medical schools place a lot of weight on this section. If there is anything about you that makes you an extraordinary or unusual applicant, it should be mentioned here. Students, I have noticed, tend to minimize their nonacademic achievements. The fact that you may have played in a symphony orchestra, were a collegiate athlete, or held a political office is relevant and worth stating. So is your involvement in school clubs and organizations, particularly if you were involved in leadership activities. Work and volunteer experience is also important, especially if it was in a health field.

A friend of mine was once employed as a hospital orderly, but neglected to say so on his medical school applications. He thought that all premeds had done some hospital work and that being a mere orderly (rather than a research assistant) was not worth mentioning. Nowadays, most premedical students have some hospital or other health care experience before going to medical school. Even if you were an ambulance driver, aide, or simply a volunteer, make certain you note it. Far from looking demeaning, it will show the admissions committee that you had the initiative to work in a medical environment before making a final decision on a medical career. For some of you, it might even have been the impetus to choose medicine as your vocation—if so, say so. Also, a person who has worked in a hospital setting has a much easier time answering the perennial question asked at the personal interviews: "Why do you want to become a physician?"

Having done hospital work is clearly advantageous. More than anything else, it helps you make up your own mind about choosing medicine. Other service-oriented work is just as important, for it shows your interest in and compassion for other people. Have you worked as a counselor in a camp for emotionally disturbed children, cardiacs, or diabetics? Were you an adviser in government-supported projects like Head Start or Upward Bound? Did you work in a day-care center or free clinic? Have you taught children or adults to do crafts? Did you do social work in a family center? Drug counseling? Tutoring? Take care of a sick grandmother? Say so!

Do not neglect to mention any science or medically related research that you have done, especially if it has been published and you have been listed as an author. Most medical school admissions officers are basic scientists and would like nothing better than to discuss an applicant's research during an interview. A successful strategy would be to send a reprint of your article to all medical schools to which you apply and request that they append it to your application. Very few premedical students have been published, so your article will get you noticed.

What Makes You Different?

Medical schools are also impressed by work that, although not dealing directly with other people, involved the completion of a task. Thus, editing your school newspaper or literary magazine, researching, writing, and publishing a paper, or being a fine artist are all relevant to your application. Indeed, anything about you that makes you different from most everyone else is precisely what *is* relevant. If you are a top basketball star, a golfer, a tournament chess player, airplane pilot, or writer, you must say so. Medical schools look for diversity in their freshman class. Diversity can mean many different things: unusual major, where you are from, where you grew up (foreign country, rural background, moved around a lot), ethnic background, economic background, special accomplishments such as those mentioned earlier. It is not hard to find students with high GPAs and MCATs—they are plentiful. It is hard to find students who bring unusual backgrounds to the study of medicine.

Besides the AMCAS personal statement, many medical schools also require additional essays. Some ask that you write about why you want to become a doctor or other specific topics, whereas others let you do with the space as you wish. In all cases, the page should be used and under no circumstances should it be returned blank. If you are coming to medicine late in your college career or after you have been out of school for a while, then you should offer some explanation. If you are from an economically disadvantaged background, are the first person in your family to attend college, or have overcome some difficult personal obstacles, you might want to talk about how this has influenced your life experience and the achievement of your educational goals. Admissions committees always want to know when and how you have decided to study medicine. You can use this space to tell them.

Dr. Woodrow W. Morris, associate dean of the University of Iowa College of Medicine, made these comments about the personal statement page on application forms quite some time ago in an issue of *The Advisor*. His comments are still applicable today.

"The way in which applicants use this blank space has already proved useful to admissions committees in the realm of affording them a little insight into the personality make-up of the writer. And some of the ways the space has been used have been wonderful to behold. Among these are: straightforward appeals for admission, autobiographical sketches, philosophical

Anything about you that makes you different from most everyone else is precisely what is relevant.

dissertations on everything from the state of mankind...to the essential qualities of the complete physician. Other uses have included doggerel verse such as the student who apparently wanted to impress the reader with his knowledge of anatomy by writing:

> The cow is of the bovine ilk,
> One end is moo,
> The other milk.

Still others have filled the space with more ambitious creative poetry, again on the various kinds of topics already listed. Perhaps the most unusual of all have been those creations produced by applicants with an artistic flair— everything from chiaroscuro productions to caricatures. Finally, it should be noted that there are occasionally those brave souls who dare look at the blank space, and leave its pristine surface alone. (This, it should be observed, often leaves admissions committees in doubt as to whether the student did not wish to reveal his [*sic*] or herself, or whether the applicant simply had nothing to say.)

"It would be a service to both applicants and admissions committees if preprofessional advisers would encourage their students to make optimum use of the opportunity provided to them for expressing their individual thoughts and talents. Similarly, it would be helpful if future AMCAS materials provided both more space for 'personal comments' and more detailed instructions concerning the use of this important space."

The essay should be typewritten and grammatically correct, at the very least. A great deal of care should be taken in organizing it. A good idea is to write a rough draft, put it away and pull it out a few days later, and see how it looks to you. In the meantime you might think of things you wish to add or delete, or you might consider a different focus to give the essay. You might also want to show your essay to a few trusted individuals for some feedback—a professor, an adviser, a med student, or a physician. This little essay is far more important than any paper you will write in college, so judge the time you spend on it accordingly. Given the fact that many incoming medical students cannot even write a coherent paragraph, a well-written essay is downright impressive.

Recommendations

After MCAT scores and GPA, recommendations are another important criterion for admission to a medical school. Although they are usually not given quite as much weight as the interview in the final analysis, recommendations are read carefully for positive, lukewarm, and negative comments that provide further insight into you as a candidate. It is true that most recommendations are positive in their appraisal of a student, but some are more positive than others, and some are just negative enough to keep you out of medical school.

The usual way of obtaining recommendations is to use the services provided by the premedical adviser at your undergraduate institution. Although this is not required and you can use the separate forms provided by each medical school and have the letters sent directly from each recommender to the schools, it is usually easier and preferable to utilize the premed office if they offer some kind of recommendation system. Many colleges have premedical advisory committees that interview applicants and write composite letters. This letter is often attached to recommendations your professors have sent in, comments are excerpted, and your qualifications are summarized in the committee letter. Some premed offices offer only a recommendation service, whereby you solicit letters that are sent to the office; the letters are kept on file, and then the collection is sent to the med schools upon your request.

The professors you choose should have had you in a class and be able to assess your academic skills, laboratory competence, character, and potential for success as a medical student and physician. If you have some question about whether or not the professor feels able to provide a positive recommendation, it is not unreasonable to ask that beforehand.

The premedical student might also want to make the faculty member whose recommendation is being solicited aware of the kind of letters medical schools like to receive—namely letters that reflect real knowledge of the student and his or her past performance. Comments that help put the student's performance in perspective and make clear the letter writer's opportunity to evaluate the student are very helpful. A comment such as "He is one of the best premedical students I have had in his laboratory class for some time" or "She ranked in the upper third of this seminar for laboratory students" help the medical schools interpret the comments made on the student. If the class is one for majors or has special qualifications for enrollment, it should be noted. The basis for evaluation—e.g., two midterm examinations and a final test, or two three-hour laboratory sessions a week throughout the quarter—helps the medical school interpret the evaluation.

Medical school admissions committees tend to think in terms of rank categories. For example, if you received an honor, they would be delighted to know just how selective an honor it was. If you were "highly recommended" by the premedical committee, what percentage of all the premeds were similarly recommended? Being elected to Phi Beta Kappa as a physics major may be more significant than gaining the same honor as a humanities student if, at your institution, it is rare for physics students to be elected. Or if, for example, you have received a highly competitive summer research fellowship, you may ask your professor to comment on the conditions of the competition. If, on the other hand, you were the only applicant for the position, the less said the better.

The student should attempt to solicit a recommendation from the faculty member with the highest professorial rank, provided that person is well enough acquainted with you. An outstanding recommendation from a full professor is much more impressive than one from a laboratory instructor, and it carries far more weight.

Some students simply have had no personal contact with their teachers and have difficulty obtaining recommendations. Medical school admissions committees feel that it is the student's responsibility to get to know professors, especially the faculty adviser. The reason is that student-teacher contact is an integral part of college education, and the good student will make an effort to establish it—even if only for the sake of getting a recommendation. Medical schools do not frown on aggressive students!

Reference letters written by relatives, clergy, or friends are not only absurdly flattering, but there is rarely any pertinent character content. These recommendations often have nothing whatever to do with your ability to perform in medical school or to be a physician, plus they are considered to be very biased. Also avoid politicians and prominent business executives who are friends of the family, unless you have actually been employed or supervised by them in some way pertinent to your career goal. Admissions committees are most interested in hearing from people who evaluate you in an objective manner.

> **Recommendations from people outside the academic sphere—the family minister, priest, or rabbi, relatives, or friends—are usually uniformly laudatory and should be avoided.**

Certain types of recommendations, however, may be helpful. If, for instance, you have worked in a research lab during your summer vacations, you might ask the director to write a recommendation for you, especially if he or she was favorably impressed with your work. A letter from any physician, health care administrator, or community service supervisor under whom you have worked in a nonacademic setting can be of use. In fact, anyone who has known you in a professional context should be considered as a source of letters of recommendation. Letters may be mailed to your school's premedical advisory committee or sent directly to the medical schools to which you have applied.

The importance of the recommendation is not merely to reaffirm your academic competence; your grades and MCAT already attest to that. Rather, recommendations serve basically to assess your character and to explain any discrepancies that may exist on your academic record. If you are a more capable student than your transcript indicates, perhaps your recommendations will state this. If your grades dropped sharply one semester because you held a part-time job to earn enough money to continue in school, your recommendations should make this clear. On the other hand, if you argued incessantly for grade changes or are an antisocial dolt with no personality, your recommendations are likely to say so, and they will be a severe handicap to your getting into a medical school.

One issue connected with recommendations concerns the confidentiality of the evaluations. When you ask each recommender to write a letter or evaluation, you are given a choice on the form to waive your right to see what is written and keep it confidential or to reserve the right to review the letter and designate it nonconfidential. Your rights are protected under the Family Educational Rights and Privacy Act of 1974. Obviously, faculty members may write different letters if they know their letters are going to be read by the student than if these comments will remain confidential. Medical schools are aware of this; therefore, it is generally to your best advantage to have confidential letters. If the letters are not confidential, admissions committees may assume that the student pulled letters they did not want sent out. Some admissions committee directors might even make a phone call to the recommender(s) to get a more candid appraisal.

Choose your recommenders carefully, go for quality, not simply quantity, and complete your recommendation file or committee evaluation early. Courtesy demands that you allow a person at least two weeks to complete a recommendation. Help your recommenders. Make a personal contact (don't just leave the request in their mailbox), volunteer information about yourself and your decision to enter medicine, and perhaps provide a brief resume and/or copy of your transcript. When you ask recommenders for a letter, give them a deadline by which *you* need to have it in—not the schools' final deadlines. Remember, medical schools are looking for these materials *before,* not on, their deadlines. Lastly, check on the receipt of your recommendations—never just assume that they have been sent in.

The Interview

According to a survey of U.S. medical schools published in July 1991 in *Academic Medicine,* the interview was ranked the highest of five preadmission criteria listed, the others being MCAT, science GPA, nonscience GPA, and letters of recommendation. When medical schools were asked to list the purpose of the interview, most responded that it was used to assess the applicant's noncognitive skills, to predict success as a medical student, to clarify written application information, to assess the applicant's fit with the individual school's mission, and to determine potential psychological problems or immaturity. Another important purpose listed was as a recruitment tool to "sell" students on attending.[7]

For the most highly qualified candidate, it is true that the interview may be somewhat of a formality; however, particularly while applicant numbers remain high, it is an important selection criterion for *all* candidates. Besides allowing the medical schools to evaluate an applicant's characteristics, as mentioned earlier, the interview also affords the candidate an opportunity to take a look at the medical school and ask whatever questions are considered pertinent. In almost all cases, interviews are required for admission.

The survey published in *Academic Medicine* also indicated that an average of 42 percent of candidates who had *completed* applications were interviewed. The percentage of students interviewed varies at each medical school, and this percentage can indeed fluctuate depending on the number of applications received at a school in any given year. At state schools, residents always have a better chance of receiving an interview than nonresidents. You also might want to note that usually the figure quoted for number of applications received is on *all* (including incomplete) applications. Many students never complete their applications and are, thus, not even considered for an interview. Today, some schools who are receiving 10,000 or more total applications may interview well over 1,000 students for an entering class of 150. So even though you've made it past a major hurdle at the interview stage, you must still convince the committee of your qualifications and desire to attend their particular school of medicine. In other words, being granted an interview is great, but your job isn't over yet.

It was pointed out at one recent medical conference dealing with admissions interviewing that too many applicants fail to realize one very important factor—physicians, by nature of their training, are professional interviewers. Doctors are experts at fishing out information from people even if these people resist initial attempts at probing. Doctors are trained to interview patients and to look for signs that a patient is holding back information or harboring false ideas about his or her individual condition. If you are unsure of yourself or unconvincing as a future doctor, then the interviewing physician will easily spot this and take note.

Actually, the interview is a humanizing aspect of the medical school admissions process. This is your chance to sell the product you know best—yourself. The interview gives you the opportunity to see the particular school and to meet some faculty members and students. Take advantage of the situation and explore the school, ask questions, and try to form an impression of the school in your own mind. The interview is a mutual exchange; make it work for you.

The interviews are established to explore several different areas of the applicants' backgrounds. They test the motivation, preparation, commitment, and sincerity of the applicant. Believe it or not, these seemingly intangible factors can be easily assessed. Motivation we have discussed before in terms of summer work and understanding the role of the physician in our society. Preparation is another important aspect of any application. The interviewers will want to know if you took the proper science courses at your college or if you substituted "physics for poets" for the required course. How well did you perform on the MCAT and did you take it seriously enough to prepare for it in advance? What is your level of commitment to medicine as demonstrated by your knowledge of the different types of specialties and practices? Do you follow newspaper articles about medical issues or is your only desire in life an MD license plate? Lastly, is your sincere desire to become a physician rooted in your own desires and intellect or are you a last-minute convert to the medical mode? How seriously have you considered the alternative health careers and why did you choose medicine as opposed to social work?

Being able to answer these questions for yourself is the primary goal here. You have to be honest with yourself before you can be honest with your probing interviewer. Review the evolution of your career decision and your qualifications. You cannot anticipate every question you will be asked nor should you have stock or memorized answers ready for your interview, but it is helpful to put in some preparation. Be aware of some of the commonly asked questions and give those some thought. Practice answering open-ended questions, such as "Tell me about yourself," and "Describe your strengths and weaknesses." Some students participate in mock interviews, some practice with a friend or adviser, some just talk to the mirror. This exercise can help you collect your thoughts, build your self-confidence, and help you be a little more at ease at the real interview.

If you are lucky enough to be invited for a personal interview, you should certainly try to learn as much as possible about the school you are visiting. Don't go to the interview ignorant. By all means read the school brochure or catalogue beforehand. It is also a good idea to skim over your application to the school to refresh your strong points. Of course, this also means that you should copy everything before you mail your applications away. Think of the mail as a conspiracy against you, and you'll see how easy it is to learn to copy everything first.

Never, never be late for an interview. If your train or plane is late, then it is your responsibility to phone the school and explain the circumstances involved. This is a signal to the school of your maturity level and coolhead-edness. Try to arrive early for your interview if possible. This way you will have some time to look around and start to relax a little. If your interviewer is late, do not make any reference to the amount of time you had to wait. Believe me, he or she was probably doing something more important at the moment than you. Don't worry, you were not forgotten.

Dress appropriately. Although this should be obvious to any college senior, you wouldn't believe what some people look like for an interview. Men don't have to look like an advertisement for Brooks Brothers, but certainly wear a suit if you can. If money is a problem, then a quiet sport coat and unobtrusive tie are in order. Avoid jeans and sweaters—they may go over well in certain parts of the country but aren't certainly going to help your case. If you generally wear glasses, then wear them to the interview; don't sit there squinting at the interviewer for the sake of vanity. Interviewers are not interested in filling a class with Robert Redford types.

For women, the rules are similar: Slack suits, no matter how appealing, should NOT be worn to a formal medical school interview. A skirt suit, tailored skirt and blouse, or conservatively cut dress is far more appropriate. Avoid frilly things, mini skirts, excessive makeup, and fancy jewelry. You won't impress anyone with that kind of approach. Dress for the seriousness of the situation, and you should come out looking just fine.

Probably the most important recommendation anyone can make is the necessity for being completely honest at an interview. If you don't know something, don't be afraid to say so. This will demonstrate your own level of self-confidence and bearing. If you have certain questions about the school's program, then voice them at the appropriate time. Be honest about your financial needs and be prepared to discuss them intelligently if the situation arises. Be prepared to discuss any deficiencies in your record and try to avoid buttering up the interviewer at all costs. Do not second-guess the person questioning you and just try to be yourself. What you say and how you say it are what counts.

Definitely try to assert your positive aspects during the medical school interview. If you are particularly proud of a certain research project you completed, then say so in an effective manner without pontificating. Try to convey your own enthusiasm for a particular field to your interviewer. If you did poorly in one course because of a teacher conflict, then tactfully explain the situation without attacking the professor involved. Never berate your own school, as this is a sign of immaturity. Of course, it is also important to be a good listener as well as talker. Keep your eyes on the person talking to you and pay attention.

Use the English language to your advantage and avoid the pitfalls of everyday usage. The interview is no place for *like* and *you know*. You don't have to sound like a walking thesaurus, but do avoid hackneyed expressions. Put your best foot forward and think before you speak. It is better to pause with silence than to say *um* twenty times in one conversation. Absolutely avoid impressing the interviewer with a small amount of medical talk you may know. This could be disastrous if he or she follows up this line of conversation and your knowledge runs out after two sentences.

Try to relax and be yourself. I realize that for some individuals this will be the most difficult part of the interviewing process. If you really are excessively nervous, then state this fact. It may help to caution the interviewer to be a little more understanding about your anxiety. If you approach the interview with PMA (Positive Mental Attitude), then you will be much cooler and self-assured without being cocky. If you are the knee-trembling type, then try this simple, proven technique used by public speakers and politicians. When sitting facing the interviewer, simply curl your toes up as tight as you can, of course without grimacing or removing your shoes! The tension created by this simple maneuver will relax the rest of your body, and the shakes will miraculously disappear. Practice this trick if you want when you go out on a first date, and you'll see your nervousness vanish. Good public speakers may be a bundle of nerves inside, but outwardly they are the essence of cool. This little trick helps you to relax and makes you more confident.

Lastly, remember to write down the names of the people who interviewed you. This serves two functions. It is always a good idea to send a brief thank-you card to an interviewer, stating the following:

> Dear Dr. _____
>   Thank you for taking the time to discuss my application for the (Name of School) on (Date). I am looking forward to hearing from you soon.
>   Sincerely,

This will help to reinforce your name in the interviewer's mind and also demonstrate your level of breeding. Good manners are *always* good policy. Secondly, if you have occasion to write to the school for more information or for another reason, don't hesitate to include your interviewer's name in the note or, even better, write directly to the admissions committee, care of that particular individual.

Questions most frequently asked at the medical school interview include those about your family background, extracurricular activities, employment or volunteer experiences (particularly those that are health-care- and community-service-related), your ability to work well with people from diverse backgrounds, your hobbies, what you do to relax, and how you handle stress. Other types of questions deal mainly with standard yet very important issues about your possible fields of interest: why medicine, and your thoughts on current issues such as AIDS, abortion, euthanasia, and health-care reform. Remember, the interviewer wants to see how you reason and how you react under fire. He or she is not concerned with your own opinion per se. Total truthfulness is the best approach for the interview confrontation.

Some students, particularly women, may be faced with questions that they feel are inappropriate or possibly discriminatory. According to a recent American Medical Student Association (AMSA) survey, 33 percent of responding students reported having experienced questions relating to such issues as gender, age, and religion. Women are sometimes asked questions regarding marriage and family plans, and in most cases these questions are considered legal if they are asked of the same number of men. Although some of these questions may be illegal, many interviewers still ask them anyway, and you have to decide how you will answer them. Outright refusal to answer may be legitimate but may not be the approach to take in this situation. Another approach might be to politely and pleasantly question the perhaps inexperienced interviewer as to the relevance of this question to your medical school application, giving them a chance to back off. Most applicants, as uncomfortable as it may be, simply answer the question as succinctly as possible in order not to jeopardize their chances for admission.[4] Some schools offer you the opportunity to provide feedback or fill out a post-interview questionnaire, and if you feel strongly that you have been asked an inappropriate question, you may report it in that manner.

Under certain circumstances, an interview can assume even greater importance. Sometimes committee members are reluctant to accept a candidate because of special questions raised by his or her application. The only advice I can give in this case is to answer all questions at the interview and to be yourself. Remember that the ultimate question is always: "Who is this human being who will someday take care of other human beings?" Make the committee feel as good about you as you feel about yourself.

NOTES

[1] American Association of Medical Colleges. *FACTS: Applicants, Matriculants, Graduates 1989–95.*

[2] American Association of Medical Colleges. *Medical School Admissions Requirements 1997–98.* 47th ed.

[3] Begun, M. S. "Legal Considerations Related to Minority Group Recruitment and Admissions." *Journal of Medical Education* 48: 556–559.

[4] Ciesielski-Carlucci, C., G. Hern, and T. K. Kushner. "A Rite Gone Wrong." *The New Physician* (November 1995).

[5] Franklin, Karen. "To Have and to Hold." *The New Physician* (March 1993): 13–18.

[6] Iserson, Kenneth V. *Getting into a Residency: A Guide for Medical Students.* 3rd ed. Galen Press, 1993.

[7] Johnson, E. K., and J. C. Edwards. "Current Practices in Admission Interviews at U.S. Medical Schools." *Academic Medicine* Vol. 66, No. 7 (July 1991).

CHAPTER 5

How Medical School Admissions Committees Evaluate Applicants

Since I have never been a member of a medical school admissions committee, my information in this chapter is admittedly secondhand. It is true that some schools do have students serving on this committee, but, in most cases, admissions committee members are recruited from the medical school faculty to serve varying periods of time, usually from one to three or four years. The assistant or associate dean of student affairs is commonly a permanent member, whereas other members rotate, for the job is time consuming and most faculty members have other obligations.

An admissions committee may have as few as five or as many as twenty-five members, selected from all areas of the clinical and basic sciences. They will try to be fair, but, like most human beings, they see the ideal applicant as someone who is quite like themselves. Therefore the more members a committee has, the greater are your chances of finding an advocate.

Can the Applicant Make It?

Medical school admissions committees look for three things when they evaluate applicants. First they ask, can he or she get through the program? This is crucial. There are many who have the desire to become physicians, are congenial enough, and have perhaps the capacity for genuine concern and empathy for others. However, unless the committee feels that an applicant has made the commitment and can do the work, they will not recommend acceptance. Medical schools are acutely aware of the need for physicians and do not want to waste a precious place on an applicant who is not likely to complete the program. Second, admissions committee members are concerned about the character of the people who will one day practice on the public. They feel it is their job to select students who will not only become competent physicians but who are also reasonably stable and responsible. Finally, they ask whether it is fair to admit a specific applicant in preference to someone else, and while all members of admissions committees will admit to personal biases about what constitutes a desirable applicant, there is a universal attempt to be fair and impartial. To avoid pressure, members of the committee often remain anonymous.

With the enormous number of applicants to medical school each year, it is not possible for every member of an admissions committee to review each application. The number of applications may vary from 1,000 to as many as 10,000 for anywhere from 50 to 200 places. Your application may be reviewed by one or several members of the committee, but certainly not by all of them.

The usual procedure is as follows: The admissions committee probably won't even consider your folder until all the numerical information is at hand. In other words, it is best to have your transcripts and MCAT scores sent to the schools as early as possible. Once all the information is assembled, your folder is completed and ready for review.

Many schools differ in their review process. Unfortunately, due to budget and personal constraints, many public medical colleges have resorted to a computerized check-off system for folders. All the numbers are fed into a computer formula, and if a certain cut-off-point is reached, the applicant is invited for a personal interview. If the cutoff point of a specific GPA and MCAT combination is not attained, the applicant is summarily rejected.

At many other schools, the situation is not as grim. The folder is assembled, and the GPA may not even be computed. The applicant may be invited for an interview based on the essay or personal comments section of the application. This is a very time-consuming process but, in an important way, is a reflection of the caliber of the school and its faculty's commitment to the students. Several schools utilize a two-stage process where the applicant is asked to first send his or her grades and MCATs and then, if satisfactory, to complete the essay portion of the application. Happily, more schools are turning to their own students for help in this area. Medical students may even serve as voting members of the admissions committee and have rights equal to full faculty members.

To review, cumulative grade point averages as well as grades obtained in science courses, scores on the MCAT, descriptions of extracurricular activities, letters of recommendation from faculty members, and letters from past employers are evaluated. If the application is given a high rating by each of the people who did the screening, the applicant will most likely be invited for the prized personal interview. At least he or she will have cleared the first hurdle.

Determining the Motivation

After a candidate clears initial screening, his or her whole application is carefully evaluated. Special attention is given to five areas. First, the admissions committee ascertains what courses went into producing the student's GPA. Required and science-related courses are noted as well as those that show breadth of education. If there is a discrepancy between GPA and MCAT scores, a candidate's coursework is looked at for a possible explanation. Basically, however, the admissions committee is interested in what turned the applicant on in college. The same can be said for extracurricular activities. However, good grades and no extracurricular activities may be indicative of a person who used up all available energy supplies just to do well academically. Students who list many extracurricular activities and have also done well in class are thought likely to be capable medical students.

Just as extracurricular activities provide the admissions committee with insight into the applicant as a human being, the personal statement also lets the student seem more of an individual. The personal statement details the applicants motivation for seeking a medical career. The expressed attitude toward service takes a particularly high priority in the committee's evaluation. If you state a strong desire to work with people but your transcript shows you took only science courses and your summer job was as a lab assistant, the committee will sense a discrepancy and will begin to doubt your suitability as a medical student. The committee must feel that society is going to profit when you become a physician, that your motives are service-oriented rather than self-aggrandizing.

Committee members are adept at judging such an amorphous concept as motivation. Ideally, they look for a certain group of characteristics in a potential physician. In an Ethics of Health Care study performed by the National Academy of Sciences, the top seven personal attributes used in the selection process were as follows: 1) humanitarian beliefs and sincerity, 2) evidence of psychological maturity, 3) initiative, perseverance, and enthusiasm, 4) ability to communicate effectively, 5) interest and knowledge of medicine, 6) general intellectual interest and cultural development, and 7) imagination or creativity. Furthermore, in the same study, faculty members on the admissions committee of a particular school endorsed *alert, conscientious, enthusiastic,* and *honest* as the adjectives used to describe the best candidates they had seen or folders they had reviewed at one time.

According to Dr. Marvin Fogel of the Mount Sinai School of Medicine, "the verbal and action offerings apparent in your credentials will be the following: the undeniable fact of your desire for knowledge and its implementation against disease; your quite evident compassion for the ill and the solving of their problems; your positive ability to work with people even under vexing circumstances; your unequivocal understanding of the continuing, unceasing education process that the practicing physician must undergo; the inescapable sacrifice of outside interest time in order to devote yourself to the 'jealous lover,' which is the profession of medicine."

Lastly, another favorite guidepost or indicator of a candidate's motivation level, is the summer activities. Were the applicant's months away from school used to get a great tan, or did he or she attempt to learn more about the complex medical field? More on this appears in Summer Programs for the Premed (beginning on page **125**); be sure to see this information before planning your next beach-bum summer!

Family background is important in only two instances. The first is if the applicant's family is poor. This is usually taken as an indication of a highly motivated student who has had to fight all the way along the line. However, the committee may want to know why this candidate decided on medicine and what the choice means financially to the family. The second case is that of a physician's son or daughter who applies to medical school. The committee may become suspicious and want to be sure that the student's decision was not influenced by family pressure. The committee knows that attrition rates for the sons and daughters of MDs are higher than for the offspring of any other professional or nonprofessional group.

Letters of recommendation from undergraduate faculty members assume great importance in the committee's evaluation of an applicant. Not all recommendations are uniformly glowing. Some are merely perfunctory, while others may be ambiguous and need clarification and still others may be unfavorable. In these letters, admissions committees look for statements regarding the candidate's motivation or commitment to medicine, his or

It gives the interviewer a chance to see the candidate
as a human being.

her integrity, originality, and dependability. Any inconsistencies between GPA, personal statement, and faculty recommendations must be explained.

On the basis of the appraisal of the application, a student may be put into one of four categories:

1- Invited for interview—if satisfactory, accepted.

2- Invited for interview—use interview to clarify problems or inconsistencies in the record. Explain red flags. Give the student an opportunity to explain parts of the record that cause committee members some concern before acceptance is offered.

3- Hold category—hold until another group of applicants has been evaluated or until additional information is received, such as grades of courses in progress.

4- Rejected on the basis of the record.

If the candidate falls into either category one or two, he or she will be interviewed.

The interview itself serves two functions. It gives the interviewer a chance to see the candidate as an individual rather than as a collection of papers in a file somewhere. Second, it enables the interviewer to clarify items in the application if that is necessary.

Being invited for a personal interview is an accomplishment in itself. Once invited, you can be assured that your folder will get a very thorough going-over. Beware, however, that an interview appointment does not mean automatic acceptance. Several hurdles lie ahead.

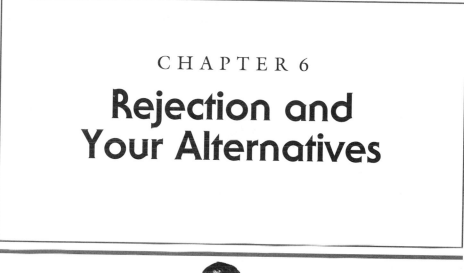

CHAPTER 6
Rejection and Your Alternatives

Rejection and Reapplication

A favorite question posed at the end of medical school interviews is, "What will you do if you don't get into a medical school?" This is not usually asked out of any genuine concern for your future but to assess the strength of your conviction to pursue medicine. Don't say, "There's always teaching biology or selling encyclopedias."

The person who really wants to become a doctor will outline specific plans to wait, perhaps do some more coursework, and reapply the next year. If again unsuccessful, a foreign medical school would be the next step. Or even more confidence can be shown and the student can say that all other alternatives are second rate, no serious consideration had ever been given to being anything other than a physician, and he or she feels perfectly capable of completing the medical school curriculum.

This is an appropriate answer to the examiner's question but is certainly not the most realistic way to think about the problem. In other countries, where medical school enrollment is open to all who have college degrees, the question of alternatives would be superfluous. Here, where demand for places in medical school far outstrips supply, the issue is crucial. To preserve your sanity, not to mention your livelihood, the issue of alternatives must be faced early in your premed career. To be sure, there are three possibilities for the rejected applicant: choose an alternative profession, reapply, or attend a foreign medical school. Although any combination of alternatives may be pursued simultaneously, it is necessary to plan for the first one well in advance of your graduation date.

To be able to select a suitable alternative career while still a premed, you must be very sure of your motives for wanting to enter medicine. This will also be an asset when, should you become a physician, it comes time to choose a field of specialization. Basically, you must have an accurate picture of *what* it is doctors actually do, and then ask yourself, "*Why* do I want to become a doctor?" The *what* problem can be taken care of by visiting medical centers and physicians' offices and observing what goes on. Work in a hospital for a summer. Read medical periodicals. Talk to physicians. Talk to patients. The *why* requires more insight, and you might avail yourself of help from a therapist in order to get it all straightened out.

Once you've got your head together, the question of alternative professions can be faced intelligently, should the need arise. If your motives for entering medicine are strictly materialistic, then for the amount of time invested, the business professions and dentistry yield much higher dividends. If the motivating force is status and prestige, law or politics is a suitable alternative. Anyone interested in basic medical research can pursue it almost as easily with a PhD as an MD. Altruistic motives will probably find gratification in the service professions—notably social work or psychology. The clinical aspects of medicine can be duplicated in nursing and in physician assistant programs as well as by training in the alternative health fields such as acupuncture, chiropractic, massage, and nutrition counseling.

Consider Reapplying

The issue of reapplication to medical school deserves some discussion. Clearly, it is more difficult to get into a medical school the second time around, although many students have entered by this route. In fact, of the 46,591 applicants in 1995–96, 14,415 were repeat applicants. These students most often have strong academic records and either applied to the wrong schools or sought admission in an especially competitive year. They are not marginal students. As a rule they are the students who are most surprised at being rejected. They fully expected to be admitted to a medical school, and their premedical advisers expected them to be as well. They are the students who can point to others with lesser credentials who were successful where they failed. For such students reapplication is feasible. The questions are when to reapply and what to do in the meantime.

Reapply to any school that has encouraged you to do so and to any school where you were interviewed or put on a waiting list. If you initially applied to the "wrong" schools, as previously defined, find out what the "right" schools are for you and apply to all of them. Reapply early. The question of what to do in the interim has various answers. A school may urge that you take additional courses or enter a special program with the incentive that if you do well enough they will accept you, reconsider you, or something in between these extremes. The choice is yours. I would only suggest that the more positive the incentive the more you should consider following the recommendation.

Many students with bachelor's degrees enter graduate school for a year as a stepping-stone to medical school. There is a growing feeling in medical schools, however, not to accept candidates in the process of obtaining a higher degree until after that degree has been earned. Thus, entering a graduate school might result in a two- to three-year delay before acceptance by a medical college. In addition, you will once again be under the same pressure to perform academically as you were when an undergraduate. I would not recommend this route to the nonscience major and would advise it only for science majors who feel the extra science will be useful to them in their medical field.

Actually, medical schools do not necessarily look favorably at students with either advanced or multiple degrees. Primarily, they wonder why the student could not find satisfaction in their first field of study. If the student has spent little or no time practicing in the area in which he or she was credentialed, then committee members may regard this as wasted education.

For example, a person licensed to practice nursing and radiology technology who does neither and then applies to medical school has deprived the health professions of two health-care workers. This person is usually viewed as a student with uncertain motivation instead of one who can achieve what he or she sets out to do.

Rejection by medical school requires a careful consideration of the applicant's weaknesses. Academic shortcomings can be remedied by repeating courses or taking extra ones as a special student. Low MCATs necessitate retaking that exam after extensive preparation. A student with a one-sided education stressing academics exclusively may find two years in the Peace Corps or performing other service-oriented jobs will prove an asset.

Reapplication to medical school is itself a testimonial to the applicant's persistence and desire to become a physician. Indeed, such students often graduate at the top of their medical school class. Before investing time in the reapplication process, an applicant must proceed from a realistic appraisal of their position. With competition for medical school places becoming stiffer each year, it would be self-defeating for someone with a weak record to stay in the race. An objective evaluation of your chances for success should be solicited from the premedical adviser or other counselor. It is important for your own mental health to know when to quit and do something else.

A past issue of the *Journal of Medical Education* offers an excellent study of unsuccessful applicants to medical schools. Using questionnaires, the authors compiled data on a group of ninety-eight rejected students. Information was solicited on the respondent's college major and accomplishments in the physical and biological sciences, MCAT scores, application patterns, the influence of various forces on the decision to enter medicine, the perceived reasons for rejection, and factors related to subsequent academic and career decisions. Of particular interest is the large percentage of rejected applicants who chose careers related to the health professions; i.e., dentist, podiatrist, optometrist, pharmacist, health educator, sanitary engineer, medical laboratory technician, medical and scientific writer, or pharmacologist.

In a similar study conducted at Johns Hopkins, some interesting results were obtained. Almost 2,000 rejected applicants were questioned about their future plans. As explained in the *National Premedical Newsletter:*

The majority of the 1,933 who responded to the questionnaire had reapplied to medical school. Of these, 27 percent had succeeded in entering either U.S. or foreign schools. Because women comprised only 12.8 percent of the total applicant group, the entire available number of unaccepted female applicants was contacted. Of all who responded—men and women—most tended to have higher MCAT scores and were more likely to gain admission when they reapplied. Of the unaccepted applicants then engaged in study in foreign schools (96), 90 percent intended to practice in the United States.

Among those who were rejected after a second try, many were still intending to reapply, a fact that would indicate that the original intention of becoming a doctor dies hard. It was found that the earlier in life the applicants had decided on a medical career, the less willing they were to give up, *especially if they had no contingency plans.*

Most of those reapplying who sought counsel from nonprofessional sources (family, friends) were urged to reapply and were more apt to do so. Such nonprofessional advisers were not apt to suggest alternatives to a medical career.

What of those who did not reapply? The study found that 53 percent of the men and 42 percent of the women were still pursuing studies in graduate or professional schools, both in health-related and nonhealth-related fields. Of those pursuing studies other than medicine but in health-related fields, 18 percent of the men were in dental school. The largest group of women were studying microbiology, bacteriology, or other medical sciences.

Most of the remaining group were employed, 55 percent of them in the health field—17 percent of the men and 31 percent of the women in clinical laboratory technology.

The doctors who conducted the survey were concerned that about half the unaccepted applicants were not attracted to alternative health careers when there is such a vital need for additional health manpower in specific geographic areas and in particular aspects of health care. If this situation is to be turned around, the doctors felt that knowledgeable counselors should be available at the undergraduate and high school levels (rather than for the applicant to rely on family and friends *after* being turned down).

They also raised questions as to whether or not medical schools are selecting appropriate numbers and types of applicants in view of current and future health-care needs. Do the paramedical health careers need to be upgraded in terms of status and income to attract the appropriate personnel? They concluded that the answers to such questions will help determine the best use of this country's qualified health-oriented labor force.

Several years ago I received a most interesting letter from a student who, by all established criteria, should have been admitted to medical school, but wasn't. His letter was the most articulate I have ever received, his questions the most serious, and his situation the most instructive. In his rejection there is a lesson for even the most outstanding applicant:

> *Dear Dr. Brown:*
>   *I'm one of your readers and have a special interest in the sixth chapter of your book* Getting into Medical School. *I've just gone through an agonizing six months of interviewing and waiting for replies from various medical schools across the country. Things have not gone well and I'm now seeking sound advice about rejection and reapplication. Unfortunately, I can't seem to find anyone I can really talk to about the matter and I thought perhaps it might be helpful to contact you.*
>   *My circumstances are a little unusual, I suppose, and that may be part of the problem, so I should fill you in on some background. I'm a graduate student in biochemistry at the University of*

Illinois at Champaign-Urbana and plan to finish my PhD in the next few months. I wish dearly to attend a good medical school and become a research physician; I feel I have the credentials to be admitted to some of the better medical schools in the country. Therefore, this past year I submitted applications to nine schools, most of them probably ranked in the top twenty in the United States, hoping to be admitted for the fall of 1984 (by which time my thesis will be complete). I got the applications in on time, not as early as I had hoped, but within the deadlines. I then received some promising news in December of last year: a letter from Washington University in St. Louis, asking for an interview and invit-ing me to apply for a Distinguished Student Scholarship, and a letter from Harvard asking for an interview. The Harvard interview came first and was held in Chicago. I felt it went well and the one interviewer, who was a member of the admissions committee, talked very encouragingly to me, though he did say he could not guarantee anything. The Washington University interviews went all right, but I was told that my application was submitted kind of late.

Next, I had interviews with representatives of the University of Miami. I felt I handled myself fairly well at the interviews but the last interviewer told me that, although I was a well-qualified applicant, I did not stand a chance of getting into a school like Harvard. He said it was obvious that I did not know how to "play the game," that the only way to get into a top school was through "contacts." His comments upset me very much, but I put them aside and hoped he was just trying to convince me that Miami was a choice I should consider (it is not among my first several choices) or that he just didn't know what he was talking about.

Disappointing news began to arrive after this point. Washington University did not accept me but placed me on a waiting list and said I might hear from them later. Yale and Cornell sent me rejections. Then two more crushing letters arrived: rejections from Harvard and Johns Hopkins. I was very discouraged by this point. Then I received news that Stanford wanted to interview me in Chicago. I went, not expecting much to come of it because it was so late in the year. Several weeks later I found out I was on their waiting list and would hear from them later if anything devel-oped. Nothing has developed.

I was accepted at Miami, but I had to turn the offer down. I knew I really did not want to go to Miami and, since the program is accelerated, it begins in mid-June and I felt I would not have completed my thesis by that time. Also, they required a nonre-fundable $1,000 deposit, which was a little steep for me.

I've read portions of your book, particularly the chapter on rejection and reapplication, and I've settled it in my own mind that I must reapply and try to get into these schools one more time. However, I think, as you pointed out, it is imperative that I understand where in the application process I fell short. Obviously, of the schools I applied to, only one accepted me and the majority outright rejected me. I've tried to discuss the matter with several people (my adviser, health professions counselors, etc.) and have even written letters to the admission directors, trying to nail down specific areas where I was not competitive in relation to the accepted candidates. Unfortunately, no one seems able or willing to give me helpful answers. The typical response I get is something like, "Such a large number of very fine applicants apply to these programs each year that it is simply not possible to accept everyone," which, of course, tells me absolutely nothing.

     What I need to know, and am hoping you can help me identify, are the factors in my application or background that hurt me the most. Obviously, since I was interviewed by some of these schools, they must have at least entertained the notion of accepting me. What factors did they look at then which caused them to say no or maybe instead of yes? I do not believe the interviews themselves were the problem; the feedback I got from the interviewers was largely positive. Also, my letters of recommendation were good and there is no indication that they presented any kind of problem. Do you think it could be my age? I realize I'm a bit older than the average applicant, but I was told that older candidates are not discriminated against so much any more and are even looked on more favorably by some schools. Was it because I did not have any "contacts" within the schools, someone who could put in a good word for me directly to admission committee members? Was the fact that I didn't have journal articles published yet considered significant (they're in preparation)? Or do medical school admissions committees simply frown on PhDs seeking a medical degree (I've heard some do)?

     It may seem a little odd that I'm trying to get advice from a stranger so far away, but I just can't seem to get substantive answers from anyone I've contacted. Perhaps it is unrealistic to hope you can provide some insights into my problems, but I felt I must try, and the invitation in the preface of your book to write caught my eye. I apologize for the length of the letter and hope I have not infringed too much on your time. I realize you cannot be absolutely conclusive about the matter. Yet, I would appreciate any ideas you might have about specific shortcomings in my application in relation to the schools to which I applied. I've included a copy of my AMCAS application to give you more information to go on. If it is more convenient for you to call than write

or if you have specific questions, please feel free to call collect.
Once again, thanks for your time.

Robert A. Mock

Mr. Mock included a copy of his AMCAS application along with his letter. It is impressive. His academic record is a compendium of A's and honors; his undergraduate GPA was 3.98 overall and his graduate GPA was 4. He had many extracurricular activities as well as interesting school-year and summer employments. His page for personal comments was extremely well written.

What went wrong? How could such an applicant be denied admission to medical school? Is there no justice in the universe? I was so intrigued that I took Mr. Mock up on his offer to call him rather than write. It proved to be well worth doing.

Over the phone, Mr. Mock came across as a sincere but unenthusiastic speaker. He spoke in flat unmodulated tones. It made me wonder if his interviewers might not have found him a bit too unemotional. But, to be fair, they might have interpreted this as being even-keeled or steadfast. On the whole, however, I feel that the interview is a place to strut your stuff. It's the time to make a lasting impression and state your case for why you should be admitted. Conveying your excitement is OK.

Actually, Mr. Mock is not so unusual an applicant. In point of fact, he is your run-of-the-mill extremely well-qualified candidate. There are hundreds like him with similar profiles—perpetual students with near perfect grade points, high test scores, obviously bright, well-motivated, and capable of becoming physicians. Many of them get admitted to medical school. Some do not.

Mr. Mock's mistake was in not realizing that the prestigious schools to which he had applied get many applications from students of his caliber. At less renowned schools, he would have been more of a standout and probably would have gained admission. Mr. Mock should have applied to more of these; although there is wide variance in this, nine is almost an insufficient number of applications when they are all to "top twenty" schools.

Mr. Mock's refusal to accept Miami's offer perplexed me and I asked him about it. Apparently, he would have had to start medical school before completing his PhD, and this he was unwilling to do. This was a mistake, I believe, since medical school places are so prized and Mr. Mock was not unusually competitive in his position (a near PhD without publications). Sometimes you can't have your cake and eat it: sacrifices must be made.

I encouraged Mr. Mock to pursue his ambition. I advised him to reapply to all schools that put him on their waiting list and to more of the less prestigious institutions. He was a strong candidate who simply applied to the wrong schools and may not have been aggressive enough at his interviews. His application timing may have been off, too. I fully expected to see him admitted the next year, after earning his PhD. His interviewer would then address him as Dr. Mock!

Attending a Foreign Medical School

For many rejected applicants, foreign medical schools offer an alternative to either giving up medicine or reapplying to U.S. medical schools. Currently, there are about 10,000 native U.S. citizens and an equal number of naturalized citizens at schools abroad. These students attend medical schools in some fifteen countries but are chiefly in Mexico, Grenada, Montserrat, and the Dominican Republic. Smaller groups are located in Belgium, France, Israel, Italy, and the Philippines. Medical schools in Canada and the British Isles rarely admit Americans. In general, foreign, nonproprietary schools using English as the language of instruction do not admit students from countries that have medical schools.

Americans who apply to foreign medical schools should know that most countries have to have at least one medical school that serves to educate native physicians. These schools are largely off limits to foreigners. Realistically, most foreign medical schools that accept Americans were not created to serve the local population; they were begun by entrepreneurs to offer medical degrees to all who could pay the price. In this respect they are similar to the proprietary type of medical school that flourished in this country in the nineteenth century. Organized for profit, these schools had low academic standards, poorly equipped laboratories, and undistinguished physicians holding the title of professor. The famous *Flexner Report* of 1910 effectively put these schools out of business, but they have resurfaced again, at least in spirit, during the last two decades. I am speaking particularly of the Caribbean Basin and Mexico, where the majority of all Americans studying abroad are enrolled.

I had the opportunity to visit the St. George's University School of Medicine in Grenada in 1995, where almost 1,500 Americans are enrolled. The school has two enrollments a year of 200 students, thus, far exceeding the number of matriculants to U.S. medical schools, which average 100 to 125

students per year. Surprisingly, I was told that they had eight applicants for every place and, although they had students from all over the world, over 85 percent were from the United States. This school, as well as other foreign medical schools popular among U.S. students, is geared to getting their students to pass the United States Medical Licensing Examination (USMLE) parts 1 and 2, which is the primary requirement of the Educational Council for Foreign Medical Graduates (ECFMG) for admission into graduate medical education (residency programs) in the United States and the gateway to obtain a full and unrestricted license to practice medicine here. However, average pass rates for these students is under 50 percent, perhaps as much because they are not good test takers (which is why they were rejected from U.S. medical schools) as because of the quality of the training. But this can be uneven from school to school, and the good news is that the exam may be taken as many times as necessary to pass.

The laboratories at St. George's were well equipped and the library had a plethora of current journals. The lecture halls were spacious and comfortable and the professors seemed primarily dedicated to teaching. There were services for students who were having academic or psychological difficulty. Housing was available. And, most important, classes and textbooks were in English. It's hard enough studying medicine in a foreign country without having to also deal with a language barrier, although most foreign medical schools do conduct their classes in the language native to their country. Unless proficient in a foreign language, Americans would be best advised to first consider those schools that cater to them. These would include most of the Caribbean and Mexican schools.

Even with classes in English, the American medical student studying abroad faces other obstacles. Financially, they are on student visas and rarely permitted to work for money. Therefore, they must be adequately financed

The language barrier is the main problem.

before they go, either from savings or loans. Medical education abroad is not cheap. In fact, tuition and living expenses rival that of onshore schools. Additionally, travel and incidental expenses would probably make the cost of foreign medical study in excess of that here. Psychologically, the U.S. student is at a clear disadvantage in a foreign country. Having been rejected from U.S. schools and not having gone abroad as a first choice, he or she may be embittered. Also, culture shock may be pronounced; living in a strange country is often an alienating experience even when there are other North Americans around, for as soon as you get off campus, you are in another world. The American student abroad may initially experience overwhelming loneliness and frustration.

Although the basic medical sciences may be taught up to a minimal standard, students need to be concerned about the adequacy of the clinical years. The third and fourth years of medical school give students exposure to patients and their illnesses. Unless clerkships give students sufficient clinical experience they may be at a disadvantage when taking part 2 of the USMLE. The smaller foreign schools have attempted to deal with this by sending their students to other countries. Grenada, for example, has clerkships in the United States and the United Kingdom, and none on that small island.

Perhaps the biggest problem studying medicine abroad is the uncertainty about what will happen afterward. For years, international medical school graduates (IMG), both U.S. citizens and not, were vital to the operation of many of our hospitals, particularly in the Northeast and Midwest. This was because there are many more residency positions than U.S. graduates to fill them. This shortage worked to the advantage of the IMG. In 1988, 3,500 IMGs entered the first postgraduate residency year—20 percent of the total of U.S. grads. By 1994 their participation had increased to 7,500. The total number of IMGs in residency programs during the same time period increased from 15.3 percent to 23.3 percent of all residents in allopathic programs. Two points of interest: this growth of IMG participation occurred without any agreed-upon targets for expansion of the U.S. physician workforce, and most of these IMGs are not native U.S. citizens. The absolute number of U.S. citizens studying abroad has decreased since 1988.

The times they are a-changing. There isn't one major medical think tank or blue-ribbon commission that does not foresee a doctor surplus sometime after the year 2000. Experts disagree as to dates, but trends predict too many physicians per capita in the near future. There are already too many physicians in some medical specialties in some locations. This will ultimately lead to too many physicians in all specialties in all locations unless the trend is checked. How do we turn down the tap and limit the flow of medical school graduates?

Already some U.S. medical schools are reducing their class sizes. No new medical schools are being built in this country. But short of closing schools now existent, little can be done nationally to reduce physician output. And, indeed, what's the point in chiseling down a few U.S. grads when schools like St. George's are turning out 400 graduates a year and the University at Guadalajara probably a similar number? These schools are unabashedly operating for profit, have capable students, and are geared toward getting their students to pass the USMLE. Most of them do and, upon graduation, are eligible to apply for those residencies that U.S. graduates find undesirable. They go to places that depend on resident physician labor, generally in the inner cities and rural areas. Places that, as a tourist, you wouldn't want to visit and as a physician you wouldn't want to train. And there's the dilemma.

If these hospitals—in cities like Newark, Detroit, Kalamazoo, Macon, Brooklyn, Hartford, and dozens of other places that even Humbert Humbert never thought to visit—don't get doctors, then they will be forced to close, thereby denying medical care to the indigent populations that they serve. Residency physicians are a cheap source of medical labor and traditionally form the house staff of teaching hospitals. Mass General and the Mayo Clinic need not worry; their positions will always fill. But Coney Island Hospital and St. Mary's in Waterbury may not be able to run without the international medical graduate. These are the kind of places that foreign graduates go to train, and the training is actually quite good because the hospitals are usually understaffed and the residents usually run them. Of course, studies show that the IMGs don't stay where they trained but seek out the same desirable locations as the U.S. graduates, leaving the inner cities still relatively deprived of physicians, and the suburbs surfeited.

I believe that we will see the closing of more and more of these hospitals as managed care makes inroads into their neighborhoods. Inpatient medicine will be handled in fewer facilities as ambulatory care centers abound. More efficient management will allow higher salaries for house staff, and they will be recruited from among the already trained specialists and generalists who are the junior members of health maintenance organizations. Furthermore, the outcry from organized medicine to shut the gates to the

IMG will be hard to oppose once there is little demand for their services and more American-trained doctors find themselves under- and unemployed. I predict that in five to ten years, the well will run dry for the foreign medical school graduate. Already there is proposed legislation that would limit the number of residency slots to 110 percent of U.S. medical school graduates. That would effectively put most of the foreign medical schools that cater to Americans out of business.

But in the meantime, foreign study remains a viable option. Another alternative, seldom mentioned, is for students to remain abroad and to practice medicine in the foreign countries in which they become licensed physicians. I have met retired people in their fifties and sixties who were studying medicine abroad with expressly that purpose in mind. They had comfortable retirement incomes and were fulfilling lifelong desires to become physicians. Furthermore, many of them brought to their study and practice of medicine technical expertise of great value in their countries of emigration. They knew that they were of an age when finding positions back home would be impossible so they learned a new language and offered their skills where they were most needed. A while ago, I received a letter from a senior citizen studying medicine in Guadalajara!

Dear Dr. Brown:

I do definitely recall reading your book and writing to you several years ago. I tried all over Europe, especially Italy and Spain, and also happened to write to the Universidad Autónoma de Guadalajara. I got accepted here at UAG and am now in my second semester. It's been real exciting for me to begin a new profession—I think I told you I was 62 years old and a retired chemical engineer. I have to be very thankful to UAG for giving me this chance. There are about 500–600 other students here from the U.S. who are also thankful for their chance to pursue medicine.

As luck would have it, UAG turns out to be a very good medical school. They have started a program for Americans in which all the basic sciences are taught in English. The program is aimed at imitating American med schools. All our tests contain national-board-type questions and the depth of each science course is modeled after American medical colleges. Actually, UAG was forced into restructuring their curricula to compete with the Caribbean schools.

My wife, who was a biology major and a licensed laboratory technician in Illinois, decided to enter medical school with me. After graduation we hope to return to the U.S. to do family

*practice residencies wherever they might be available. We
would love to return to California, since we are both natives, but
that looks extremely impossible at the moment, as I'm sure you
know. However, I am confident we will find an area of the U.S.
where doctors are needed. Louisiana sent a representative
down here to recruit good students for residencies in pediatrics
and family practice because of physician shortages in their
poorer areas. We have read of great health care needs among
migrant workers in Utah. Also, we would not be unhappy
remaining in Mexico since service is our ultimate goal.*

Jim Watts

I know of no evidence that it is easier to get into an American medical
school after a year in a foreign one compared to taking an advanced degree,
more coursework, or simply reapplying. To recapitulate briefly: Going to a
foreign medical school is better than going to none at all, if you are determined to become an MD. Graduate school should not be entered unless
you sincerely want to earn a degree in one of the basic sciences. Extra
coursework should be followed to correct obvious weaknesses. Work in
medical areas is a definite plus. Simply reapplying the next year is a prerog-
ative for the strongest applicants who, I would suggest, take the year for
personal growth.

CHAPTER 7

Amazing Success Stories

several years ago I had a novel idea for another book for premeds: a compilation of incredible stories from students with unusual backgrounds who had managed to get accepted into medical school despite overwhelming odds. I wasn't thinking merely of the nonscience-majoring applicant, nor strictly of the minority or older student. Nor did I have in mind women (who were then a minority in most medical school classes), nor Doogie Howser types. I was thinking of *extreme* types: the grandmother who got into medical school, students without college degrees who got in, students who talked their way in; felons, deaf or mute students, amputees, impaired students, former alcoholics and drug abusers . . . All right, perhaps not *that* extreme. But I honestly did not know what to expect when I started running classified ads in the *Journal of the American Medical Association,* the *New England Journal of Medicine,* and *The New Physician.* The ads said simply: "Seeking unusual stories of how physicians got into medical school for forthcoming book." I also sent out similar requests to premedical advisers and medical school admissions directors.

The response was not overwhelming, but neither was it negligible; I received twenty or so letters of varying lengths from people who thought that they had unusual stories to tell. Many weren't, but some were *truly amazing.* I thought that my story was exceptional, but some of these people's were stranger than fiction. Unfortunately, I was not able to collect enough of them for a book, so I filed them away, awaiting a suitable opportunity to publish. This book's revision has provided me with that chance.

I have elected, at times, to change names, places, and dates to protect confidentiality, but have left the basic facts unaltered. If it's inspiration to continue pursuing your dream of medical school acceptance that you're looking for, then, pilgrim, your search has ended. These students beat the odds. Anyone who isn't heartened by their stories would probably do better to switch to a business or computer major. If you can top them, write to me; you will make it into the tenth edition.

Dear Dr. Brown:

I received your letter the other day. I am anxious to tell you my story hoping that it will be published. Perhaps other premeds might learn from some of the difficulties and mistakes that I encountered.

In order to understand my unusual circumstances, it is necessary to realize that I was a competitive figure skater. My attachment to the sport turned out to be both my demise and greatest asset in regards to my application to medical school.

I entered college in 1976 as a premed with a biomedical engineering major. I was a strong math/science student in high school and thought that I would have a stronger interest in the School of Engineering. My first quarter included the basic premed courses (calculus, chemistry, and biology) and I was still a competitive skater. This necessitated numerous hours at the rink for practice and also involved missing as much as two weeks of a nine-week quarter to attend competitions.

That quarter I won a bronze medal at the U.S. National Championships. Upon returning to school, I faced numerous midterms and unfortunately I either failed or did poorly on most of them. It was at that point that I had to decide whether to continue with school or to skate full time. I struggled with this decision and decided to dedicate myself to academics.

I continued in the School of Engineering for three years. Eventually I took six courses in calculus, numerous chemistry (general, organic, physical, and biochemistry) and upper-level biology/physiology courses. The quarter courseloads were rigorous because the majority of these were taken simultaneously and, as a result, my grade point average was mediocre. A crucial point came during the fall quarter of my junior year, in which I was taking biochemistry, mechanics, neurophysiology, and psychopathology. Additionally, I was working as an oral surgical assistant and teaching skating fifteen hours per week. The results of that quarter were disastrous. The courses proved too difficult to take simultaneously and I realized that I'd practically ruined all my chances of ever getting into medical school. My grade point average plummeted, and I was told point-blank by the premedical adviser, "Mr. Belmonte, you're never going to be a doctor." Those words will never be forgotten.

I subsequently switched to a major in biology. I rounded out my sciences with liberal arts courses and my grade point average improved steadily. I also got involved in student musical productions. I was in the school's premiere annual production, which involved many hours of rehearsals, yet I managed to keep up with my courses and two jobs. Unfortunately, I had an even bigger problem coming up—the MCAT. As luck would have it, the opening performance turned out to be the same day as the MCAT. I was excused from the afternoon performance, took the MCAT, and performed on stage that evening. It may have been exhilarating, but it was also unwise, since the results turned out average on the MCAT.

That summer I started applying to medical schools. I applied to nineteen of them. As I was filling out my AMCAS application, I sensed an impending doom. I was applying with a 2.73 grade point average with MCATs at or slightly below national means.

By senior year I was getting rejected by medical schools left and right. I knew that my academic credentials were not impressive, yet I was hoping that admissions committees would see past them. Even though my average was low, I had taken extremely difficult courses above and beyond the recognized standard. Many were graduate level in the sciences and math. Also in my favor were the experiences in the medical field. I had worked as an oral surgical assistant and even had one-to-one patient contact as a biofeedback therapist in a headache clinic with a prominent neurologist. I was hoping that these attributes would at least get me an interview, at which point I could prove to the committees that I had more potential than my numbers indicated. Eventually I did get an interview. However, after looking at my file, the interviewer bluntly stated that he didn't think I would get into their school. It really seemed hopeless.

I retook the MCAT, but my scores were basically unchanged. At this point, it was hard to keep everything in perspective. I continually agonized over skating. For the three years following my amateur retirement, my former competitors that I defeated in 1977 were gaining national prominence and eventually went on to win a silver medal in the 1984 Olympics. When graduation came around, I found myself holding a bachelor's degree and sixteen rejection letters. Worst of all, I gave up a chance at the 1980 or 1984 Olympics for a career in medicine. Unfortunately, neither of the two was going to come true.

I considered applying to foreign schools, even received applications from several of them, but decided it would be best to work for a year to help pull my shattered ego back together. I found a job in a cardiologist's office. I learned a tremendous amount there—the most important lesson being that I wanted to be the doctor, not work for one, as I had done so often in the past. I knew that I would eventually reapply to medical school, though I didn't know when, or how I was going to change my academic profile.

That year my life took a big change. A touring company of the Ice Capades was in town and holding auditions. I read about this in the local newspaper and auditioned on a whim. One month later I had a contract in my hand. I would join them in three months at the start of their new season. I joined as a member of the chorus and emerged three years later as one of their soloists. It was a chance to finish my unfulfilled skating career. Yet, in the back of my mind, I knew that I wanted to be a doctor, but was at a loss as to when I would try again. Three years later, when my contract came up for negotiation, I realized it was time once again to begin my quest for medical school.

It became apparent that the only way that anyone would remotely consider my application would be if something improved drastically. As I already had my degree, the most natural thing to improve would be my MCAT. Having been out of school for four years, the thought of studying for them was horrifying. Yet I spent three entire months, five days a week, taking a review course and becoming a very serious student. I studied seven hours a day after teaching skating in the morning. My scores improved tremendously, with my highest score in the 94th percentile.

I spent the year applying to several allopathic and three osteopathic schools. By December, I had two interviews—one at each type of school. Ironically, medical schools found my background as a skater very impressive and a definite asset. They realized very little as to how my skating hindered my previous application. Later that month, I was accepted at the osteopathic school and was placed on the alternate list at the allopathic medical school.

I was ecstatic, but yet still had sincere hopes of entering the allopathic school. Although I realized that the practice of osteopathy is much the same as "traditional" medicine, my heart was intent on becoming an MD and not a DO. I rationalized many months over this, realizing that at least I would be able to practice medicine in either case.

In July I was still on the alternate list and the time was rapidly approaching in which I'd have to matriculate at the osteopathic school. Eventually I matriculated and finally began my medical career. I was extremely insecure about being able to handle the academic load. I spent many hours studying the first week, being so paranoid after being out of school for such a long time. I made many close friends, yet only confided in a few of them that I was still on an alternate list elsewhere. On the day of our first biochemistry exam I was notified that I'd been accepted at my state medical school. I was torn by leaving my good friends and also faced the loss of $8,000 of my $13,000 tuition. I was back in Chicago the following day.

Unbelievably, the academics went relatively smoothly and I studied diligently. Even when the pressures and workload were intolerable, I would never take for granted the fact that I was finally in med school. I've done well enough to be in the top half of my class. This is ironic, as according to all other stats from AAMC I really should never have been admitted, much less survived the ordeal. As a matter of fact, I just finished with the basic sciences two days ago and will begin my clinical training tomorrow.

I feel that my story might be inspirational to many struggling premeds. I've faced adversity, but my perseverance was paramount in achieving my goal. Retrospectively, I was not honest with myself in college. I let many of my extracurricular activities detract from my priorities and failed to realistically assess my average performance by rationalizing that I had such tremendously difficult courseloads. Unfortunately, I learned how inconsequential my schedule really was. One must get past the numbers game before an admissions committee will consider motivation, potential, and past medical experiences. I would have been much better off taking standard courses, doing well, and maintaining a decent GPA. One needs to maintain this objectivity.

At times, I visit my undergraduate campus to study for my final exams, and I overhear many premeds speaking of the same concerns that I faced eight years previously. I will never forget my premed adviser telling me that I would never become a doctor. I proved him wrong.

Sincerely,
Ray Belmonte

Dear Dr. Brown:

If you are looking for strange stories, how about this one?

I graduated from high school and went to the University of Texas in Austin. I started out with advanced placement, having tested for placing out of seventeen hours of Spanish and three of chemistry.

As a long-haired, pinko, radical type, I never went to classes (or studied either, for that matter). I was also working as a paramedic starting my second year and as a research assistant in the department of zoology.

By the end of my second year or start of my third year, I was a full-pledged frat-rat (I must admit in all honesty that Animal House was very reminiscent of my fraternity days).

By now I was putting in even more hours working as a paramedic and less at anything connected with school.

During all this I was constantly taking off during weekends (almost every one during the summer and one or two per month during the rest of the year) to go to Native American Indian pow-wows (i.e., Indian dances).

I had started Indian dancing and craft work at age 13 and I must admit I am quite an expert in the field. In the middle of my fourth year in Austin, I was kicked out of school for having taken a Spanish achievement test for one of my fraternity brothers. At the time we did it, we thought it was rather funny. Unfortunately, the dean of students did not think so.

So I returned to Houston to work and think things over.

Well, I decided I really wanted to be a doctor above all things and registered for school at the University of Houston. Meanwhile, I was working in a pulmonary functions lab at the Methodist Hospital there. The University of Texas called me and told me they had decided to change my one-year suspension to a six-month one and I could come back, but I decided to stay.

When I arrived at U. of H. to speak to the premed adviser, he looked at my record—approximately 115 hours with a GPA of 2.05. He laughed and told me to beat it and I was totally wasting my time. I convinced him to approve my schedule and started school.

I took all upper-divisional science courses, taking six to ten hours a semester with a 3.65 GPA. During the same time I

—Became certified as a cardiopulmonary technician.

—Took over a research project from a pulmonary fellow. It eventually was presented at the ACCP meeting and will likely have a follow-up publication.

—Went to work at the University of Texas Medical School as a
research assistant.

—Did extensive work helping people out with various technical
problems in research projects and got my name on several
abstracts and presentations.

—Started (with my brother) a DJ business playing music at par-
ties. In three years it became so successful that, working
part-time at this, I was making almost as much as my salary
as a technician.

As the years passed my premed adviser laughed less and less.
Finally, with his help and the very invaluable help of several
friends on the faculty who were very supportive to me at work,
I was accepted and started medical school at the University of
Texas Medical School in Houston.

Now I'm doing a surgical residency that I started at age 30.
I don't make Indian powwows like I used to (or party like I used
to), but I'm still happy with myself and doubt I'd change anything I
ever did.

Sincerely,
Eddie LaRouche

Dear Dr. Brown:

My mother taught me and encouraged me to pursue any field of study that interested me. In junior high and high school, I found myself very involved in music and science. Both of my brothers were into science, one receiving a degree in physics and the other in mathematics. I, on the other hand, decided that my career would be in music. Specifically, I had decided to become a bassoonist. Bassoonists are a rare commodity for most orchestras and bands, so I had ample opportunity to pursue my musical interests. My mother, who had been a widow since I was seven years old, encouraged me in music. The support of my private music instructor also strengthened my desire. When it came time to enter college in 1977, I had chosen to attend the University of Southern California as a music performance major in bassoon.

My four years at USC were a tremendous musical experience. I was able to play in the USC Trojan Marching Band (as a tenor saxophonist) each year as well as perform in the school's highly regarded performing ensembles. As a senior, I competed in the Coleman National Chamber Music Competition with the USC Woodwind Quintet. We won second place in the competition and subsequently performed in the winners' concert the following day. I graduated from USC in 1981 and received the award of outstanding graduate in the wind and percussion area. A career in music appeared imminent.

However, instead of immediately beginning work or graduate school, I chose to serve a mission for the Church of Jesus Christ of Latter-day Saints (Mormon). I was called to serve a full-time proselytizing mission to France in September 1981. My mission helped me reevaluate my career and life goals. I began having doubts about becoming a professional musician. In addition, my mother was killed in a bicycle accident while I was in France. The sadness I felt at that time caused me to reflect on a career in dealing with the health of others. Still, medicine had not yet really entered my mind.

I returned to the United States in the spring of 1983. I worked for several months in Los Angeles before entering graduate studies at Brigham Young University. Still unsure as to my future plans, I was pursuing a master's degree in music. Perhaps a career in academic music would be of interest to me. In April of 1984, after two semesters, I first approached the idea of medicine as a profession.

I am still uncertain as to how exactly I came to the decision to attempt getting into medical school. I do remember an incident that occurred at my fiancé's apartment. A couple of students were visiting her and her roommates while I was there. One of them mentioned that he had a married friend with children who had suddenly decided to go back to college and try to get into medical school. The fellow talking thought his friend was crazy. I, on the other hand, was motivated to find out what I needed to do to go to medical school.

This was a very radical idea for me. I was about as far away from a premedical student on the educational spectrum as one can be. Not only was I in music, but I had not even taken a science course as a college student. In high school, I had taken physics, chemistry, and calculus, but it stopped there. In addition, my GPA at USC was a none-too-impressive 2.95. My goal had been to come out of USC as a fine bassoonist, not an honors student. The fact that my graduate adviser and the professors in my specialty area would not be pleased with such a choice clouded the situation. I disregarded these complications for the moment and went to see the premedical counselor. I was not aware of how much my life would change starting with that important step.

I felt very inadequate as I sat at the desk of the premedical counselor and explained to him my desire to go to medical school. He listened intently as I explained to him that, even though I had woefully neglected my classes at USC, I felt I could do well in the required science studies. I believe he was intrigued by the opportunity to work with a musician. With restrained encouragement, he wrote out a schedule and timetable: between June 1984 and August 1985 I would complete the courses required for the MCAT. The list included such standards as inorganic and organic chemistry, noncalculus-based physics, and biology. He also recommended anatomy, genetics, and physiology. The goals were a September 1985 MCAT, a 3.5 (or better) GPA, and a fall 1986 acceptance to a medical school. He emphasized that a good MCAT score was a must. I was, in general, encouraged and excited about my chances.

I took two courses (inorganic chemistry and anatomy) during the summer term in 1984. At the end of August, I returned to my counselor's office and emphatically (and naively) told him that I would take the calculus-based physics course starting in the fall. He was less than encouraging and clearly doubtful of my calculus skills (as was I, though I didn't admit it!). Nevertheless, he told me which class to take and added that if I were able to do reasonably well in that specific course, he would be favorably impressed.

The next two semesters for me were very challenging. I took twelve credit hours of science classes each semester in addition to continuing work on my degree in music. I had decided to finish my degree, as that had been my original goal. This meant that I spent about twelve hours in rehearsals each week in addition to scheduled concerts. I also found it necessary to work between ten and fifteen hours each week. In addition to my schedule, my new wife and I were adjusting to the first year of married life. Despite the busy schedule, five-hour physics exams, and memorizing organic chemistry reactions, I really enjoyed myself during those two semesters. I had the feeling that the choice to pursue a medical career was the correct one.

The summer of 1985 was considerably less taxing. I was taking no music classes and was completing organic chemistry, taking physiology, and preparing for the MCAT. I also filled out my applications and sent them in near the beginning of July. I feel that the decision to get my applications in early was crucial. Despite not having my MCAT scores, most schools (I applied to nine) sent me supplementary applications. When my MCAT scores were available in early November, most schools then had a complete file for me. This kept me from being too far behind the applicants who had taken the April MCAT.

The application process was certainly not a simple task. Two of the schools I applied to did not accept the AMCAS (American Medical College Application Service) forms, so additional time was required to fill out their applications. In order to satisfy the requirements of my premedical committee and the medical schools, I solicited no less than six letters of recommendation. In addition, almost every school required a supplementary application. My decision to be very prompt and complete in completing and returning these items was, as I have mentioned, important to the success of my overall application.

In November of 1985, I received my MCAT scores. At that time, I evaluated my records to assess my competitiveness as an applicant. I had attained a 64 cumulative on the MCAT and my science GPA was 3.54. My overall GPA had crawled up to about 3.20 (including my undergraduate grades). Despite the latter statistic, I felt that I had a chance at several of the schools to which I had applied.

My first interview offer came from the University of Utah in December of 1985. As a Utah resident, Utah was the only public school to which I applied. Utah gave me two interviews during my visit, both of which I enjoyed very much. I was, as was to be expected, nervous. One interviewer went down my list of classes at USC and asked me about each of my low grades. I was also asked about such topics as euthanasia, my favorite composer, what books I had read recently, Einstein's theory of relativity, and trichinosis. Within two weeks, on Christmas Eve, I had a letter of acceptance from the University of Utah School of Medicine. That was a wonderful Christmas present!

Within the next several months, I withdrew from two schools and received interview invitations from five other schools and a rejection from one school. I accepted only one of the interviews, at the University of Rochester, after my acceptance to Utah. At Rochester I had three very positive and enjoyable interviews. In contrast to Utah, the interviewers at Rochester had not seen my application and therefore approached me without any prior knowledge. It was interesting for me to compare and contrast the two different interviewing philosophies. In each case, the interviewers were very positive about my background in music and all seemed to feel that it would not be a detriment to my success in medicine.

I had to make a difficult decision in the summer of 1986 when Rochester accepted me. I finally decided to attend Utah. Upon receiving my master's degree in music at BYU in August I enrolled, at the age of 27, as a first-year medical student at the University of Utah School of Medicine. I am a little older and certainly a little out of the ordinary when compared with most of my classmates.

My first year of medical school will soon be completed and I have enjoyed it very much. I have found time to spend at home with my wife and daughter and to play in the Salt Lake Symphony Orchestra. I feel quite certain that the challenging premedical schedule I had helped me cope with the rigorous coursework I've had this year. Playing in the orchestra, spending time with my family, and remaining active in my church have proved to be very effective stress relievers.

The entire process of preparing, applying for, and beginning a medical education is a great challenge. I suppose the future will prove to be no less of a challenge. I would, however, not change the way I approached my premedical and present medical education. I am convinced that many medical schools are looking for a diverse student body and for a variety of experiences in a student's background. In my situation, I was acutely aware of the need to prove myself in basic science skills, but I believe all applicants must somehow do the same. Once this is accomplished, all other interesting and extraordinary life experiences tend to add dimension to the medical school applicant.

Sincerely,
Ray Patterson

Several replies to my ad came from premedical advisers, from among which I have selected these two vignettes.

Dear Dr. Brown:

You may be interested in interviewing one of our graduates, Portia Smith. She is now a second-year student at the Philadelphia College of Osteopathic Medicine.

Portia is black, in her mid-late thirties, and the mother of five children. She saw her husband through school, had her children, and then began her college career. Portia first completed an associate's degree at Philadelphia Community College and then transferred to our campus to pursue the baccalaureate in premedicine. She commuted approximately eighty miles round trip a day to and from Philadelphia to our suburban campus on public transportation. This required the use of three to four vehicles and a good hike. Money was always scarce. Her husband was usually unemployed. Once she apologized to me for missing class because she did not have sufficient money for transportation. In spite of this and other almost insurmountable obstacles, she told no one of her circumstances, never asked for special consideration, and proved to be a solid student. She was recognized as an outstanding continuing education student by the Common-wealth of Pennsylvania in her last year here.

Portia's story would make most students count their blessings and would encourage many others to pursue their goals despite obstacles.

Sincerely,
Barbara Hoffman, PhD
Premedical Adviser

Dear Dr. Brown:

Hooray! Brian Smothers got in; he's gonna be a doctor!

Brian was a high school dropout in the tenth grade; he became a bricklayer. The story of this amazing young man's eventual progress into medical school is heartwarming and inspiring. At age 30, Brian received his acceptance last weekend.

I had wanted to write you in response to your card last October but decided I'd better wait until I knew for sure Brian would make it. I had a pretty strong inkling as his premed adviser, but you need genuine success stories for your new book.

A few more details on Brian: he injured his back as a bricklayer and went to a chiropractor. While undergoing treatment, it occurred to him that the chiropractor made a lot more money with a lot less work than he as a bricklayer. He got his GED, gained two years of spotty college work, and entered chiropractic school. There, he decided the profession was, shall we say, hokey, was not impressed with its quality and dropped out. Totally lost as to what to do with his life, he retired to a log cabin on an Indian reservation in Montana for two years, basically living off the land. There, he met the reservation doctor. That did it. Brian finally knew.

Returning to the University of Arizona, Brian's goals were clear, and the change in his grades and success was dramatic. His record shows 3.85 and 4.0 consistently. He works in the lab of a major research biochemist who was, at first, reluctant to take on this unlikely assistant. But the letter that biochemist wrote the med school in recommendation is the most glowing I have ever read. Brian has become a top student and researcher.

The medical school wisely overlooked his checkered background and focused on his steady recent achievements.

Finally, there is one other story, Karen's, of a 39-year-old woman whose interest in how people learn led her into psychology, then neurology, thence, to med school. She proved herself by taking twenty-four units one semester of premed requirements, earning a 4.0. The med school overlooked her low MCATs, as she had not even completed the coursework before the exam. It's a story I use to encourage my older students and to illustrate the value of a truly focused purpose in attending medical school. It is my observation that an older applicant is more successful if he/she has a specific goal in mind, a specific topic of research, for example, rather than a vague desire for a career change "in order to help people."

Sincerely,
Christine Jones
Prehealth Professions
Program Adviser

Next, the most amazing success story of them all. My writer was rejected by all medical schools to which he applied the first time around. He was shocked, but was told by a medical school dean that they felt he needed another year to prepare himself. He didn't quite know what he needed to prepare himself for; he already had a master's degree. But he took a job as a research assistant in a molecular genetics lab and continued to plug away. He made early application to the same state medical school that had rejected and then encouraged him, was the first person interviewed that year, but got another rejection letter "on Friday, October 13." He was crushed and thought his life was at an end. But he was also astounded and furious that they had again rejected him. This second rejection prompted him to write back to the admissions committee the following letter:

Gentlemen:

I believe that your recent decision to reject my application for a place in the class of 1983 was hastily made. It is my opinion that I am deserving of a closer and more thorough evaluation. Therefore, I respectfully request that you reconsider my application. There are several factors that lead me to ask for this reexamination.

First, I felt that my interview did not allow me the opportunity to verbally express my sincere desire and motivation toward the study and practice of medicine. The brevity of it led me to believe that my character could not have been easily evaluated. Further, it may not have provided an unbiased evaluation of my more subjective qualities. I feel that a second interview would allow me the opportunity to express myself, answer pertinent questions, and provide you with another opinion of my personality.

Second, I prefer you not consider my grades as an entity unto themselves. They are inextricably linked to my need to provide for myself, thus, explaining the cause of the obvious disparity between my test scores and grades. I believe my MCAT scores should be the measure of my innate knowledge. Allow my academic and work experiences to provide you with a clear picture of my ability to work long hours, beyond the capacity of most individuals. Consider how well I could perform if my extracurricular employment were reduced to zero.

As a state resident, of course I desire to attend your school. My AMCAS form clearly indicates my desire to serve my state, biasing other schools against me. At present, I work about eighty hours per week because I desire to bear as much of the financial burden as

possible. I wish to devote my life to the study and practice of med-
icine here in this state, in an area where those services are
needed. I want your school to provide me with the education nec-
essary to do this. It is my honest and sole intention to attend your
school and excel.

Finally, I am acutely aware of the fact that my application is
atypical. As you reconsider it, be aware of the difficult road I have
traveled. Take into account my willingness to sacrifice and my
intense desire to excel in your program. It is my belief that,
allowed to direct the totality of my personal energy to the study of
medicine, my ability to excel cannot be doubted.

Respectfully yours,
Ronald L. Perry

Basically, Mr. Perry said that he felt the admissions committee had made a mistake and they ought to take a better look at him. They did this and, lo and behold, he received his acceptance in the mail shortly thereafter:

Dear Mr. Perry:

It is with with very great pleasure that the Committee on
Admissions is able to offer you a place in the Class of 1983,
entering the School of Medicine in August 1979. This offer is con-
tingent upon satisfactory completion of the requirements of
entrance as stated in our current catalog and the satisfactory com-
pletion of all college courses as stated in your application. The
Committee assumes that you will maintain your present high
level of scholarly achievement.

A reply to this offer, at your earliest convenience, would be
appreciated. This offer does expire two weeks from the above
date. In order to matriculate, a remittance of fifty dollars ($50), by
check or money order should be returned
to the Committee.

This remittance, an advanced deposit of $50 on your tuition,
will be credited to your first-semester charges when you register. In
the event that you withdraw before registration, it will be returned
upon request.

You will receive a receipt for the amount sent us. This receipt
must be presented to the Comptroller's Office at the time of
registration in order that it can be credited to your first semester's
charges.

For the purpose of tuition, our records show you to be classified as a resident.

Prior to matriculation in September, the University requires that you have sent to this Office, official transcripts of all courses taken in college including those to be completed this academic year.

It is with great pleasure that we are looking forward to having you with us at the School of Medicine.

Sincerely yours,
Committee on Admission

My own personal story is topical too, and should be somewhat inspiring to those of you who have been advised to plan for alternative careers following medical school rejection. For I still believe that if you are aggressive, persevering, and a wee bit lucky, you can gain admission to a medical school.

When I decided that I wanted to become a physician I had just graduated from college. I had been an English major and had taken not one premed course. Naturally, I hadn't taken the MCAT—I hadn't even heard of it. I didn't know any science professors I could ask for recommendations. My undergraduate GPA was 2.96. I had no experience working in a medical environment. Is it any wonder that when I finally found the premedical adviser, he told me to forget it? I would have, too, if I hadn't been obsessed. That was fall 1968. Less than one year later, I began my freshman year of medical school.

In retrospect, it seems incredible even to me. Yet, when I think about it, my approach to the problem of how to convince a medical school to accept me was perfectly sensible. My success at it was in part a tribute to my rationality and in part a tribute to my good luck. The luck I didn't worry about; it was beyond my control. However, I took a lot of care to be rational.

In 1968, I was a totally unqualified college graduate wanting to go to medical school. Well, perhaps I wasn't totally unqualified. It's true I didn't have any premedical coursework or experience, but I did have confidence. Why? Because I had edited my college literary magazine my senior year and almost singlehandedly put all 128 pages of it together. To me it was a monumental achievement and although it didn't satisfy any premedical requirements, it showed me that I had the tenacity to complete a task. And getting into medical school was going to be one gargantuan task.

That summer, I decided that it was important to work in a medical environment. I didn't want to do it to impress a medical school of my sincerity;

I wanted to do it to convince myself that I was on the right track. Deciding to become a physician was a bit of an epiphany for me and I wanted to be sure I could trust my revelations. Luckily I had a friend who worked as an assistant administrator at a large metropolitan hospital. I called him to ask if there was anything that I could do to gain medical experience. I was ready to be an orderly, a lab-runner, anything. My friend had an idea. Knowing I had been an English major he asked me if I would like to write a health publication on lead poisoning for their outpatient clinics. Childhood lead poisoning was becoming epidemic and there was then no preventive information for parents. I said, "When can I start?"

I was hired with the undistinguished title of clerk, paid $2 an hour, and left to my own devices. Six weeks later, I had managed to complete my project and, in the process, was able to check out most of the hospital, which was so large that they had separate emergency facilities for men and women. I met physicians, medical students, and patients. I observed clinics and wards. I made home visits with medical personnel. It all served to strengthen my resolve; I made plans to return to school in the fall to begin premedical coursework.

In the meantime, the cartoon coloring book on lead poisoning I had written and designed and a friend had illustrated was becoming popular in the clinics. The finished product was somewhat primitive; text was typed onto the illustrated pages and then photocopied and stapled. It was a low-budget operation from beginning to end, but it worked. It even received some media coverage in the local papers. Later, it would accompany my applications to medical school to give credibility to my attempt to project myself as a different type of applicant. Medical schools, I came to learn, welcome the nontraditional applicant to add depth and diversity to the incoming class. However, admissions committees must be convinced of that applicant's ability to survive the basic medical sciences. They pay careful attention to performance in premedical courses and on the Medical College Admission Test. Here was my next challenge.

Doing well in premedical courses was somewhat worrisome for me. After all, I had majored in the humanities. I had met only my university's minimal science requirement for graduation—one year. I had taken oceanography and astronomy, neither of which gave me any premedical credits. They were known as science courses for nonscience majors—mickey-mouse but interesting, and nonintimidating. Fortunately, they were offered by the physics and biology departments as well. Naturally, I signed up. As far as I and medical schools were concerned, mickey-mouse biology was Bio 101-102, period. Grades were all.

Chemistry was a different kettle of fish. There was no chemistry for non-chemistry majors. Chem 101 included biology majors, budding chemists, engineers, and premeds. It had the reputation of being absurdly difficult, for its purpose was to separate science majors from the chaff. Realizing that anything less than a grade of B would effectively eliminate me as a contender for medical school, I enrolled in introductory chemistry in night school at a local community college. Even that wasn't easy, but at least I had a fair chance.

While waiting for my premedical courses to start, I made a trip to the local hospital to seek part-time employment. By this time I was coming to enjoy the hospital environment. Again, I was ready to accept any kind of work. Luckily, I was hired by the department of social services, which consisted of one full-time worker, to do part-time medical social work. My lack of experience was no obstacle; she was willing to train me. She wanted a student and I wanted a job. It worked out perfectly.

I divided my time between the department of physical rehabilitation and the cerebral palsy clinic, and I came to see patients differently. Rather than focusing on disease, as I was later taught to do in medical school, I was made to appreciate the impact the disease had on patient and family. Initially, I would do the intake interview and then discuss my impressions with my supervisor. Invariably she would show me how unaware I was of what was really going on. It was humbling. But, eventually, I began to get better at it. I also learned how to do direct service, finding my way through the bureaucracy to get canes, wheelchairs, braces, home health care, educational instruction, and other concrete things that patients required.

Meanwhile, I decided to apply to medical schools for the following fall. I admit I really did this just to energize my interest in my premedical activities. I had no expectations of being considered a serious candidate anywhere. After all, I still had not even completed my first-semester sciences. I had taken the old MCAT and done well on the general information and verbal sections. I was in the 50th percentile in mathematics and the 25th percentile in science. But I considered this a surprising score, since I was competing with science majors. With two months of introductory biology I had outdone 25 percent of them. I was impressed. Yet I had no illusions about medical schools. As far as they were concerned, I had nothing academic to show. Nevertheless, all they could do was say no, and at least I would have had the experience of applying.

I applied to seven medical schools, most of which were in my home state. I was rejected by five of them quickly, including the one attached to the hospital where I had done my health education project. The sixth school waited a little longer to reject me. The seventh requested an interview.

Sometime in February 1969 I boarded an airplane and flew to Milwaukee, Wisconsin, to be interviewed at what was then the Marquette University School of Medicine (now the Medical College of Wisconsin). Little did I know then that my extracurricular work had impressed a member of the admissions committee and he wanted to know me better. I had two interviews; one was perfunctory, the other more interesting and inti-

mate. It went overtime, and when we were done I believed I had an advocate on the committee. God knows, I needed one.

The next three months went by without any response from Marquette. What was up? I had no idea, except that I felt I was fast becoming a mailbox junkie. In the meantime I had completed first-semester biology, chemistry, and physics, earning all B's, and started the second semester of the same. By the end of the second semester (again, straight B's) I had heard nothing more than that my application was being processed and they would notify me as soon as possible. I hadn't been accepted, I hadn't been rejected, and

I hadn't been put on a waiting list. Now I had a decision to make: whether to take the masochistic organic chemistry course that summer and be done with it or postpone it for the fall. I opted for the summer. That way I wouldn't be tying up the whole next year and, if Marquette was still considering me for the September class, I would have fulfilled all requirements.

My next decision was where to take it. Being keenly aware of my aversion for cutthroat competition I avoided the course at Columbia, Harvard, and Berkeley. I selected the University of Minnesota, and on the way out to Minneapolis I conveniently revisited Milwaukee. There I learned, from my advocate, that the admissions committee was still not convinced that I could do medical school work. They were holding a place, waiting to see what grade I earned in organic. That was it. Do or die.

Minneapolis was delightful that summer and the course was civilized. There were five morning lectures and three morning labs. We were out by noon every day. I was competing with premeds, but also with prepharmacy and prenursing and chem majors. On the great bell curve I made another B, proving at least my consistency in science. Fortunately this was sufficient to allay the fears of the other committee members and on July 26, 1969, I received notification that I had been accepted into the freshman class at Marquette. Of course I had to complete the second semester of organic, which I did, earning another B. Medical school began four days after my course ended.

I do not mean to suggest that it was all downhill from there. Now I was forced to compete with all those premedical science majors that I had so assiduously avoided during my college career. These characters had already been exposed to many of the first-year medical school courses in college—anatomy, histology, and physiology, for instance. All I had done was run the obstacle course of the basic premedical requirements. These, it turned out, had minimal relevance to first-year medical school. How I survived that, however, makes for another story.

Where my sympathies lie must be obvious. They're with students, like myself, who have taken a nontraditional route to medicine. Medical schools still accept a preponderance of science majors with high GPAs and MCAT scores. But they accept people like me, too. And if me, why not you?

CHAPTER 8

The Future of Medicine?

For the past twenty-five years I have been in the unique position of being both a family physician and an adviser to premedical students. However, until recently I held no official advising position; my advice was solicited mostly through the mail by readers of books that I wrote to encourage the nontraditional applicant, having been a bit atypical myself. And for most of the twenty-five or so years that my books have been in print, I have been able to advise my readers that what awaited them at the end of their arduous endeavors was worth the effort. This was necessary because even in its halcyon days, going into medicine still entailed more postgraduate education than any other professional training and required more sacrifice. Premeds and medical students, who spent most of their lives studying and delaying gratification, realized this. But the good news was that, after much time and expense, they became highly trained and well-paid professionals with limitless possibilities for employment. I could and did say that it did get better and it was worth it. Today, I am not as optimistic.

During the last fifteen years, and, particularly, during the last several, there have been cataclysmic changes in the way medicine is practiced in this country and in the way health care is being delivered. In retrospect, it was predictable. The now almost passé fee-for-service system of reimbursement had a faulty foundation; it was based on what you did to the patient and therefore encouraged doing more. Furthermore, in the old days, physicians were paid what they billed. Although this system nurtured the doctor-patient relationship, it did nothing to contain costs or foster wellness. There was no incentive to do either, and the health-care budget rose at double-digit rates, easily tripling the yearly rate of inflation. It was clearly a process that could not go on indefinitely. It was also significant that, over the past forty or fifty years, most Americans got health insurance to pay their medical bills, and mostly through their workplace. This served to consolidate the payers for health care into large insurance companies, which then became even larger, were able to amass the necessary actuarial data, and continue making the insuring of people's health profitable.

There were some early attempts at reform. Kaiser, the nation's first major HMO, started enrolling patients after the Second World War and was predicated on correct principles. They offered people low-cost health insurance at fixed rates and took care of them in their own hospitals with their own doctors. Physicians were salaried, so there was no incentive for them to do more than what was necessary, as any additional procedures or care would not benefit either them or their organization financially. Criticism of this type of plan is that it is often difficult to get to see your physician, or any physician, and that patients may be undertreated. But the cost of care is hard to beat and, in recent times, patient satisfaction has generally been high.

The government also has been pruning the Medicare program. Initially strongly opposed by organized medicine as socialistic, it was subsequently embraced as it paid physician bills in toto and became an important source of operating revenues for hospitals and medical schools. However, politicians and health-care administrators, aware that the well could run dry, began instituting reforms in the 1980s, beginning with the relative value system. Under this plan, hospitals were paid a flat rate per diagnosis, regardless of how long it took the patient to get well and be discharged. Reform of physician fees soon followed. Other insurance companies soon began to emulate these models and produced their own fee schedules for doctors and hospitals. The days of carte blanche billing were over; the people who paid the bills were now calling the shots. The payers had become the players, and physicians and hospitals had become minor characters in the unfolding drama.

It doesn't take an economist to realize that not only can health-care costs be contained but that health care can, in and of itself, be profitable. Indeed, to a businessman, health care is just another industry to be micromanaged, and the potential for profits are enormous. All the elements are in place for a corporate takeover of the profession; excess waste and tremendous possibilities for cost savings; many years' worth of actuarial data on which to base pricing; an abundance of workers, including physicians, from which to draw a relatively cheap labor pool; and industry with the dollars to spend to ensure that their employees received adequate health care. The era of managed care had arrived.

The recent spate of acquisitions of hospitals, medical practices, medical supply services, computerized billing services, and pharmaceutical drug services by parvenu health-care conglomerates is testimony to the exponential rate of change in the profession. There is no going back. The old paradigms are dead; new models are forming at an accelerating rate. The actual practice of medicine, which remained unchanged for generations, is now changing so rapidly that it would be hard to hazard a guess what it might be like to practice in the next century.

What I find of great interest and concern is that through all the ferment, the selection and training of physicians has not changed very much at all. Premeds still take the same required courses and the medical school curriculum remains immutably intact. Furthermore, the factors that once motivated the best and brightest students to go into medicine are still operational—the need for prestige, independence, high remuneration, security, mobility, intellectual challenge, and service. But the playing field has been leveled by managed care. The times call for different motivations for entering medicine if our premeds are to be happy and successful. The fact that many premeds have not given credence to this is explained by what the great economist Thorstein Veblen described as "habits of thought," or the persistence of beliefs that are no longer useful after the institutions that fostered those beliefs die.

Let me use myself as an example to demonstrate how much medicine has changed over the past twenty-five years—in practice, although not necessarily in perception. First off, when I was a medical student, medical school was cheap; it cost me only $2,000 per year for tuition. I didn't have to borrow money and I graduated from medical school with only a small debt accrued from some college loans. A rotating internship, completed in 1974, was all I needed to work, and I was able to find employment in emergency rooms, clinics, and even doing some epidemiological research. Private practice was also an option, and I could have hung out my shingle just about anywhere and been busy.

As things turned out, I did part-time work for several years in the city and then relocated to the country, where I found employment in a rural hospital emergency room, and I did open a private practice. Without board certification, I was given hospital staff privileges in all services and continue to hold them today except in obstetrics, which I voluntarily stopped doing twelve years ago when the price of insurance became too high. I remain self-employed and have been able to set my own working hours—two days a week in the office and one weekly shift in the ER. I own the building I practice in and, as the managed care revolution has not yet reached us, still have the ability to choose my private patients, as they have the option of whether or not to select me as their physician. The result has been that I enjoy my work and believe that, in my case, the doctor-patient relationship is alive and well.

How would my style of practice fare today? In the first place, I could not have afforded medical school without taking out a large loan. If my debt had been typical, I would have graduated owing $65,000. This would have dampened my enthusiasm about taking time off for personal growth and I probably would have opted for a residency, as the rotating internship has been long defunct and one year of postgraduate medical education is no longer the union card necessary for employment. Nowadays, three to five years of residency training is one of the prerequisites for going to work.

Another prerequisite is rapidly becoming board certification. Because board eligibility in many areas requires not only the completion of a residency but so many years in practice as well, it has become a problematic catch-22 for many doctors looking for their first job. How can they get hired if they don't have their boards? How can they get their boards if they don't practice? The places where I cut my teeth are no longer options for new graduates unless they have board certification in emergency medicine or family practice. Although one year of postgraduate education still qualifies for licensure, the only place I can imagine such an individual could find work would be as a doc-in-the-box in an ambulatory care clinic.

My hospital will no longer accept medical staff applications from non-boarded people and positions in the emergency room have been long since filled. The community, once in need of practitioners, has become saturated and I would be unable to find work here today. Even were I fully papered, I would still have to look for another location to ply my skills. Probably it would not be where I wanted to live but where there was a job. And, in all likelihood, I would be an employee, not self-employed. I would be on salary with prescribed work hours and vacation time. My income would be limited by contractual arrangement. My performance would be monitored with careful attention to the bottom line—costs. With a plethora of doctors, I would be a surplus commodity, easily replaced and able to count on little or no patient loyalty. Just another worker in the organization.

Nothing is intrinsically wrong with physicians being treated like any other kind of worker. Indeed, that is the pattern in most of the world. However, there grew up an entirely different tradition in this country with entirely different expectations. Until recently, most doctors were self-employed and independent. They were able to earn more by working more, could do what they felt was best for the patient without worrying about getting authorization, and could see as many or as few patients as they were comfortable seeing without worrying about whether they were meeting their assigned quota. They were able to practice medicine the way they felt was best. People who selected medical careers treasured their autonomy, were self-directed, and tended to like to have things their way. They liked to give orders, not get them. They liked to be in control.

Current applicants are a lot like this, but the medical world they will be preparing to enter has changed. It will now reward the team player, not the entrepreneur. It will favor people who can play by the rules and not question them. It will no longer represent job security but will be a more and more insecure livelihood as American and international medical schools continue to crank out graduates to fill residency positions. It will favor people of independent wealth because of the high costs of medical education and the projected shrinking salaries of physicians. (Thus, we will see the reemergence of the gentleman doctor who doesn't have to work for money but just wants to work to be of service.) The need to serve, to be useful, to make a difference in other people's lives will still be a prime motivation, but there will be many more constraints on the way health care is delivered, which will prove to be frustrating to people who will wonder why, after seven to ten years of postgraduate education to get their MDs, they are having to take orders from people who spent two years after college getting their MBAs.

The crux of the problem is, simply, that there is no mechanism other than the market to regulate physician supply in the face of diminishing demand for physician services. Managed care is extremely efficient and tolerates no waste. Already many established physicians have been given notice and have either moved to other locales to practice, retired early, dropped out, or retooled into a primary care specialty. It's no secret that physician dissatisfaction is high, and many say they would not do it over again if they could. Many are discouraging to premeds, who are almost universally idealistic. But it may not be registering; more students are applying to medical schools today than ever have before.

The job of the premedical adviser is not only to assist students in their quest to gain admission to a medical school but also to describe what the actual practice of medicine is like. Because advisers are almost never physicians, they too may labor under many of the same myths as their students. Medicine is just not their workaday world. Even the proverbial soldier in the trenches, such as myself, would have a hard time hazarding a guess about what medicine will be like in ten to fifteen years, about the time it will take my readers, most of whom are high school and university students, to pass through college, medical school, residency training, and be ready to enter the job market.

It is possible that, because the institutions that control the demand for physicians (managed care organizations) are not the same as those that control the supply (colleges and universities, medical schools, and residency training programs), doctors could become a surplus commodity in the labor market to the extent that some will be unemployed. Competition for available positions will be intense, the same way competition among PhDs is intense for university faculty positions, the more so the more desirable the location. The number of applicants will diminish as people realize that medicine is no longer a guaranteed secure profession, but there will always be more applicants than there are places and so many students in the pipeline that doctors will never have the collective bargaining power that they once possessed. Market demands will dictate specialty choice but, because of a declining need for physician services, it will be hard to predict, for more than a year or two at a time, which medical specialties will experience shortages. And, because of the long training programs that residents are locked into, new graduates may begin a residency optimistic of future employment only to find a surfeit of their kind three to five years later.

Until the people who supply the jobs control the selection and training of physicians, there will continue to be a lack of central planning. But managed care conglomerates have no incentive to control the selection and education process; it gives the appearance of impropriety and is unnecessary from management's point of view. Without any outside interference, the existing system will continue to produce a cheap labor pool, which will only benefit the corporate providers of health care. Turf wars between special interest groups will make mutual cooperation difficult besides. It will all work to the detriment of the newly minted MDs, who will wonder how on earth they are going to begin to pay back their debts while living on the salaries offered them.

Perhaps it won't be so bad, although I read in a recent issue of the *AMA News* that, for the first time ever, physician's incomes declined, that HMO enrollment is projected to near 65 million Americans—up more than 25 percent from 50 million members a few years ago—that Columbia/HCA, the country's largest managed care behemoth, is on a buying spree and anticipates acquiring more hospitals, and that "good communication saves time and money in a managed care world." Another article from the *Associated Press* proclaims, "Managed care forcing demoralized physicians to quit," and goes on to explain that doctors are "hanging up their stethoscopes in frustration over red tape and loss of control." It is the practice of medicine dictated by the business of medicine that is today's front page news.

Should you be a premed? Should you go to medical school? Yes, if you're truly fascinated by medicine, if you really want to make sick people well or prevent disease and disability, if your true mission is service, if you want a job with a fair amount of prestige, decent income, and regular hours (workaholics beware—you will not be allowed to put in 80- to 100-hour work weeks and will have to spend more time with your family or develop other interests). Yes, if you want a challenging career, crave opportunities for intellectual growth and diversity, prefer working with a group of peers. And, of course, yes, if nothing else will do. But no, if you treasure your independence, if you want to be your own boss, need to do it your way, or prefer working alone. No, if you have zero tolerance for bureaucracies and red tape. No, if income is of primary importance, or the ability to choose what you will do and where you will do it is. No, if you can't live with having an education loan as large as your house mortgage. And especially no if you are counting on medicine to be a secure profession.

There will always be sick people, and we will always need physicians to care for them. But let's have physicians that are happy and satisfied in their work and not physicians who feel trapped in a job that they have too much time, energy, and money invested in to leave, although it may not suit their temperament.

APPENDIX I

Summer Programs for the Premed

Now that you've read the entire book and are a step ahead of the other students who haven't, there is one final important area to discuss. It has already been stated that candidates who have worked in a medical environment are judged to be motivated and thought to make capable future physicians by admissions committee members. How then can you gain this valuable experience?

You have to go where the action is—to hospitals, laboratories, and research institutions. Summer employment at a medical center is fun, exciting, and educationally beneficial because it gives you a chance to see physicians and scientists at work. In addition, it may help to strengthen your career choices and to better define your own personal goals. This, in turn, will enable you to speak with some degree of authority about what medicine means to you and why you are contemplating such a career.

There are two ways in which you can become involved with a program that will introduce you to the medical field. The first is by getting a job or volunteering at your local hospital. Most hospitals in the United States have some sort of volunteer program that you can join. As a hospital volunteer, you will be able to see and interact with patients as well as the medical staff. A second option is to apply for a summer position with an institution that provides summer work experience for students. The following is a list of current summer programs that provide excellent opportunities to discover the world of medicine, learn laboratory procedures, and have a great summer too (some material is borrowed heavily from brochures describing individual programs).

SEP—Advanced
c/o Dr. Georgiana Aboko-Cole, Director
Center for Pre-professional Education
Howard University
PO Box 473
Administration Building
Washington, DC 20059
Tel: (202) 806-7231/2/3

The Summer Health Careers Advanced Enrichment Program at Howard University is a rigorous six-week program designed for disadvantaged students, although anyone may apply. Participants will learn the skills necessary for success in the health professions. They will also review the fundamental principles in the sciences in preparation for the more advanced courses and prepare for professional school entrance examinations (DAT, MCAT, PCAT). The program is highly structured and academically challenging, and the student is expected to attend classes on human anatomy, biochemistry, physiology, skills for learning, clinical experience, admissions workshops, and excursions.

To be eligible for the program, a participant must be a citizen or permanent resident of the United States, have earned a minimum overall GPA of 2.5, and have completed the basic courses required by the health professions schools (juniors and rising seniors).

Mellon Summer Research Program in Psychiatry for Undergraduates
Western Psychiatric Institute and Clinic
3811 O'Hara Street
Pittsburgh, PA 15213

The annual Mellon Summer Research Program in Psychiatry for undergraduates provides six to eight fellowships to outstanding college juniors and seniors with an eight-week research experience in psychiatry that includes participation in clinical activities. This involves close collaboration with faculty who are conducting investigations in clinical and basic psychiatric research. Fellowships are open to students with junior or senior standing by a specified date. Criteria for selection are the student's career goals and their relevance to this research program. Western Psychiatric Institute and Clinic, which houses the Department of Psychiatry of the University of Pittsburgh School of Medicine and is also the psychiatric specialty hospital of the University Health Center of Pittsburgh, provides a broad range of programs and activities dedicated to education, research, and patient care in western Pennsylvania. The institute offers comprehensive continuity of care through inpatient-outpatient services. Research at the institute focuses primarily upon developing methods and technology for the diagnosis and treatment of severe mental disorders. The stipend is $1,200 plus travel expenses. Housing can be arranged through the Western Psychiatric Institute and Clinic. Inquiries should be directed to Carol Kaufman, MEd, Assistant Director of Research, at the address indicated earlier.

Research Participation Program
Roswell Park Memorial Institute
666 Elm Street
Buffalo, NY 14263
Tel: (716) 845-2339

The Research Participation Program is a national program designed for students who have completed their junior year and who have research interests in science. The objectives of the program are "(1) to expose the participant to an atmosphere of intensive research where he is in constant contact with scientists, and continually challenged by them, (2) to help develop his own scientific creativity, and (3) to aid in planning his career." Stipends are available to both out-of-town and local students. Applications are made available every year on November 15 and are due February 15. Inquiries should be directed to the preceding address.

Strachan Donnelley, PhD
Director of Education
Associate for Environmental Ethics
The Hastings Center
255 Elm Road
Briarcliff Manor, NY 10510

The Student Intern Program is open to any student actively pursuing a degree who is interested in doing serious and independent research on ethical issues in medicine, the life sciences, and the professions. Internships typically last from two to six weeks. The overall aim of the program is ethical exploration and the overarching purpose is mutual benefit. The program looks for students who are lively, interesting, and ethically committed with substantively important projects and personal experiences. They are expected to be colleagues who will join in the daily life, which importantly includes bioethics discussions over lunch as well as conferences and research project meetings. Both scholars and interns are asked to give periodic formal presentations on their research during the in-house luncheon program. The Student Intern Program is meant for advanced students of bioethics, whether undergraduate or graduate, who are actively pursuing a well-focused research topic in biomedical or environmental ethics.

Jo Ann Wilson, PhD
UC—Davis Medical Center
Department of Pathology
Education Office
Edmondson Fellowship Program
4825 Second Avenue
Sacramento, CA 95817
Tel: (916) 734-0231

The Edmondson Fellowship Program is an opportunity for those having an interest and aptitude in the health science field and the desire to participate in research. The program offers experiences in areas of the department of pathology including toxicology, hematology, chemistry, cancer research, microbiology, immunology, immunohematology, and anatomical pathology. Fellows participate in significant research projects with professionals in pathology. Extensive interaction with other fellows in problem-based learning exercises promotes investigative thinking. This full-time summer opportunity offers a $2,000 stipend and is open to college/university students with a 3.0 GPA and high school seniors with a 3.5 GPA. The program runs from mid-June to mid-August.

Robert Thomas
Summer Student Program
Science Education Center, Bldg. 438
Brookhaven National Laboratory
Upton, NY 11973
Tel: (631) 282-4385
Fax: (631) 282-5832

The Summer Student Program offers several ten-week research appointments to undergraduate students at the junior or senior level. Students majoring in applied mathematics, physical and life sciences, engineering, and scientific journalism from all colleges and universities are eligible to apply. Participants are associated with members of the scientific and professional staff in an educational training program developed to give research experience in areas of chemistry, biology, nuclear medicine, science writing, and others. To be eligible, a student must be a U.S. citizen or permanent resident alien, be at least 18 years of age, and have completed his or her junior or senior year by June with a B average or better. Stipends are available with round-trip travel expenses reimbursed at lowest cost airfare. The application deadline is January 31. The laboratory's multidisciplinary programs, staff, and unique research facilities have fostered a worldwide reputation.

Jackie Plummer, Summer Employment Program Administrator
PO Box 5510, L-725
Livermore, CA 94551
Fax: (510) 423-0894
E-mail: plummer1@llnl.gov
Internet: http://www.llnl.gov/

Each year the Lawrence Livermore Laboratory in Livermore, California, offers twelve-week summer appointments to undergraduates, graduate students, and faculty members through the Summer Employment Program. The program has a twofold objective. First, it permits such summer employees to apply their academic backgrounds to practical research problems resulting in worthwhile work experience. Second, it benefits the laboratory by bringing new ideas and fresh approaches to current scientific research problems. Assignments for summer appointees are distributed among all of the major departments and research programs. It is expected that there will

be openings in experimental physics, theoretical physics, computer pro-
gramming, chemistry, biology and medicine, and hazards control.
Supplementary brochures describing the work of these groups in more
detail may be obtained through the placement office. Selections and assignments are based on academic achievements, prior experience, technical
interest, and number of positions available. Application forms may be
obtained from the placement office or by writing directly to the laboratory.

Amigos de las Americas
5618 Star Lane, Dept. CS
Houston, TX 77057
Tel: (713) 782-5290 or (800) 231-7796
Fax: (713) 782-9267
Contact Person: Celdie Sencion, Director, Operations

Amigos de las Americas is an international, nonprofit, private, nonsectarian
voluntary organization. Through Amigos, young volunteers are provided
leadership development opportunities while serving in public health projects in Latin America and the Caribbean. Teams of Amigos volunteers are
assigned to live and work in rural villages in Mexico, the Caribbean, and
Central and South America. They live with local families or are housed in
schools or clinics. The mayor, local doctor, or town priest is responsible for
the volunteers' needs and safety, and in the field staff visits regularly with
supplies and mail. Amigos programs currently include community sanita-
tion, dental hygiene, human immunization, rabies vaccination, and
environmental education. The cost to participants ranges between $2,595
and $3,080, including international transportation. Fund-raising materials
are provided and some scholarships are available.

Bruce L. Ballard, MD, Associate Dean
Cornell University Medical College
Travelers Summer Research Fellowship Program
1300 York Avenue, D-119
New York, NY 10021
Tel: (212) 746-1057

The Travelers Summer Research Fellowship Program for Premedical
Minority Students is designed to give participants deeper insights into the
wide range of options that exist for minority physicians. Twenty-five minor-

ity premedical college students get a preliminary look at medical school life. Through the experiences of laboratory or clinical research, classroom lectures, seminars on public health issues, practical discussions by physicians from different specialties, and observations of hospital care, the college students gain a clearer picture of both the demands and the opportunities they will encounter in medicine as a career. While at Cornell, the college students' major activity is the fellowship research project, which enables each student to pursue a specific research problem under the supervision of a faculty member. A lecture series will explore topics in cardiovascular physiology. Students receive a $120-a-week cost-of-living allowance and are housed rent free in the dormitory for medical students.

ABL-Basic Research Program
Personnel Department/SS
NCI-FCRDC
PO Box B, Bldg. 428
Frederick, MD 21702-1201
Tel: (301) 846-1539 or 846-1166

The ABL-Basic Research Program is dedicated to basic research in virology, molecular biology, biochemistry, crystallography, genetics, and organic chemistry. A vigorous seminar program, implemented by formal and informal arrangements with the National Institutes of Health, Johns Hopkins University, University of Maryland, and other research and academic institutions, provides opportunities for extensive interaction within the scientific community. The scope of current projects is indicated by the research interests of the senior scientists. The Summer Undergraduate Fellowships are paid positions designed to provide undergraduate students of science with firsthand laboratory experience under the guidance of a senior research scientist. Outstanding students interested in pursuing careers in science are invited to apply. The program lasts approximately ten weeks, beginning in May, and is flexible to the student's vacation schedule. The application deadline is March 15.

Levon O. Parker
Director, Summer Program in the Neurological Sciences
National Institutes of Health
Building 31, Room 8A-19
31 Center Dr., MSC 2540
Bethesda, MD 20892-2540
Tel: (301) 496-5332
Fax: (301) 402-2818
E-mail: 1p33s@nih.gov
E-mail: lop@cu.nih.gov

Learning about the brain and nervous system—how they work to provide for learning, memory, and performance, and how they fail when damaged by trauma, stroke, genetic disorders, and brain cell degeneration—is the objective of the research program of the National Institute of Neurological Disorders and Stroke (NINDS), National Institutes of Health (NIH). The NINDS, located in Bethesda, Maryland, supports and conducts research and research training on the brain and nervous system, and neurological and neuromuscular disorders. Examples of these disorders include brain and spinal cord trauma, cognitive disorders, Parkinson's disease, Huntington's disease, epilepsy, stroke, aphasia, brain amyotrophic lateral sclerosis, and sleep disorders. This program provides hands-on neuroscience research training for academically talented high school, undergraduate, graduate, and medical students contemplating a career in biomedical research or academic medicine. Students attend lectures and seminars concerning the latest advances in brain and nervous system research. Students receive a biweekly or monthly salary or stipend. The deadline for applications is January 15.

Summer Fellowship Program
University of Connecticut School of Dental Medicine
Office of Student Affairs MC 3905
Farmington, CT 06030-1905

The purpose of the Summer Fellowship Program is to provide a research enrichment experience and some exposure to clinical medicine or dental medicine. A faculty sponsor will be identified for each student. Faculty develop and make available suitable project descriptions. The student meets with the faculty sponsor and develops a research protocol in April or May.

The student commits approximately thirty hours per week for the project and will work with the faculty sponsor or his/her designates. A $2,000–$2,500 stipend is provided. Undergraduate college students interested in careers in dental medicine and biomedical research are invited to apply. Students completing their junior year are given preference. Applicants should have completed some college coursework in biology and chemistry (preferably through organic chemistry). Previous laboratory experience is desirable. A variety of projects is available. Applicants must submit an application, transcript, standardized test scores, and two letters of recommendation. A $25 application fee should also be submitted.

Glenn Goldfinger, MA, PT
Program Director, Health Career Opportunity Program
400 East 34th Street
New York, NY 10016

This program provides both a realistic work experience in a rehabilitation hospital environment and an educational/study component. The Health Career Opportunity Program is divided into three four-week sessions during June, July, and August. Applicants must be over 17 years old and either a senior in high school or enrolled in college in a degree program. Separated into clinical and research divisions, students have a full-time placement in one department but learn about the others through the lecture program. Most fellowships are for one session; however some eight-week fellowships are available in selected departments. There are many departments to choose from, as the Rusk Institute of Rehabilitation Medicine is one of the largest rehabilitation centers in the United States. Students are given the opportunity to observe and participate in the following clinically oriented areas: nursing, orthotics and prosthetics, recreational therapy, occupational therapy, physical therapy, horticulture therapy, pharmacy, clinical nutrition, radiation oncology, special education, and animal facility. Students may do research such as data collection, library research, and lab work. Some of the research is patient oriented, whereas some is directed toward the basic sciences.

Summer Program in Pediatrics
Attn: Dr. Charles J Graham
Arkansas Children's Hospital
800 Marshall Street
Little Rock, AR 72202

Dr. Richard Drake
UAMS College of Medicine
4301 West Markham, Slot 516
Little Rock, AR 72205

Student Summer Research Fellowship
Dr. Charles Winter, Associate Dean For Research
UAMS College of Medicine
4301 West Markham, Slot 718
Little Rock, AR 72205

Brenda S. Sprite
Educational Programs Coordinator,
Michigan State University
Office of International Education Exchange/Overseas Study
108 International Center
East Lansing, MI 48824-1035
Tel: (517) 353-8920
Fax: (517) 432-2082
E-mail: ovr06@msu.edu.

The last is a program on medical ethics and the history of health care, held in London, England, and is sponsored by Michigan State University.

The American Academy of Family Physicians (AAFP) has compiled a directory of preceptorship opportunities for premedical students. It lists over eighty programs in thirty-four states that offer premeds the chance to observe patient care in family practice residency programs. These shadow programs allow premeds to work with physicians, residents, medical students, and other premeds for upward of eight weeks throughout the year. Many include seminars, assigned readings, research, group participation, and supervised patient management. Some offer stipends, lodging, and a food allowance. Many are open to high school students as well as college premeds and accept students from out of state. A complete listing can be had by requesting the entire directory from the AAFP at 8880 Ward Parkway, Kansas City, MO 64114-2797, c/o the Student Interest Department.

These summer programs should interest many premedical students from numerous colleges and universities. If you are unsuccessful in obtaining entrance to these programs, as they are becoming more competitive, here are some other words of advice from the Career Planning Offices of Bryn Mawr and Haverford colleges:

"Look in the phone book for a list of hospitals and then send away for information from those hospitals which interest you. Ask them if they sponsor internships, research-oriented or otherwise, for undergraduates, or if they are willing to hire you, or accept you as a volunteer, for some position in their hospital. It may not be an internship, but it is an excellent way to become familiar with hospitals, medicine, and what the discipline of medicine requires from those who practice it.

"Another worthwhile reference source is the journals of the various health professions. Thumb through these journals, looking specifically for articles describing an ongoing research program that might be of interest to you. Write down the names of the people conducting the research and the address of the institution sponsoring the research project; mail them a letter stating your interest in their program, telling how you heard about it and asking whether they sponsor internships or would like to hire someone with your qualifications."

Remember to point out that you are interested in a medical career and hope to gain something out of the classroom or real-world experiences. Be honest and you'll be surprised at the warmth of the reactions you'll receive.

Directory of American Medical Schools

The following directory of American medical schools provides a beginning for your search for a medical school. These schools are all accredited by the Liaison Committee on Medical Education (LCME), an accrediting agency sponsored by the Association of American Medical Colleges and the American Medical Association.

For additional information on admissions policies and programs of study at these schools, you should check *Medical School Admission Requirements: United States and Canada,* 2000–01 edition, published by the Association of American Medical Colleges, Washington, DC, and the *AAMC Curriculum Directory* and the *AAMC Directory of Medical Education,* also published annually by the AAMC.

Schools are designated by their membership in AMCAS (see page **57** for complete explanation) and/or in WICHE, the Western Interstate Commission for Higher Education, a thirteen-state student exchange program under which students from Alaska, Montana, and Wyoming can attend the participating schools and pay only the in-state tuition at a public school or a reduced fee at a private school.

Each profile in the directory includes the following data:

- The correct name and address of the medical school; whether the MCAT is required for admission
- Both the overall GPA and the science GPA, if available.
- Information about the medical school: the founding date; under public or private control; special programs.

- Enrollment data and costs, in approximate figures.
- Information about the application, notification, and response dates; amount of deposit; early decision plan; state residency preference; admissions criteria; and the person or office to whom admissions correspondence should be sent.
- Information about minority students, including percentage of the total and first-year student classes, percentage receiving aid, special programs, aid application deadlines, and the person or office to whom aid inquiries may be addressed; the application fee.

Albany Medical College*
47 New Scotland Avenue
Albany, NY 12208
Tel: (518) 262-5521
http://www.amc.edu

MCAT: required

GPA: 3.4

FOUNDED: 1839; *private*. The Medical College, in conjunction with Rensselaer Polytechnic Institute, sponsors the Accelerated Biomedical Program, a 6-year program leading to the BS and MD degrees.

ENROLLMENT: 64 men, 64 women (first-year).

TUITION & FEES: Resident, $30,797; Nonresident, $30,797.

APPLICATIONS: Should be submitted between June 1 and November 15; the application fee is $75. Notification begins October 15; response must be received within 2 weeks; A deposit is required to reserve place in class. In recent years, approximately 50% of entering students have been state residents. Admission factors include academic record, MCAT scores, and personal qualifications as evaluated from letters of recommendation and a personal interview. *Correspondence to:* Office of Admissions.

MINORITY STUDENTS: Comprise 5% of the first-year class; most of these students receive aid. The Medical College offers a special orientation program and introduction to the basic Medical Sciences for entering students who exhibit special academic needs. Tutorial assistance is available during the academic year. *For additional information:* Office of Minority Affairs. Information regarding application for financial assistance is made available in mid-November.

---

*member AMCAS

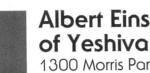

Albert Einstein College of Medicine of Yeshiva University*

1300 Morris Park Avenue
Bronx, NY 10461
Tel: (718) 430-2106
http://www.aecom.yu.edu

MCAT: required

GPA: 3.61

FOUNDED: 1955; *private.*

ENROLLMENT: 83 men, 97 women (first-year).

TUITION & FEES: Resident, $30,350; Nonresident, $30,350.

APPLICATIONS: Should be submitted between June 1 and November 1; the application fee is $85. Notification begins January 15; response must be received within 2 weeks until May 1, within one week thereafter, a deposit is needed to hold place in class. Early Decision plan is available. While no strict preference is given to state residents, about 50% of the entering class have been New York residents in recent years. Admission criteria include academic performance, MCAT results, letters of recommendation, and personal qualifications as judged by the Committee on Admissions. *Correspondence to:* Office of Admissions.

MINORITY STUDENTS: 9% of the first-year class; most of these students receive aid. *For additional information:* Office of Minority Student Affairs. Applications for aid are available from the Student Financial Officer.

---

*member AMCAS

Baylor College of Medicine

One Baylor Plaza
Houston, TX 77030
Tel: (713) 798-4842
http://www.bcm.tmc.edu

MCAT: required

GPA: 3.8

FOUNDED: 1900, moved to Houston in 1943; *private*. An MD/PhD program is offered with the Graduate School of Biomedical sciences. A biomedical engineering program with Rice University and a structural and computational biology program with Rice University and the University of Houston are also available.

ENROLLMENT: 86 men, 81 women (first-year).

TUITION & FEES: Resident, $7,513; Nonresident, $20,613.

APPLICATIONS: Should be submitted between June 1 and November 1; the application fee is $35. Notification begins October 15, response must be received within 2 weeks; a deposit is needed to secure a position in the class. Early Decision plan is available. Some preference is given to state residents, 77% of a recent freshman class were residents of Texas. Admission factors include collegiate curriculum and performance, MCAT scores, and personal qualifications as evaluated in letters of recommendation and the personal interview. *Correspondence to:* Office of Admissions.

MINORITY STUDENTS: Comprise 21% of the first-year class; most of these students receive aid. The $35 application fee may be waived. The College of Medicine also sponsors a summer work-study program for minority premedical students. *For additional information:* Associate Dean. Applications for aid should be requested within 2 weeks of submission of application.

Boston University*

School of Medicine
715 Albany Street
Boston, MA 02118
Tel: (617) 638-4630
http://www.bumc.bu.edu/

MCAT: required

GPA: 3.52

FOUNDED: 1873 as the New England Female Medical College; *private.* Special programs include a 7-year Liberal Arts–Medical Education Program that admits students after the senior year of high school.

ENROLLMENT: 97 men, 53 women (first-year).

TUITION & FEES: Resident, $35,975; Nonresident, $35,975.

APPLICATIONS: Should be submitted between June 1 and November 15; the application fee is $95. Notification begins in February; response must be received within 2 weeks. A deposit is needed to hold place in class. Early Decision plan is available. Selection factors include scholastic record, college recommendations, involvement in college and community activities, as well as personal qualifications. *Correspondence to:* Admissions Office.

MINORITY STUDENTS: Comprise 15% of the first-year class; most of these students are receiving aid. The Office of Minority Affairs organizes programs for the recruitment and support of minority students. These include a special prematriculation summer program in the medical sciences. *For additional information:* Associate Dean for Student and Minority Affairs.

----

*member AMCAS

Brown University

School of Medicine
97 Waterman Street
Providence, RI 02912-9706
Tel: (401) 863-2149
http://www.brown.edu

MCAT: required only for Brown-Dartmouth Medical Program

GPA: 3.47

FOUNDED: 1975; *private.* Eight-year combined BA–MD program; certain students also accepted to 4-year degree-granting program, entering in the fourth year of the 8-year program. Students in the Brown-Dartmouth Medical Program spend the first 2 years at Dartmouth and the last 2 years at Brown (contact the Dartmouth Medical School Admissions Office for more information).

ENROLLMENT: 28 men, 37 women (first-year).

TUITION & FEES: Resident, $29,027; Nonresident, $29,027.

APPLICATIONS: Should be submitted between August 15 and March 1; the application fee is $65. Notification begins March 15; response must be received within 3 weeks; no deposit is required to hold place in class. Admission factors weighted most heavily include GPA, letters of recommendation, personal qualities, and the interview. *Correspondence to.* Office of Admissions and Financial Aid.

MINORITY STUDENTS: Comprise approximately 18% of the first-year class. *For additional information:* Associate Dean. Application for aid should be made upon acceptance.

Case Western Reserve University*

School of Medicine
10900 Euclid Avenue
Cleveland, OH 44106-4920
Tel: (216) 368-3450
http://mediswww.cwru.edu/

MCAT: required

GPA: 3.6

FOUNDED: 1943; *private.*

ENROLLMENT: 80 men, 65 women (first-year).

TUITION & FEES: Resident, $31,400; Nonresident, $31,400.

APPLICATIONS: Should be submitted between June 1 and October 15; the application fee is $60. Notification begins October 15; response must be received within 4 weeks; no deposit needed to hold place in class. Early Decision plan is available. Preference is given to state residents. Admission factors include academic performance, MCAT results, verbal skills, letters of recommendation, and the personal interview. *Correspondence to:* Associate Dean for Admissions and Student Affairs.

MINORITY STUDENTS: Comprise 15% of the first-year class; most students receive aid. *For additional information:* Office of Minority Programs.

*member AMCAS

Columbia University*
College of Physicians and Surgeons
630 West 168th Street
New York, NY 10032
Tel: (212) 305-3595
http://cpmcnet.columbia.edu/dept/ps

MCAT: required

GPA: 3.75

FOUNDED: 1767; *private.*

ENROLLMENT: 88 men, 64 women (first-year).

TUITION & FEES: Resident, $29,548; Nonresident, $29,548.

APPLICATIONS: Should be submitted between June 15 and October 15; application fee is $75. Notification begins February 1; response must be received within 3 weeks; no deposit required to hold place in class. Admission factors include academic record, letters of recommendation, the personal interview, nonacademic achievements and activities, and personal qualifications. *Correspondence to:* Admissions Office.

MINORITY STUDENTS: Comprise 11% of the first-year class. Tutorial assistance is available to all students who require such help. *For additional information:* Associate Dean for Minority Affairs.

Creighton University*
School of Medicine
2500 California Plaza
Omaha, NE 68178
Tel: (402) 280-2799
http://medicine.creighton.edu

MCAT: required

GPA: 3.73

FOUNDED: 1892; *private.*

ENROLLMENT: 57 men, 58 women (first-year).

TUITION & FEES: Resident, $28,010; Nonresident, $28,010.

APPLICATIONS: Should be submitted between June 1 and December 1; application fee is $65. Notification begins October 1; response must be received within 2 weeks; a deposit is needed to hold place in class. Early Decision plan is available. Some preference is given to residents of those states without medical schools and to Creighton University graduates. Admission factors counted heavily include GPA, MCAT, and recommendations from academic professors or premedical committee. *Correspondence to:* Office of Admissions.

MINORITY STUDENTS: Comprise 6% of the first-year class; most of these students receive aid. The application fee may be waived. *For additional information:* Director of Minority Affairs for Health Sciences. Submit application for financial aid after acceptance.

----

*member AMCAS

Dartmouth Medical School*

3 Rope Ferry Road
Hanover, NH 03755-3833
Tel: (603) 650-1505
http://www.dartmouth.edu/dms/

MCAT: required

GPA: 3.6

FOUNDED: 1797; *private.* Students in a special program spend the first 2 years at Dartmouth and then transfer to Brown University for the last 2 years.

ENROLLMENT: 40 men, 37 women (first-year).

TUITION & FEES: Resident, $27,355; Nonresident, $27,355.

APPLICATIONS: Should be submitted between June 1 and November 1; the application fee is $60. Notification begins December 15. Response must be received within 2 weeks of notification; no deposit needed to hold place in class. Some preference is given to state residents and applicants from northern New England. Admission factors include consideration of both academic and personal qualifications. *Correspondence to:* Office of Admissions.

MINORITY STUDENTS: Comprise 10% of the first-year class. The application fee may be waived. The Committee on Equal Opportunity, which includes minority students and faculty members, is involved in the evaluation and selection of minority applicants. *For additional information:* Assistant Dean, Minority Affairs. Application for aid should be made upon acceptance.

----
*member AMCAS

Duke University*
School of Medicine
Duke University Medical Center
PO Box 3710
Durham, NC 27710
Tel: (919) 684-2985
http://www.mc2duke.edu/depts/som/

MCAT: required

GPA: 3.69

FOUNDED: 1930; *private.*

ENROLLMENT: 55 men, 45 women (first-year).

TUITION & FEES: Resident, $30,714; Nonresident, $30,714.

APPLICATIONS: Should be submitted between July 1 and December 1; the application fee is $65. Notification begins February 28; response must be received by school within 3 weeks; $100 deposit needed to hold place in class. In-state students receive special consideration. Admission factors include academic record, MCAT results, extracurricular activities, faculty evaluations, and the personal interview. *Correspondence to:* Committee on Admissions.

MINORITY STUDENTS: Comprise 25% of the first-year class; almost all of these students receive aid. *For additional information:* Associate Dean, Medical Education. Application materials for financial aid are available upon acceptance.

---

*member AMCAS

East Carolina University*
School of Medicine
Greenville, NC 27858-4354
Tel: (252) 816-2202
http://www.med.ecu.edu/

MCAT: required

GPA: 3.5

FOUNDED: 1977; *publicly controlled.*

ENROLLMENT: 39 men, 33 women (first-year).

TUITION & FEES: Resident, $3,286; Nonresident, $22,968.

APPLICATIONS: Should be submitted between June 1 and November 15; the application fee is $35. Notification begins October 15; response must be received within 3 weeks; $100 deposit needed to hold place in class. Early Decision plan is available. Preference is given to state residents. Admission factors include academic record, MCAT scores, and personal qualifications as evaluated in letters of recommendation and two personal interviews. *Correspondence to:* Associate Dean, Office of Admissions.

MINORITY STUDENTS: Comprise 24% of the first-year class. *For additional information:* Assistant Dean for Student Affairs.

----
*member AMCAS

Eastern Virginia Medical School*
of the Medical College of Hampton Roads

721 Fairfax Avenue
Norfolk, VA 23507
Tel: (757) 446-5812
http://www.evms.edu

MCAT: required

GPA: 3.41

FOUNDED: 1973; *private.*

ENROLLMENT: 57 men, 45 women (first-year).

TUITION & FEES: Resident, $16,847; Nonresident, $28,347.

APPLICATIONS: Should be submitted between June 1 and November 15; the application fee is $85. Notification begins October 15; response must be received within 2 weeks; a deposit is needed to hold place in class. Early Decision plan is available. Preference given to state residents. Admission criteria include academic achievement, MCAT results, written evaluation, personal interview, and evidence of sustained motivation. *Correspondence to:* Office of Admissions.

MINORITY STUDENTS: Comprise 4% of the first-year class; almost all of these students receive aid. The Medical School sponsors a remedial assistance program for students requiring such help during the academic year. *For additional information:* Assistant Dean, Minority Affairs.

---

*member AMCAS

East Tennessee State University*

James H. Quillen College of Medicine
PO Box 70580
Johnson City, TN 37614-0580
Tel: (423) 439-6221
http://qcom.etsu.edu

MCAT: required

GPA: 3.5

FOUNDED: 1974; *publicly controlled.*

ENROLLMENT: 30 men, 30 women (first-year).

TUITION & FEES: Resident, $9,666; Nonresident, $18,614.

APPLICATIONS: Should be submitted between June 1 and December 1; the application fee is $25. Notification begins October 15; response must be received within 2 weeks; a deposit is needed to hold place in class. Early Decision plan is available. Preference is given to state residents. Selection factors include both academic and personal qualifications. *Correspondence to:* Office of Student Affairs.

MINORITY STUDENTS: Comprise 42% of the first-year class. *For additional information:* Associate Dean, Student Affairs.

---

*member AMCAS

Emory University*
School of Medicine
Woodruff Health Sciences Center
   Administration Building
Atlanta, GA 30322
Tel: (404) 727-5600
http:/www.emory.edu/WHSC/MED/index.html

MCAT: required

GPA: 3.75

FOUNDED: 1915; *private.*

ENROLLMENT: 59 men, 52 women (first-year).

TUITION & FEES: Resident, $27,459; Nonresident, $27,459.

APPLICATIONS: Should be submitted between June 1 and October 15; the application fee is $60. Notification begins October 15; response must be received within 3 weeks; no deposit is needed to hold place in class. Preference given to state residents; approximately one half of the entering students are Georgia residents. The remaining positions are filled by out-of-state applicants, with some preference for residents of the southeastern states. Selection factors include academic performance, fitness and aptitude for the study of medicine, and personal qualifications. *Correspondence to:* Medical School Admissions, Room 303, Woodruff Health Sciences Center Administration Building.

MINORITY STUDENTS: Comprise 20% of the first-year class; most of these students receive aid. The application fee may be waived. *For additional information:* Director, Office of Minority Affairs. Applications for aid should be submitted upon acceptance.

----

*member AMCAS

Finch University of Health Sciences*

The Chicago Medical School
3333 Green Bay Road
North Chicago, IL 60064
Tel: (847) 578-3204
http://www.finchcms.edu

MCAT: required

GPA: 3.3

FOUNDED: 1912; *private.*

ENROLLMENT: 103 men, 63 women (first-year).

TUITION & FEES: Resident, $33,527; Nonresident, $33,527.

APPLICATIONS: Should be submitted between June 1 and November 15; the application fee is $85. Notification begins October 15; response must be received within 2 weeks; a deposit is needed to reserve place in class. Early Decision plan is available. Admissions decisions are based on the MCAT, GPA, recommendations, character, motivation, and a personal interview. *Correspondence to:* Office of Admissions.

MINORITY STUDENTS: Comprise 8% of first-year students. The application fee may be waived. The Medical School sponsors a special orientation program for minority students; tutorial assistance and counseling are also available. *For more information:* Associate Dean, Ancillary Programs. Financial aid is available, apply after notification of acceptance.

----

*member AMCAS

Georgetown University*

School of Medicine
3900 Reservoir Road, NW
Washington, DC 20007-2195
Tel: (202) 687-1154
http://www.dml.georgetown.edu/schmed

MCAT: required

GPA: 3.58

FOUNDED: 1851; *private.*

ENROLLMENT: 100 men, 71 women (first-year).

TUITION & FEES: Resident, $28,683; Nonresident, $28,683.

APPLICATIONS: Should be submitted between June 1 and November 1; the application fee is $90. Notification begins October 15; response must be received within 3 weeks; a deposit is required to hold place in class. Admission factors include scholastic record, MCAT scores, personal qualifications, letters of recommendation, and the personal interview. *Correspondence to:* Office of Admissions.

MINORITY STUDENTS: Comprise 2% of the first-year class; most of these students receive aid. A year-long prematriculation program is available to qualified students; priority is given to residents of the District. *For additional information: Dr. Arthur H. Hoyte,* Director, Office of Minority Affairs. Application for aid should be made upon acceptance.

---

*member AMCAS

The George Washington University*
School of Medicine and Health Sciences
2300 Eye Street, NW
Washington, DC 20037
Tel: (202) 994-3506
http://www.gwumc.edu/smns/

MCAT: required

GPA: 3.57

FOUNDED: 1825; *private.*

ENROLLMENT: 80 men, 71 women (first-year).

TUITION & FEES: Resident, $32,800; Nonresident, $32,800.

APPLICATIONS: Should be submitted between June 1 and December 1; the application fee is $75. Notification begins October 15; response must be received within 2 weeks; no deposit is needed to hold place in class. Early Decision plan is available. Some preference is given to residents of the District of Columbia and the surrounding metropolitan area. Admission factors include academic record, trends in performance, MCAT scores, extracurricular activities and work experiences, letters of recommendation, the personal interview, and the essay portion of the application. *Correspondence to:* Office of Admissions.

MINORITY STUDENTS: Comprise 14% of the first-year class; more than half of these students are receiving aid. Tutorial assistance is available to all students who require help. Minority students and faculty members serve on the Committee on Admissions. *For additional information:* Associate Vice President for Graduate Medical Education. Financial aid information and applications are available upon acceptance.

----

*member AMCAS

Harvard Medical School*
25 Shattuck Street
Boston, MA 02115
Tel: (617) 432-1550
http://www.hms.harvard.edu/

MCAT: required

GPA: 3.8

FOUNDED: 1782; *private.*

ENROLLMENT: 90 men, 75 women (first-year).

TUITION & FEES: Resident, $27,000; Nonresident, $27,000.

APPLICATIONS: Should be submitted between June 1 and October 15; the application fee, due with request for application, is $75. Response after notification must be received within 3 weeks; no deposit needed to hold place in class. Admission criteria include the MCAT, extracurricular activities, summer occupations, and letters of recommendation. Also considered are personal integrity, judgment, maturity, and aptitude. *Correspondence to:* Office of the Committee on Admissions.

MINORITY STUDENTS: Comprise 18% of the first-year class. Some tutorial assistance is available to those in need of such help. *For additional information:* Dr. Alvin F. Poussaint, Associate Dean for Student Affairs. Application for aid should be made upon acceptance.

---

*member AMCAS

Howard University*
College of Medicine
520 W Street, NW
Washington, DC 20059
Tel: (202) 806-6270
http://www.howard.edu/

MCAT: required

GPA: 3.2

FOUNDED: 1868; *private (federal government supported).* Special programs include the Early Entry Medical Education Program, which admits students after 2 or 3 years of college work; a 6-year combined BS-MD program; and a 5-year curriculum schedule for students who need extra time to complete the requirements.

ENROLLMENT: 56 men, 54 women (first-year).

TUITION & FEES: Resident, $17,433; Nonresident, $17,433.

APPLICATIONS: Should be submitted between June 1 and December 15; the application fee is $45. Notification begins October 15; response must be received within one month; a deposit is needed to reserve place in class. Admission factors include academic record, MCAT scores, motivation and personal qualifications, letters of recommendation, and an interview. *Correspondence to:* Admissions Office.

MINORITY STUDENTS: Comprise 72% of the first-year class. Most receive aid. *For additional information:* Sterling M. Lloyd, Jr., Assistant Dean, Student Affairs.

---

*member AMCAS

Indiana University*

School of Medicine
1120 South Drive, Fesler Hall 213
Indianapolis, IN 46202-5113
Tel: (317) 274-3772
http://www.medicine.iu.edu

MCAT: required

GPA: 3.68

FOUNDED: 1907; *publicly controlled.* The University School of Medicine has first- and second-year medical programs on seven college campuses in the state.

ENROLLMENT: 169 men, 111 women (first-year).

TUITION & FEES: Resident, $14,347; Nonresident, $34,432.

APPLICATIONS: Should be submitted between June 1 and December 15; the application fee is $35. Notification begins October 15, response must be received within 3 weeks; no deposit needed to hold place in class. Early Decision plan is available. Strong preference is given to state residents; recently, fewer than 6% of the entering class were nonresidents. Admission criteria include the MCAT, scholarship, character, and residence. *Correspondence to:* Medical School Admissions Office, Fesler Hall 213.

MINORITY STUDENTS: Comprise 4% of the first-year class; tutorial and financial assistance are available, as is a 2-week prematriculation program. *For additional information:* Admissions Office.

---

*member AMCAS

Jefferson Medical College of Thomas Jefferson University*

1025 Walnut Street
Philadelphia, PA 19107
Tel: (215) 955-6983
http:/jeffline.tju.edu/CWIS/JMC/jmc.html

MCAT: required

GPA: 3.5 science

FOUNDED: 1824; *private*. A cooperative program with the Pennsylvania State University leads to a combined BS-MD degree; the Physician Shortage Area Program is designed to recruit and educate medical students to enter family medicine and practice in rural communities and inner cities of Pennsylvania (physician shortage areas).

ENROLLMENT: 112 men, 111 women (first-year). Up to 40 places in each class may be filled from the cooperative program; 20 more places are usually set aside for Delaware residents through a special program with the state.

TUITION & FEES: Resident, $28,376; Nonresident, $28,376.

APPLICATIONS: Should be submitted between June 1 and November 15; the application fee is $65. Notification begins October 15; response must be received within 2 weeks; a deposit is needed to hold place in class. Early Decision plan is available. Preference may be given to state residents. Admission factors include consideration of undergraduate college attended, academic performance, MCAT scores, letters of recommendation, and a personal interview. *Correspondence to:* Associate Dean for Admissions.

MINORITY STUDENTS: Comprise ½% of the first-year class; most of these students receive aid. Application for aid should be made by April 1. *For additional information:* Assistant Dean for Student Affairs.

---

*member AMCAS

The Johns Hopkins University

School of Medicine
720 Rutland Avenue
Baltimore, MD 21205
Tel: (410) 955-3182
http://www.med.jhu.edu/admissions

MCAT: not required

GPA: not available

FOUNDED: 1893; *private*. In addition to the 4-year program, an optional 3-year program is offered. A combined MD/PhD program in all disciplines and master's and doctoral programs in public health are available.

ENROLLMENT: 71 men, 49 women (first-year).

TUITION & FEES: Resident, $27,290; Nonresident, $27,290.

APPLICATIONS: Should be submitted between July 1 and November 1; the application fee is $60. Notification begins November 1, response must be received within 3 weeks; no deposit needed to hold place in class. Early Decision plan is available. Admission factors include academic record, MCAT scores, extracurricular activities, and personal qualifications. *Correspondence to:* Committee on Admission.

MINORITY STUDENTS: Comprise 11% of the first-year class. An advising system is available to students that permits the selection of both preclinical and clinical faculty advisers. A faculty member is also designated as minority student adviser. *For additional information:* Dr. Roland T. Smoot, Assistant Dean for Student Affairs.

----

*member AMCAS

Loma Linda University*†

School of Medicine
Loma Linda, CA 92354
Tel: (909) 588-4467
http://www.llu.edu

MCAT: required

GPA: 3.66

FOUNDED: 1909; *private.* Seventh-Day Adventist Church.

ENROLLMENT: 91 men, 69 women (first-year).

TUITION & FEES: Resident, $27,124; Nonresident, $27,124.

APPLICATIONS: Should be submitted between June 1 and November 1; the application fee is $75. Notification begins December 1; response must be received within 30 days; a deposit is needed to hold place in class. Preference is given to Seventh-Day Adventists. Admission factors include GPA, MCAT scores, letters of recommendation, and the personal interview. *Correspondence to:* Associate Dean for Admissions.

MINORITY STUDENTS: Comprise 7% of first-year class. *For additional information:* Assistant Dean for Clinical Affairs.

----

*member AMCAS
†member WICHE

Louisiana State University*
School of Medicine in New Orleans
1901 Perdide Street
New Orleans, LA 70112
Tel: (504) 568-6262
http://www.medschool.lsumc.edu/admissions

MCAT: required

GPA: 3.4 science

FOUNDED: 1931; *publicly controlled.*

ENROLLMENT: 95 men, 72 women (first-year).

TUITION & FEES: Resident, $6,827; Nonresident, $20,347.

APPLICATIONS: Should be submitted between June 1 and November 15; the application fee is $50. Notification begins October 15; response must be received within 2 weeks; a deposit is needed to hold place in class. Strong preference is given to state residents; recently 100% of the entering class were Louisiana residents. Admission factors include the MCAT, scholastic performance, extracurricular activities, character, attitude, and interest. *Correspondence to:* Admissions Office.

MINORITY STUDENTS: Comprise 11% of the first-year class. A broad program of student aid is administered by the Student Financial Aid Office to help students financially through awards, scholarships, and loans. *For additional information:* Assistant Dean, Minority Affairs.

---

*member AMCAS

Louisiana State University*
School of Medicine in Shreveport
1501 Kings Highway, PO Box 33932
Shreveport, LA 71130
Tel: (318) 675-5190
http://www.sh.lsumc.edu/

MCAT: required

GPA: 3.6

FOUNDED: 1966, admitted first class in 1969; *publicly controlled.*

ENROLLMENT: 59 men, 41 women (first-year).

TUITION & FEES: Resident, $6,827; Nonresident, $20,345.

APPLICATIONS: Should be submitted between June 1 and August 1; the application fee is $50. Notification begins October 15; response must be received within 2 weeks; a deposit is needed to hold place in class. Strong preference given to state residents. In recent years, admission has been limited to Louisiana residents. Selection factors include academic record, MCAT scores, recommendations, and personal interviews. *Correspondence to:* Office of Student Admissions, LSU Medical Center.

MINORITY STUDENTS: Comprise 7% of the first-year class; most of these students receive aid. The application fee may be waived. *For additional information:* Director, Multicultural Affairs. Applications for aid are available after acceptance.

---

*member AMCAS

Loyola University of Chicago*

Stritch School of Medicine
2160 South First Avenue
Maywood, IL 60153
Tel: (707) 216-3229
http://www.meddean.luc.edu/

MCAT: required

GPA: 3.6

FOUNDED: 1870; *private.*

ENROLLMENT: 70 men, 59 women (first-year).

TUITION & FEES: Resident, $29,455; Nonresident, $29,455.

APPLICATIONS: Should be submitted between June 1 and November 15, the application fee is $50. Notification begins October 15; response must be received within 2 weeks; no deposit is needed to hold place in class. Early Decision Plan is available. Some preference is given to state residents and to applicants committed to the needs of the Illinois health care system. Admission factors weighted most heavily are the MCAT, GPA, character, evidence of community service and motivation. *Correspondence to:* Office of Admissions, Room 1752.

MINORITY STUDENTS: Comprise 9% of the first-year class. The application fee may be waived. *For additional information:* Dr. Michael Rainey, Associate Dean for Student Affairs. Applications for aid should be made upon acceptance.

----

*member AMCAS

Marshall University*
School of Medicine
1600 Medical Center Drive, Suite 3400
Huntington, WV 25701
Tel: (304) 691-1738
musom.marshall.edu/

MCAT: required

GPA: 3.5

FOUNDED: 1972; *publicly controlled.*

ENROLLMENT: 24 men, 24 women (first-year).

TUITION & FEES: Resident, $9,476; Nonresident, $23,456.

APPLICATIONS: Should be submitted between June 1 and November 15; the application fee is $40 for residents, $80 for nonresidents. Notification begins October 15; response must be received within 2 weeks of notification; no deposit needed to hold place in class. Preference is given to state residents. Selection factors include academic records, MCAT scores, and personal qualifications. *Correspondence to:* Admissions Office.

MINORITY STUDENTS: Comprise 19% of the first-year class. *For additional information:* Associate Dean for Student Affairs.

----

*member AMCAS

Mayo Medical School*
200 First Street, SW
Rochester, MN 55905
Tel: (507) 284-3671
http://www.mayo.edu/mms/

MCAT: required

GPA: 3.8

FOUNDED: 1972; *private,* academic affiliation with University of Minnesota, associated with the Mayo Clinic.

ENROLLMENT: 17 men, 25 women (first-year).

TUITION & FEES: Resident, $4,925; Nonresident, $9,850.

APPLICATIONS: Should be submitted between June 1 and November 1; the application fee is $60. Notification begins October 15; response must be received within 2 weeks; a deposit is required to hold place in class. Early Decision plan is available. Slight preference is given to state residents. Admission factors counted most heavily include GPA, MCAT, interviews, and letters of recommendation. *Correspondence to:* Admissions Committee.

MINORITY STUDENTS: Comprise 7% of the first-year class. The medical school offers preadmission laboratory experiences and tutoring programs for students of disadvantaged backgrounds. *For additional information:* Associate Dean for Student Affairs. Application for aid should be made upon acceptance.

---

*member AMCAS

MCP Hahnemann University School of Medicine*

2900 Queen Lane
Philadelphia, PA 19129
Tel: (215) 991-8202
http://www.mcphu.edu/medschool/medschl.html

MCAT: required

GPA: 3.41

FOUNDED: 1850; *private.* Combined baccalaureate-MD program available for high school graduates; special arrangements with Lehigh University and Villanova University.

ENROLLMENT: 92 men, 143 women (first-year).

TUITION & FEES: Resident, $27,560; Nonresident, $27,560.

APPLICATIONS: Should be submitted between June 1 and December 1; the application fee is $65. Notification begins October 15; response must be received within 3 weeks; a deposit is needed to hold place in class. Early Decision plan is available. Preference is given to state residents. Admission criteria include evidence of intellectual excellence, integrity, emotional maturity, motivation, as well as GPA and MCAT scores. *Correspondence to:* Admissions Office.

MINORITY STUDENTS: Comprise 18% of the first-year class, most of these students receive aid. *For additional information:* Director of Minority Affairs. Upon acceptance, students may apply for aid.

---

*member AMCAS

Medical College of Georgia*
School of Medicine
1120 Fifteenth Street
Augusta, GA 30912
Tel: (706) 721-3186
www.mcg.edu

MCAT: required

GPA: 3.56

FOUNDED: 1828; *publicly controlled;* a unit of the University System of Georgia.

ENROLLMENT: 118 men, 62 women (first-year).

TUITION & FEES: Resident, $5,828; Nonresident, $24,200.

APPLICATIONS: Should be submitted between June 1 and November 1; Application fee was not available. Notification begins October 15; response must be received within 2 weeks; a deposit is required to hold place in class. Early Decision plan is available for Georgia residents only. Preference is given to state residents; a maximum of 5% of first-year places is open to nonresidents. Admission factors include academic aptitude and performance, MCAT scores, potential to practice medicine as evaluated by premedical adviser, personal references, and the personal interview. *Correspondence to:* Associate Dean for Admissions.

MINORITY STUDENTS: Comprise 6% of the first-year class; most of these students are receiving aid. The School of Medicine sponsors a summer program for premedical minority students as part of its recruitment program for such students. *For additional information:* Associate Dean, Special Academic Programs.

----

*member AMCAS

Medical College of Ohio*

3045 Arlington Ave.
Toledo, OH 43614
Tel: (419) 383-4229
http://www.mco.edu/

MCAT: required

GPA: 3.51

FOUNDED: 1964; *publicly controlled.*

ENROLLMENT: 88 men, 52 women (first-year).

TUITION & FEES: Resident, $13,673; Nonresident, $27,717.

APPLICATIONS: Should be submitted between June 1 and November 1; the application fee is $50. Notification begins October 15; response must be received by school within 2 weeks; no deposit needed to hold place in class. Early Decision plan is available to Ohio residents only. Preference is given to state residents. *Correspondence to:* Admissions Office.

MINORITY STUDENTS: Comprise 12% of the first-year class. *For additional information:* Dr. Barry Richardson, Associate Dean of Minority Affairs.

*member AMCAS

Medical College of Wisconsin*

8701 Watertown Plank Road
Milwaukee, WI 53226
Tel: (414) 456-8246
http://www.mcw.edu/acad/

MCAT: required

GPA: 3.71

FOUNDED: 1890s; *private.*

ENROLLMENT: 129 men, 75 women (first-year).

TUITION & FEES: Resident, $17,359; Nonresident, $27,450.

APPLICATIONS: Should be submitted between June 1 and November 1; the application fee is $60. Notification begins October 15; response must be received within 2 weeks; a deposit is needed to hold place in class. Early Decision plan is available. Preference given to state residents; about half of recent entering classes have been from Wisconsin. Admission criteria include GPA, MCAT, candidate's statement in application, academic recommendations, personal interview, and suitability for the medical profession. *Correspondence to:* Office of Admissions and Registrar.

MINORITY STUDENTS: Comprise 3% of the first-year class. Two students per class from underrepresented minority backgrounds may be eligible for the Tuition Forgiveness Program. *For additional information:* Associate Dean for Academic Affairs. Students may apply for aid as soon as they have been accepted and indicate their intent to enroll.

----

*member AMCAS

Medical University of South Carolina*

College of Medicine
171 Ashley Avenue
Charleston, SC 29425-2970
Tel: (843) 792-3283
www.musc.edu/

MCAT: required

GPA: 3.49

FOUNDED: 1824; *publicly controlled.*

ENROLLMENT: 75 men, 64 women (first-year).

TUITION & FEES: Resident, $9,000; Nonresident, $25,852.

APPLICATIONS: Should be submitted between June 1 and December 1; the application fee is $55. Notification begins October 15 response must be received by school within 2 weeks; a deposit is needed to hold place in class. Early Decision plan is available . Strong preference is given to state residents. Admission factors counted most heavily are the MCAT, GPA, recommendations, and personal characteristics. *Correspondence to:* Office of Enrollment Services.

MINORITY STUDENTS: Comprise 24% of the first-year class. The Postbaccalaureate Reapplication Education Program is designed to further prepare South Carolina students interested in MUSC. *For additional information:* Dr. Thaddeus J. Bell, Assistant Dean, Minority Affairs.

---

*member AMCAS

Meharry Medical College*

School of Medicine
1005 D. B. Todd Boulevard
Nashville, TN 37208
Tel: (615) 327-6223
www.mmc.edu

MCAT: required

GPA: 3

FOUNDED: 1876; *private*, with support from states participating in the Southern Regional Educational Board (AL, FL, GA, LA, MD, MS, NC, TN, and VA).

ENROLLMENT: 29 men, 51 women (first-year).

TUITION & FEES: Resident, $25,822; Nonresident, $25,822.

APPLICATIONS: Should be submitted between June 1 and December 15; the application fee is $45. Notification begins October 15; response must be received by school within 3 weeks; a deposit is needed to hold place in class. Early Decision plan is available. Preference is given to residents of states that are members of the Southern Regional Educational Board. Admission factors weighted most heavily include GPA, MCAT scores, recommendations, and interest in primary health care. *Correspondence to:* Director, Admissions and Records.

MINORITY STUDENTS: Comprise 78% of the first-year class; most of these students receive aid; most remain to graduate. The School of Medicine sponsors recruiting seminars and a Summer Biomedical Science Program for minority and disadvantaged students. Tutorial assistance is available during the academic year. *For additional information:* Associate Dean for Student Affairs. Application for aid should be made after acceptance, prior to July 15.

*member AMCAS

Mercer University*
School of Medicine
1550 College Street
Macon, GA 31207
Tel: (912) 752-2524
http://www.mercer.edu/

MCAT: required

GPA: 3.2

FOUNDED: 1982; *private.*

ENROLLMENT: 32 men, 24 women (first-year).

TUITION & FEES: Resident, $21,778; Nonresident, $21,778.

APPLICATIONS: Should be submitted between June 1 and December 1; the application fee is $25. Notification begins October 15; response must be received within 10 days; a deposit is needed to reserve place in class. Early Decision plan is available for Georgia residents only. Admission factors include academic and personal potential, letters of recommendation or premedical committee evaluation, and personal interview. *Correspondence to:* Office of Admissions and Student Affairs.

MINORITY STUDENTS: Comprise 2% of the first-year class. *For additional information:* Associate Dean for Admissions.

---

*member AMCAS

Michigan State University*

College of Human Medicine
East Lansing, MI 48824-1317
Tel: (517) 353-9620
http://www.chm.msu.edu

MCAT: required

GPA: not available

FOUNDED: 1964; *publicly controlled.*

ENROLLMENT: 60 men, 46 women (first-year).

TUITION & FEES: Resident, $16,790; Nonresident, $34,706.

APPLICATIONS: Should be submitted between June 1 and November 15; the application fee is $55. Notification begins October 15; response must be received within 2 weeks; a deposit is needed to reserve place in class. Early Decision plan is available. Preference given to state residents; approximately 80% of recent first-year students have been Michigan residents. Admission criteria include academic performance and trends, MCAT scores, letters of recommendation, relevant work experience, suitability for the MSU program, and the personal interview. *Correspondence to:* Office of Admissions, A-239 Life Sciences.

MINORITY STUDENTS: Comprise 27% of the first-year class; many of these students receive aid. *For additional information:* Director of Student Affairs.

Morehouse School of Medicine*

720 Westview Drive, SW
Atlanta, GA 30310
Tel: (404) 752-1650
http://www.msm.edu/

MCAT: required

GPA: not available

FOUNDED: 1978; *private.*

ENROLLMENT: 13 men, 27 women (first-year).

TUITION & FEES: Resident, $21,774; Nonresident, $21,774.

APPLICATIONS: Should be submitted between June 1 and December 1; the application fee is $45. Notification begins December 20; response must be received within 2 weeks; a deposit is needed to hold place in class. Early Decision plan is available for Georgia residents only. Admission factors are MCAT scores, undergraduate curriculum and record, extent and nature of extracurricular activities, and personal qualifications. Preference given to residents of Georgia, but well-qualified nonresidents are encouraged to apply. *Correspondence to:* Admissions and Student Affairs.

MINORITY STUDENTS: Comprise 84% of the total student body, 85% of the first-year class. *For additional information:* Student Affairs.

---

*member AMCAS

Mount Sinai School of Medicine of the City University of New York*

1 Gustave L. Levy Place—Box 1002
New York, NY 10029
Tel: (212) 241-6696
www.mssm.edu

MCAT: required

GPA: 3.63

FOUNDED: 1963; *private, affiliated with CUNY.*

ENROLLMENT: 54 men, 51 women (first-year).

TUITION & FEES: Resident, $24,425; Nonresident, $24,425.

APPLICATIONS: Should be submitted between June 1 and November 1; the application fee is $100. Notification begins November 15; response must be received within 2 weeks; no deposit needed to hold place in class. Early Decision plan is available. *Correspondence to:* Director of Admissions, Room 5-04, Annenberg Building.

MINORITY STUDENTS: Comprise 14% of the first-year class. The School of Medicine offers a preentrance summer program for accepted students in addition to tutorial assistance during the academic year. *For additional information:* Assistant Dean, Student Affairs. Applications for aid should be made upon acceptance.

*member AMCAS

New York Medical College*
Valhalla, NY 10595
Tel: (914) 594-4507
http://www.nymc.edu

MCAT: required

GPA: 3.5

FOUNDED: 1860; *private.*

ENROLLMENT: 97 men, 87 women (first-year).

TUITION & FEES: Resident, $29,770; Nonresident, $29,770.

APPLICATIONS: Should be submitted between June 1 and December 1; the application fee is $100. Notification begins October 15; response must be received within 2 weeks; a deposit is needed to hold place in class. Early Decision plan is available. Admission factors include the MCAT, GPA, a premedical curriculum, recommendations, motivation, and integrity. *Correspondence to:* Admissions Office.

MINORITY STUDENTS: Comprise 5% of the first-year students. Financial assistance is available, 85% of the students receive aid. *For additional information:* Dr. Anthony A. Clemendor, Associate Dean for Student Affairs. Applications for aid should be made as early as possible.

---

*member AMCAS

New York University

School of Medicine
550 First Avenue
New York, NY 10016
Tel: (212) 263-5290
http://www.med.nyu.edu

MCAT: required

GPA: 3.6

FOUNDED: 1841; *private.*

ENROLLMENT: 86 men, 74 women (first-year).

TUITION & FEES: Resident, $27,605; Nonresident, $27,605.

APPLICATIONS: Should be submitted between August 15 and December 1; the application fee is $75. Notification begins December 20; response must be received within 2 weeks; a deposit is needed to secure position in the class. Selection criteria include academic performance, MCAT results, letters of recommendation, the personal interview, aptitude, and motivation. *Correspondence to:* Office of Admissions.

MINORITY STUDENTS: Comprise 21% of the first-year class; most of these students are receiving aid. The application fee may be waived. *For additional information:* Office of Minority Affairs. Accepted students are eligible to file applications for financial assistance.

Northeastern Ohio Universities*

College of Medicine
4209 State Route 44
PO Box 95
Rootstown, OH 44272
Tel: (330) 325-6270
http://www.neoucom.edu

MCAT: required

GPA: 3.3

FOUNDED: 1973: *publicly supported.* Special programs include a combined BS-MD program for high school graduates.

ENROLLMENT: 17 men, 8 women (first-year).

TUITION & FEES: Resident, $10,842; Nonresident, $15,348.

APPLICATIONS: Should be submitted between June 1 and November 1; the application fee is $30. Notification begins October 15; response must be received within 2 weeks; no deposit needed to hold place in class. Early Decision plan is available. Preference is given to state residents. Selection factors include academic records MCAT scores, personal qualifications, and demonstration of sincere motivation for the practice of medicine. *Correspondence to:* Office of Admissions.

MINORITY STUDENTS: Comprise 8% of the first-year class. *For additional information:* Dr. Kenneth B. Durgans, Special Assistant to the President for Minority Affairs and Affirmative Action.

---

*member AMCAS

Northwestern University*
Medical School
303 East Chicago Avenue
Chicago, IL 60611
Tel: (312) 503-8206
http://www.nums.nwu.edu/

MCAT: required

GPA: 3.7

FOUNDED: 1859; *private.* Special programs include an Honors Program in Medical Education leading to the MD degree after 3 years of undergraduate work at the Evanston campus and 4 years at Northwestern.

ENROLLMENT: 92 men, 78 women (first-year). 60 members of each class are admitted from the Honors Programs.

TUITION & FEES: Resident, $30,417; Nonresident, $30,417.

APPLICATIONS: Should be submitted between June 1 and October 15; the application fee is $60. Notification begins November 15; response must be received within 2 weeks; no deposit is necessary to hold a place in class. Early Decision plan is available. Preference is given to state residents; one half of students admitted must be Illinois residents, inclusive of the Honors program. Admission factors include academic performance, personal qualifications and achievements, and a personal interview. *Correspondence to:* Associate Dean for Admissions.

MINORITY STUDENTS: Comprise 6% of the first-year class. *For additional information:* Assistant Dean for Minority Affairs. Applications for aid may be submitted only upon acceptance to the school; deadline July 1.

----

*member AMCAS

Ohio State University*

370 West Ninth Avenue
Columbus, OH 43210-1200
Tel: (614) 292-7137
http://www.med.ohio-state.edu

MCAT: required

GPA: 3.6

FOUNDED: 1914; *publicly controlled.* The Independent Study Program provides the option of completing the MD degree requirements within 3 calendar years.

ENROLLMENT: 127 men, 83 women (first-year).

TUITION & FEES: Resident, $12,771; Nonresident, $33,429.

APPLICATIONS: Should be submitted between June 1 and November 1; the application fee is $30. Notification begins October 7; response must be received within 2 weeks; no deposit needed to hold place in class. Early Decision plan is available. Preference is given to state residents. Admission criteria include GPA, MCAT, letters of recommendation, the personal interview, and nonacademic achievements. *Correspondence to:* Admissions Office.

MINORITY STUDENTS: Comprise 9% of the first-year class. Academic assistance programs are available to students who exhibit special academic needs. *For additional information:* Office of Minority Affairs.

----

*member AMCAS

Oregon Health Sciences University*†
School of Medicine
3181 SW Sam Jackson Park Road
Portland, OR 97201-3098
Tel: (503) 494-2998
http://www.ohsu.edu/som-dean/admit.html

MCAT: required

GPA: 3.6

FOUNDED: 1887; *publicly controlled.*

ENROLLMENT: 56 men, 40 women (first-year).

TUITION & FEES: Resident, $17,123; Nonresident, $30,960.

APPLICATIONS: Should be submitted between June 1 and October 15; the application fee is $60. Notification begins November 1; response must be received by school within 2 weeks; no deposit needed to hold place in class. Preference is given to state residents, residents of neighboring western states without medical schools (Alaska, Montana, and Wyoming), and underrepresented minorities. Admission factors include preprofessional training, evidence of scholarship, MCAT scores, evaluations from premedical instructors, evidence of good moral character, and the personal interview. *Correspondence to:* Director of Admissions.

MINORITY STUDENTS: Comprise 3% of the first-year class. *For additional information:* Director, Multicultural Affairs. Applications for aid should be submitted upon acceptance, prior to March 1.

---

*member AMCAS
†member WICHE

Pennsylvania State University*
PO Box 850
Hershey, PA 17033
Tel: (717) 531-8755
http://www.collmed.psu.edu

MCAT: required

GPA: 3.61

FOUNDED: 1964; *publicly controlled.*

ENROLLMENT: 63 men, 45 women (first-year).

TUITION & FEES: Resident, $16,824; Nonresident, $24,550.

APPLICATIONS: Should be submitted between June 1 and November 15; the application fee is $40. Notification begins October 1; response must be received by school within 2 weeks; a deposit is needed to hold place in class. Early Decision plan is available. Preference is given to state residents. Selection factors include GPA, MCAT, letters of recommendation, and an interview. *Correspondence to:* Office of Student Affairs.

MINORITY STUDENTS: Comprise 18% of first-year students; most of these students receive aid. The College of Medicine has organized a special recruitment program for minorities and students from disadvantaged backgrounds. *For additional information:* Dr. Alphonse E. Leure-duPree, Associate Dean for Student Affairs.

---

*member AMCAS

Ponce School of Medicine*
PO Box 7004
Ponce, PR 00732
http://aafg.org/clerkships/479.html

MCAT: required

GPA: 3.3

FOUNDED: 1980 (originally Catholic University of Puerto Rico School of Medicine); *private.*

ENROLLMENT: 35 men, 30 women (first-year).

TUITION & FEES: not available.

APPLICATIONS: Should be submitted between June 1 and December 15; the application fee is $50. Notification begins October 15; response must be received within 4 weeks; a deposit is necessary to hold place in class. Early Decision plan is available. Admission decisions are based on the MCAT score, GPA, recommendations, and personal interview. Preference is given to residents of Puerto Rico; since courses are taught in both English and Spanish, students must have functional knowledge of both languages. *Correspondence to:* Admissions Office.

----

*member AMCAS

Rush Medical College of Rush University*
600 South Paulina Street
Chicago, IL 60612
Tel: (312) 942-6913
http://www.rushu.rush.edu/medcol/

MCAT: required

GPA: 3.54

FOUNDED: 1837, closed 1943 and reopened in 1971; *private*.

ENROLLMENT: 61 men, 58 women (first-year).

TUITION & FEES: Resident, $27,940; Nonresident, $27,940.

APPLICATIONS: Should be submitted between June 1 and November 15; the application fee is $45. Notification begins October 15; response must be received within 2 weeks; a deposit is needed to hold place in class. Early Decision plan is available. Admission criteria include academic performance, MCAT results, letters of recommendation, and the personal interview. *Correspondence to:* Office of Admissions, 524 Academic Facility.

MINORITY STUDENTS: Comprise 8% of the first-year class; most of these students receive aid. The application fee may be waived. *For additional information:* Chairperson, Committee on Admissions. Applications for aid may be made upon acceptance.

---

*member AMCAS

Saint Louis University*
Health Sciences Center
1402 South Grand Boulevard
St. Louis, MO 63104
Tel: (314) 577-8205
http://www.slu.edu/colleges/med/

MCAT: required

GPA: 3.62

FOUNDED: 1836; *private.*

ENROLLMENT: 79 men, 72 women (first-year).

TUITION & FEES: Resident, $31,112; Nonresident, $31,112.

APPLICATIONS: Should be submitted between June 1 and December 15; the application fee is $100. Notification begins October 15; response must be received within 2 weeks; a deposit is needed to hold place in class. Early Decision plan is available. Admissions qualifications include the MCAT, GPA, demonstrated scientific ability, character, and motivation. *Correspondence to:* Admissions Committee.

MINORITY STUDENTS: Comprise 14% of the first-year class; most of these students receive aid. The application fee may be waived. *For additional information:* Associate Dean, Admissions and Student Affairs.

---

*member AMCAS

Southern Illinois University*
School of Medicine
PO Box 19624
Springfield, IL 62794-1226
Tel: (217) 524-6013
http://siumed.edu

MCAT: required

GPA: 3.51

FOUNDED: 1969; *publicly controlled.*

ENROLLMENT: 39 men, 33 women (first year).

TUITION & FEES: Resident, $16,549; Nonresident, $46,633.

APPLICATIONS: Should be submitted between June 1 and November 15; the application fee is $50. Notification begins October 15; response must be received within 15 days; a deposit is required to hold place in class. Early Decision plan is available. Nonresidents must apply EDP. Admission requirements include GPA, MCAT, interviews, and letters of academic recommendation. *Correspondence to:* Office of Student and Alumni Affairs.

MINORITY STUDENTS: Comprise 10% of the first-year class. The School of Medicine sponsors a Medical Education Preparatory Program (MEDPREP) to aid minority students in preparing for medical school. *For additional information:* Director, MEDPREP.

---

*member AMCAS

Stanford University*†

School of Medicine
851 Welch Road
Palo Alto, CA 94304-1677
Tel: (650) 723-6861
http://www.stanford.edu

MCAT: required

GPA: 3.76

FOUNDED: 1908; *private;* a flexible curriculum allows completion of the MD program in 3 to 5 years.

ENROLLMENT: 40 men, 46 women (first-year).

TUITION & FEES: Resident, $29,348; Nonresident, $29,348.

APPLICATIONS: Should be submitted between June 1 and November 1; the application fee is $55. Notification begins October 15; response must be received within 2 weeks; no deposit needed to hold place in class. Early Decision plan is available. Selection factors include academic record and demonstrated motivational and personal qualifications for medicine. *Correspondence to:* Office of Admissions, Room 154.

MINORITY STUDENTS: Comprise 14% of the first-year class; most of these students receive aid. The School of Medicine has a strong commitment to recruit women and minority students. *For additional information:* Associate Dean for Student Affairs. Applications for aid are available after acceptance.

---

*member AMCAS
†member WICHE

State University of New York*
Downstate Medical Center
450 Clarkson Avenue
Brooklyn, NY 11203-2098
Tel: (718) 270-4315
http://www.hscbklyn.edu

MCAT: required

GPA: 3.56

FOUNDED: 1860 (acquired by state system in 1950); *publicly controlled.*

ENROLLMENT: 98 men, 91 women (first-year).

TUITION & FEES: Resident, $11,485; Nonresident, $22,585.

APPLICATIONS: Should be submitted between August 1 and December 15; the application fee is $65. Notification begins October 15; response must be received within 2 weeks; a deposit is needed to hold place in class. Strong preference given to state residents. Admissions decisions are based on college records, letters of recommendation, MCAT scores, the interview, and community service. *Correspondence to:* Director of Admissions.

MINORITY STUDENTS: Comprise 11% of first-year students. Various scholarships, work-study programs, and loans are available; most students receive assistance. The application fee may be waived. *For additional information:* Associate Dean for Minority Affairs.

---

*member AMCAS

State University of New York*

Health Science Center at Syracuse
College of Medicine
155 Elizabeth Blackwell Street
Syracuse, NY 13210
Tel: (315) 464-4570
http://www.hscsyr.edu

MCAT: required

GPA: 3.57

FOUNDED: 1834 (acquired by state system in 1950); *publicly controlled.*

ENROLLMENT: 91 men, 61 women (first-year).

TUITION & FEES: Resident, $11,250; Nonresident, $22,350.

APPLICATIONS: Should be submitted between June 1 and November 1; the application fee is $60. Notification begins October 15; response must be received within 2 weeks; no deposit needed to hold place in class. Early Decision plan is available. Strong preference given to state residents. Admission factors include scholastic and scientific aptitude and performance, MCAT scores, letters of recommendation, personal qualifications, and the personal interview. *Correspondence to:* Admissions Committee.

MINORITY STUDENTS: Comprise 6% of the first-year class; most of these students receive aid. The College of Medicine sponsors Project 90, which supports the academic needs of students of disadvantaged backgrounds. *For additional information:* Office of Multicultural Resources. Application for aid should be made upon acceptance.

---

*member AMCAS

State University of New York at Buffalo*

School of Medicine and Biomedical Sciences
45 Biomedical Education Building
3435 Main Street
Buffalo, NY 14214
Tel: (716) 829-3466
smbs.buffalo.edu/one

MCAT: required

GPA: 3.6

FOUNDED: 1846 (acquired by state system in 1962); *publicly controlled.*

ENROLLMENT: 62 men, 76 women (first-year).

TUITION & FEES: Resident, $11,790; Nonresident, $22,890.

APPLICATIONS: Should be submitted between June 1 and November 1; the application fee is $65. Notification begins October 15, response must be received within 2 weeks; a deposit is needed to hold place in class. Strong preference given to state residents. Admission factors weighted most heavily include GPA, MCAT, letters of recommendation, and the personal interview. Candidates should also demonstrate such personal qualifications as a habit of critical analysis, a spirit of inquiry, and a sense of understanding and sympathy for those who suffer. While admission decisions are based on merit, the percentage of women enrolled has traditionally been greater than the percentage of women in the applicant pool. *Correspondence to:* Office of Medical Admissions.

MINORITY STUDENTS: Comprise 10% of the first-year class. The School of Medicine sponsors a special summer program for minority and disadvantaged students. Remedial sessions are provided for all students during the academic year. *For additional information:* Director, Minority Affairs. Applications for aid are provided upon acceptance.

---

*member AMCAS

State University of New York at Stony Brook*

Health Sciences Center
School of Medicine
Stony Brook, NY 11794-8434
Tel: (631) 444-2113
http://www.informatics.sunysb.edu

MCAT: required

GPA: 3.55

FOUNDED: 1971; *publicly controlled.*

ENROLLMENT: 52 men, 49 women (first-year).

TUITION & FEES: Resident, $11,310; Nonresident, $22,190.

APPLICATIONS: Should be submitted between June 1 and November 15; the application fee is $65. Notification begins on October 15; response must be received within 15 days; no deposit needed to reserve place in class. Early Decision plan is available. Strong preference given to state residents. Admission decisions are based on MCAT, GPA, recommendations of premedical adviser, and personal abilities. *Correspondence to:* Committee on Admissions.

MINORITY STUDENTS: Comprise 7% of first-year students. Students may avail themselves of a variety of state, federal, and private programs of financial assistance administered by the Office of Student Services. The application fee may be waived. *For additional information:* Dr. Aldustus E. Jordan, Associate Dean.

---

*member AMCAS

Temple University*
School of Medicine
3400 North Broad Street
Philadelphia, PA 19140
Tel: (215) 707-3656
http://www.temple.edu/medschool/

MCAT: required

GPA: 3.42

FOUNDED: 1901; *state-related.*

ENROLLMENT: 134 men, 72 women (first-year).

TUITION & FEES: Resident, $23,708; Nonresident, $28,900.

APPLICATIONS: Should be submitted between June 1 and December 1; the application fee is $55. Notification begins October 15; response must be received by school within 2 weeks; a deposit is needed to hold place in class. Early Decision plan is available. Preference is given to state residents. Selection factors include academic performance, extracurricular activities, MCAT scores, recommendations, and the interview. *Correspondence to:* Admissions Office.

MINORITY STUDENTS: Comprise 17% of the first-year class; most of these students receive aid. The School of Medicine operates the Recruitment, Admissions, and Retention (RAR) Program, which actively identifies potential minority applicants and provides special follow-up services and financial aid during the term of their medical education. Matriculation summer program is offered for accepted minority students. *For additional information:* Charles S. Ireland, Jr., Assistant Dean.

- -

*member AMCAS

Texas A & M University

Health Science Center
College of Medicine
College Station, TX 77843
Tel: (409) 845-7743
tamushsc.tamu.edu/

MCAT: required

GPA: 3.64

FOUNDED: 1971; *publicly controlled.*

ENROLLMENT: 34 men, 44 women (first-year).

TUITION & FEES: Resident, $7,817; Nonresident, $20,917.

APPLICATIONS: Should be submitted between May 1 and October 15; the application fee is $45. Notification begins November 15; response must be received within 2 weeks; no deposit needed to hold place in class. Preference is given to state residents. Admission factors include academic records, MCAT scores, personal qualifications, and demonstration of motivation. *Correspondence to:* Associate Dean for Student Affairs and Admissions.

MINORITY STUDENTS: Comprise 10% of the total student body, 9% of the first-year class. *For additional information:* Coordinator, Minority Access to Medical Careers.

---

*member AMCAS

Texas Tech University
School of Medicine
3601 4th Street
Lubbock, TX 79430-0001
Tel: (806) 743-2297
http://www.ttuhsc.edu

MCAT: required

GPA: 3.5

FOUNDED: 1969; *publicly controlled.*

ENROLLMENT: 78 men, 45 women (first year).

TUITION & FEES: Resident, $8,040; Nonresident, $21,140.

APPLICATIONS: Should be submitted between May 1 and October 15; the application fee is $55. Notification begins October 15; response must be received by school within 2 weeks; a deposit is needed to hold place in class. Early Decision plan is available. Strong preference is given to state residents. Admissions decisions are based on MCAT, GPA, breadth and strength of undergraduate curriculum, letters of recommendation, and the personal interview. *Correspondence to:* Office of Admissions.

MINORITY STUDENTS: Comprise 10% of first-year students. Upon acceptance students may apply for aid. *For additional information:* Assistant Dean for Minority Affairs.

Tufts University*
School of Medicine
136 Harrison Avenue
Boston, MA 02111
Tel: (617) 636-6571
www.tufts.edu/med

MCAT: required

GPA: 3.59

FOUNDED: 1852; *private.*

ENROLLMENT: 95 men, 73 women (first-year).

TUITION & FEES: Resident, $34,180; Nonresident, $34,180.

APPLICATIONS: Should be submitted between June 1 and November 1; the application fee is $95. Notification begins December 1; response must be received within 2 weeks of notification; a deposit is needed to hold place in class. Early Decision plan is available. Admission factors counted most heavily include GPA, MCAT, caliber of college work, personality, and motivation. *Correspondence to:* Office of Admissions.

MINORITY STUDENTS: Comprise 4% of the first-year class. The application fee may be waived. *For additional information:* Assistant Director of Student Services. Applications for aid are available upon acceptance.

---

*member AMCAS

Tulane University*
School of Medicine
1430 Tulane Avenue
New Orleans, LA 70112
Tel: (504) 588-5187
http://www.mcl.tulane.edu/departments/admiss

MCAT: required

GPA: 3.53

FOUNDED: 1834; *private.*

ENROLLMENT: 87 men, 65 women (first-year).

TUITION & FEES: Resident, $30,007; Nonresident, $30,007.

APPLICATIONS: Should be submitted between June 1 and December 15; the application fee is $95. Notification begins October 15; response must be received before May 15; a deposit is required to hold place in class. Admission factors weighted most heavily include GPA (overall and science), MCAT scores, faculty recommendations, special accomplishments and talents, substance of undergraduate programs, and trends in academic performance. *Correspondence to:* Office of Admissions.

MINORITY STUDENTS: Comprise 21% of the first-year students; a majority of these students receive aid. A prematriculation summer enrichment program is available to entering minority and other disadvantaged students, as are tutorial and counseling services. *For additional information:* Dr. Anna Cherrie Epps, Associate Dean for Student Services.

---

*member AMCAS

Uniformed Services University of the Health Sciences*

F. Edward Hébert School of Medicine
4301 Jones Bridge Road
Bethesda, MD 20814-4799
Tel: (301) 295-3101
http://www.usuhs.mil

MCAT: required

GPA: 3.53

FOUNDED: 1972; *publicly controlled.* The school aims to prepare men and women for careers as medical corps officers.

ENROLLMENT: 122 men, 43 women (first-year).

TUITION & FEES: There are no tuition charges, and books and supplies are also furnished without charge.

APPLICATIONS: Should be submitted between June 1 and November 1; there is no application fee. Notification begins November 1; response must be received within 2 weeks; no deposit required to hold place in class. Selection factors include letters of reference, personal statement, and a service preference statement. Transcripts should not be submitted until requested. *Correspondence to:* Admissions Office; Room A-1041.

MINORITY STUDENTS: Comprise 10% of first-year students. The School of Medicine operates the Accession of Qualified Underrepresented Applicants (AQUA) program to increase the number of qualified minority and women applicants. *For additional information:* Director of Admissions/Registrar.

---

*member AMCAS

Universidad Central del Caribe*

School of Medicine
Ramón Rúiz Arnau University Hospital
Call Box 60-327
Bayamón, PR 00960-6032
http://www.uccaribe.edu/medical

MCAT: required

GPA: 3.1

FOUNDED: 1976; *private.*

ENROLLMENT: 35 men, 30 women (first-year).

TUITION & FEES: not available

APPLICATIONS: Should be submitted between June 1 and December 15; the application fee is $50. Notification begins in February; response must be received within 10 days. A deposit is needed to hold place in class. Early Decision plan is available. Admission factors include undergraduate academic record, GPA, MCAT, personal interview, and letters of recommendation. *Correspondence to:* Office of Admissions.

---

*member AMCAS

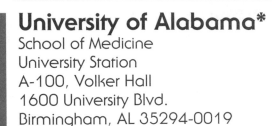

University of Alabama*
School of Medicine
University Station
A-100, Volker Hall
1600 University Blvd.
Birmingham, AL 35294-0019
Tel: (205) 934-2433
ua.edu/uasom

MCAT: required

GPA: 3.62

FOUNDED: 1859; *publicly controlled.*

ENROLLMENT: 97 men, 63 women (first-year).

TUITION & FEES: Resident, $10,409; Nonresident, $24,547.

APPLICATIONS: Should be submitted between June 1 and November 1; the application fee is $65. Notification begins October 15; response must be received within 2 weeks; a deposit is needed to hold place in class. Early Decision plan is available for Alabama residents only. Preference is given to state residents. Admission factors weighted most heavily include GPA, MCAT scores, letters of recommendation, the personal interview, and personal qualifications. *Correspondence to:* Assistant Dean for Student Services for Admissions.

MINORITY STUDENTS: Comprise 10% of the first-year class; most of these students receive aid. The application fee may be waived. The Office of Minority Student Affairs and the Admissions Committee provide counsel to minority students interested in the study of medicine. *For additional information:* Coordinator, Minority Enhancement Program. Applications for aid should be made by March 1.

----

*member AMCAS

University of Arizona*†
College of Medicine
PO Box 245075
Tucson, AZ 85724
Tel: (520) 626-6214
http://www.medicine.arizona.edu/

MCAT: required

GPA: 3.64

FOUNDED: 1967; *publicly controlled.*

ENROLLMENT: 58 men, 42 women (first-year).

TUITION & FEES: Resident, $8,436; Nonresident,not applicable.

APPLICATIONS: Should be submitted between June 1 and November 1; there is no application fee. Notification begins January 30; response must be received within 2 weeks; no deposit needed to hold place in class. Only residents of Arizona and WICHE-certified residents of Alaska, Montana, or Wyoming are considered for admission. Admissions decisions are based on the MCAT, GPA, letters of recommendation, personal interview, character, and motivation. *Correspondence to:* Admissions Office.

MINORITY STUDENTS: Comprise 24% of the first-year class. Various types of financial assistance are available as is a Summer Prematriculation Program. *For additional information:* Dr. Andrew M. Goldner, Associate Dean for Student Affairs. Application for aid may be made after acceptance.

---

*member AMCAS
†member WICHE

University of Arkansas*
College of Medicine
4301 West Markham Street
Little Rock, AR 72205
Tel: (501) 686-5354
http://www.uams.edu

MCAT: required

GPA: 3.6

FOUNDED: 1879; *publicly controlled.*

ENROLLMENT: 100 men, 50 women (first-year).

TUITION & FEES: Resident, $9,103; Nonresident, $18,031.

APPLICATIONS: Should be submitted between June 1 and November 15; the application fee is $50. Notification begins December 15; response must be received within 2 weeks; no deposit required to hold place in class. Preference is given to state residents. Admission factors counted most heavily include GPA, MCAT, premedical advisory committee and faculty evaluation, and medical faculty interview. *Correspondence to:* Office of Student Admissions, Slot 551.

MINORITY STUDENTS: Comprise 7% of the first-year class. *For additional information:* Associate Dean for Minority Affairs. Application for aid should be made after acceptance and prior to matriculation.

----
*member AMCAS

University of California, Davis*†
School of Medicine
One Shields Avenue
Davis, CA 95616
Tel: (530) 752-2717
http://www.med.ucdavis.edu

MCAT: required

GPA: 3.4

FOUNDED: 1963, admitted first class in 1968; *publicly controlled.*

ENROLLMENT: 42 men, 51 women (first-year).

TUITION & FEES: Resident, $9,900; Nonresident, $19,248.

APPLICATIONS: Should be submitted between June 1 and November 1; the application fee is $40. Notification begins October 15; response must be received within 2 weeks; no deposit required to secure place in class. Preference is given to state residents. Admission factors include academic record, MCAT results, and motivation and personal qualifications as judged from letters of recommendation and personal interview. *Correspondence to:* Admissions Office.

MINORITY STUDENTS: Percentage of the first-year class was not available. The application fee may be waived. The School of Medicine sponsors special recruitment and orientation programs for students of disadvantaged social and educational backgrounds. *For additional information:* Assistant Dean for Minority Affairs. Applications for aid may be made after acceptance.

---

*member AMCAS
†member WICHE

University of California, Irvine*†

College of Medicine
Medical Education Bldg. 802
Irvine, CA 92691-4089
Tel: (949) 824-5388
http://www.ucihealth.uci.edu/

MCAT: required

GPA: 3.67

FOUNDED: 1965; *publicly supported.*

ENROLLMENT: 50 men, 42 women (first-year).

TUITION & FEES: Resident, $10,806; Nonresident, $19,806.

APPLICATIONS: Should be submitted between June 1 and November 1; the application fee is $40. Notification begins November 15; response must be received within 2 weeks; no deposit needed to hold place in class. Preference given to state residents. Admission factors include GPA, MCAT, letters of recommendation, and a personal interview. *Correspondence to:* Office of Admissions.

MINORITY STUDENTS: Comprise 14% of first-year students. Tutorial assistance and counseling are available to students. The college provides financial aid in the form of scholarships, grants, and loans. The application fee may be waived. *For additional information:* Assistant Dean, Outreach Student Affairs. Application for aid should be made after acceptance.

---

*member AMCAS
†member WICHE

University of California, Los Angeles*†

UCLA School of Medicine
Center for Health Sciences
Los Angeles, CA 90095
Tel: (310) 825-6081
http://www.medstudent.ucla.edu/admiss/

MCAT: required

GPA: 3.66

FOUNDED: 1951; *publicly supported.*

ENROLLMENT: 58 men, 63 women (first-year).

TUITION & FEES: Resident, $10,032; Nonresident, $19,804.

APPLICATIONS: Should be submitted between June 1 and November 1; application fee is $40. Notification begins January 15; response must be received within 2 weeks; no deposit needed to secure place in class. Admission criteria include GPA, MCAT results, evaluation of accomplishments and character in letters of recommendation, and the personal interview. *Correspondence to:* Office of Student Affairs.

MINORITY STUDENTS: Comprise 49% of the first-year class; most of these students receive aid. The application fee may be waived. A subcommittee of the Admissions Committee, which includes minority faculty and students, is responsible for the evaluation of all applications from minority and disadvantaged students. *For additional information:* Director, Office of Student Support Services. Applications for aid are forwarded to entering freshmen prior to May.

---

*member AMCAS
†member WICHE

University of California, San Diego*†

School of Medicine
La Jolla, CA 92093
Tel: (858) 534-3880
medicince.ucsd.edu

MCAT: required

GPA: 3.65

FOUNDED: 1968; *publicly controlled.*

ENROLLMENT: 74 men, 48 women (first-year).

TUITION & FEES: Resident, $10,324; Nonresident, $20,128.

APPLICATIONS: Should be submitted between June 1 and November 1; the application fee is $40. Notification begins October 15; response must be received within 2 weeks; no deposit required to hold place in class. Preference given to state residents. Admission factors most heavily weighted include GPA, MCAT, letters of recommendation, personal interviews, and the nature of scholarly and extracurricular activities. *Correspondence to:* Office of Admissions, Medical Teaching Facility.

MINORITY STUDENTS: Comprise 44% of the first-year class; most of these students receive aid. The application fee may be waived. *For additional information:* Dr. Percy J. Russell, Associate Dean. Application for aid may be filed only upon acceptance.

----

*member AMCAS
†member WICHE

University of California, San Francisco*†
School of Medicine
San Francisco, CA 94143
Tel: (415) 476-4044
http://www.som.ucsf.edu

MCAT: required.

GPA: 3.75

FOUNDED: 1864; *publicly controlled.*

ENROLLMENT: 64 men, 77 women (first-year).

TUITION & FEES: Resident, $10,188; Nonresident, $19,992.

APPLICATIONS: Should be submitted between June 1 and November 1; the application fee is $40. Notification begins November 15; response must be received within 2 weeks; no deposit needed to secure place in class. Preference is given to state residents. Admission factors include academic record, MCAT scores, evidence of motivation towards medicine, and personal qualifications. *Correspondence to:* School of Medicine, Admissions, C-200, Box 0408.

MINORITY STUDENTS: Comprise 13% of the first-year class; most of these students receive aid. The Health Sciences Minority Program provides admission assistance, financial aid, a comprehensive orientation program, and other services for socioeconomically disadvantaged students. *For additional information:* Admissions Office. Application for aid should be made after acceptance.

---

*member AMCAS
†member WICHE

University of Chicago*
Pritzker School of Medicine
924 East 57th Street, BLSC 104
Chicago, IL 60637
Tel: (773) 702-1937
http://pritzker.bsd.uchicago.edu

MCAT: required

GPA: 3.61

FOUNDED: 1927; *private.*

ENROLLMENT: 52 men, 52 women (first-year).

TUITION & FEES: Resident, not available; Nonresident, $26,780.

APPLICATIONS: Should be submitted between June 1 and November 15; the application fee is $60. Notification begins October 15; response must be received within 4 weeks; a deposit is needed to hold place in class. Early Decision plan is available. No preference given to state residents, though approximately 40% of recent entering classes have been from Illinois. Selection factors include scholastic record, MCAT results, personal qualifications, and extracurricular activities. *Correspondence to:* Office of Dean of Students.

MINORITY STUDENTS: Comprise 13% of the first-year class; most of these students receive aid. *For additional information:* Director of Student Programs. Applications for aid may be submitted upon acceptance.

----

*member AMCAS

University of Cincinnati*

College of Medicine
PO Box 670552
Cincinnati, OH 45267-0552
Tel: (513) 558-7314
http://www.med.uc.edu

MCAT: required

GPA: 3.55

FOUNDED: 1819; *publicly controlled.*

ENROLLMENT: 99 men, 60 women (first-year).

TUITION & FEES: Resident, $13,173; Nonresident, $23,106.

APPLICATIONS: Should be submitted between June 1 and November 15; the application fee is $25. Notification begins October 15; response must be received by school within 2 weeks; no deposit needed to hold place in class. Early Decision plan is available. Preference is given to state residents. *Correspondence to:* Office of Student Affairs/ Admissions.

MINORITY STUDENTS: Comprise 4% the first-year class; most of these students receive aid. The College of Medicine maintains prematriculation and tutorial programs for students of disadvantaged backgrounds. *For additional information:* Assistant Dean for Admissions. Applications for aid should be made by May 31.

---

*member AMCAS

University of Colorado*†

School of Medicine
4200 East Ninth Avenue
Denver, CO 80262-0297
Tel: (303) 315-7361
http://www.uchsc.edu

MCAT: required

GPA: 3.6

FOUNDED: 1883; *publicly controlled.*

ENROLLMENT: 60 men, 62 women (first-year).

TUITION & FEES: Resident, $13,029; Nonresident, $56,423.

APPLICATIONS: Should be submitted between June 1 and November 15; the application fee is $70. Notification begins October 15; response must be received within 2 weeks; a deposit is needed to hold place in class. Early Decision plan available. Preference is given first to Colorado residents and then to residents of western states without medical schools—Wyoming, Montana, and Alaska. Admission factors counted most heavily include GPA, MCAT, the interview, and references. *Correspondence to:* Medical School Admissions.

MINORITY STUDENTS: Comprise 16% of the first-year class; most of these students receive aid. The application fee may be waived. *For additional information:* Center for Multicultural Enrichment.

---

*member AMCAS
†member WICHE

University of Connecticut*
School of Medicine
263 Farmington Avenue
Farmington, CT 06030-1905
Tel: (860) 679-4713
http://www.uchc.edu

MCAT: required

GPA: 3.6

FOUNDED: 1968; *publicly controlled.*

ENROLLMENT: 34 men, 43 women (first-year).

TUITION & FEES: Resident, $13,210; Nonresident, $25,155.

APPLICATIONS: Should be submitted between June 1 and December 15; the application fee is $60. Notification begins October 15; response must be received within 2 weeks; a deposit is required to hold a place in class. Early Decision plan is available. Preference given to state residents. Admission factors include GPA, MCAT scores, undergraduate curriculum, extracurricular activities, and letters of recommendation. *Correspondence to:* Office of Admissions and Student Affairs.

MINORITY STUDENTS: Comprise 16% of the first-year class; most of these students receive aid. *For additional information:* Associate Dean, Minority Student Affairs.

---

*member AMCAS

University of Florida*
College of Medicine
J. Hillis Miller Health
Gainesville, FL 32610
Tel: (352) 392-4569
http://www.med.ufl.edu/

MCAT: required

GPA: 3.71

FOUNDED: 1956; *publicly controlled.*

ENROLLMENT: 43 men, 31 women (first-year).

TUITION & FEES: Resident, $10,952; Nonresident, $29,485.

APPLICATIONS: Should be submitted between June 1 and December 1; there is no application fee. Notification begins October 15; response must be received within 2 weeks; no deposit needed to hold place in class. Preference is given to Florida residents. Admissions decisions are based on the MCAT, GPA, personal interview, and character. *Correspondence to:* Chair, Medical Selection Committee, Box 100216.

MINORITY STUDENTS: Comprise 9% of first-year students. Many types of financial assistance are available; students should apply upon enrollment. *For additional information:* Assistant Dean for Minority Relations.

---

*member AMCAS

University of Hawaii*†
John A. Burns School of Medicine
1960 East-West Road
Honolulu, HI 96822
Tel: (808) 956-8300
http://www.hawaiimed.hawaii.edu/

MCAT: required

GPA: 3.57

FOUNDED: 1965 as a 2-year institution, introduced 4-year program in 1973; *publicly controlled.*

ENROLLMENT: 33 men, 25 women (first-year).

TUITION & FEES: Resident, $10,939; Nonresident, $24,643.

APPLICATIONS: Should be submitted between June 1 and December 1; the application fee is $50. Notification begins October 15; response must be received within 2 weeks; no deposit required to hold place in class. Early Decision plan is available for residents of Hawaii. Preference given to state residents. Admission factors weighted most heavily include GPA, MCAT, interview, and letters of recommendation. *Correspondence to:* Office of Admissions.

MINORITY STUDENTS: Diverse ethnic backgrounds are represented in the faculty and student body. The School of Medicine sponsors 2 programs for students unable to enter directly into the normal medical program: a remedial program in the premedical sciences and a decelerated program permitting the student 3 years, with tutorial assistance, to complete the work normally completed in 2 years. These programs are designed primarily for, but are not limited to, persons of Hawaiian, part Hawaiian, Filipino, Samoan, and Micronesian ancestry. There is no application fee. *For additional information:* Student Affairs. Application for aid may be made upon acceptance.

----

*member AMCAS
†member WICHE

University of Illinois*
College of Medicine
808 South Wood Street m/c 783
Chicago, IL 60612
Tel: (312) 996-5635
http://www.uic.edu/depts/mcam/

MCAT: required

GPA: 3.41

FOUNDED: 1881; *publicly controlled.* College of Medicine programs are offered in four cities: Chicago, Urbana-Champaign, Peoria, and Rockford.

ENROLLMENT: 168 men, 118 women (first-year).

TUITION & FEES: Resident, $15,442; Nonresident, $38,288.

APPLICATIONS: Should be submitted between June 1 and December 1; the application fee is $40. Notification begins November 1; response must be received within 2 weeks; a deposit is required to reserve place in class. Early Decision plan is available for residents of Illinois. Strong preference is given to state residents. Admission factors counted most heavily include GPA, MCAT, letters of academic recommendation, and the personal statement in the AMCAS application. *Correspondence to:* Office of Admissions.

MINORITY STUDENTS: Comprise 24% of the first-year class; most of these students receive aid. Preadmissions counseling is provided and tutorial assistants are available to those students requiring additional instruction during the academic year. The application fee may be waived. *For additional information:* Associate Dean and Director of Urban Health Program. Application for aid should be made upon acceptance.

*member AMCAS

University of Iowa*
College of Medicine
100 Medicine Administration Building
Iowa City, IA 52242
Tel: (319) 335-8052
http://www.medicine.uiowa.edu/

MCAT: required

GPA: 3.66

FOUNDED: 1850; *publicly controlled.*

ENROLLMENT: 130 men, 45 women (first-year).

TUITION & FEES: Resident, $10,275; Nonresident, $26,079.

APPLICATIONS: Should be submitted between June 1 and November 1; the application fee is $30. Notification begins October 15; response must be received within 2 weeks; a deposit is needed to hold place in class. Early Decision plan is available. Preference is given to state residents. Admission factors include GPA (science and overall), MCAT scores, and personal qualifications as judged from recommendations. *Correspondence to:* Office of Admissions.

MINORITY STUDENTS: Comprise 26% of the first-year class; most of these students receive aid. The application fee may be waived. The College of Medicine sponsors the Educational Opportunity Program, which provides financial and academic assistance for minority and disadvantaged students. A summer program is offered for entering students. *For additional information:* Program Associate for Equal Opportunity Programs.

---

*member AMCAS

University of Kansas*
School of Medicine
3901 Rainbow Boulevard
Kansas City, KS 66160-7301
Tel: (913) 588-5245
http://www.kumc.edu/som.html

MCAT: required

GPA: 3.6

FOUNDED: 1899 as a 1-year institution, introduced 4-year program in 1906; *publicly controlled.*

ENROLLMENT: 101 men, 74 women (first-year).

TUITION & FEES: Resident, $10,000; Nonresident, $24,000.

APPLICATIONS: Should be submitted between June 1 and October 15; the application fee is $40 for nonresidents. Notification begins February 1; response must be received within 2 weeks; a deposit is needed to reserve place in class. Early Decision plan is available. Preference is given to state residents; the class is first filled with Kansas residents, after which a few highly qualified nonresidents are accepted. Admission factors weighted most heavily include GPA, MCAT, premedical adviser's evaluation, interview, performance in required premedical courses, and trends in academic performance. *Correspondence to:* Office of Admissions.

MINORITY STUDENTS: Comprise 8% of the first-year class. The School of Medicine sponsors a prematriculation Summer Enrichment Program and an ongoing recruitment program, in addition to its tutorial and counseling programs for matriculated minority students. *For additional information:* Associate Dean for Minority Affairs. Applications for aid should be made upon acceptance.

----

*member AMCAS

University of Kentucky*
College of Medicine
UK Chandler Medical Center
800 Rose Street
Lexington, KY 40536-0084
Tel: (859) 323-6161
www.cmc.uky.edu/

MCAT: required

GPA: 3.55

FOUNDED: 1956; *publicly controlled.*

ENROLLMENT: 54 men, 41 women (first-year).

TUITION & FEES: Resident, $10,284; Nonresident, $25,674.

APPLICATIONS: Should be submitted between June 1 and November 1, the application fee is $30. Notification is rolling; response must be received within 2 weeks; a deposit is needed to hold place in class. Early Decision plan is available. Preference given to state residents. Admission factors weighted most heavily include GPA, MCAT scores, premedical letters of recommendation, extracurricular activities, exposure to medicine, and the personal interview. *Correspondence to:* Admissions, Room MN-102.

MINORITY STUDENTS: Comprise 9% of the first-year class; most of these students receive aid. The College of Medicine sponsors a prematriculation program—Med Prep—in which selected students participate in a 1-year academic and work experience in preparation for entering medical school. The Office of Special Student Programs maintains recruitment programs for minorities and women. Tutorial assistance is available during the academic year. *For additional information:* Assistant Dean for Education. Application for aid should be made in April (prior to matriculation).

---

*member AMCAS

University of Louisville*
School of Medicine
Health Sciences Center
Louisville, KY 40292
Tel: (502) 852-5193
http://www.louisville.edu

MCAT: required

GPA: 3.6

FOUNDED: 1833, acquired by state in 1970; *publicly controlled.*

ENROLLMENT: 75 men, 68 women (first-year).

TUITION & FEES: Resident, $10,176; Nonresident, $25,566.

APPLICATIONS: Should be submitted between June 1 and November 1; the application fee is $25. Notification begins October 1; response must be received within 2 weeks; a deposit is needed to hold place in class. Early Decision plan is available. Preference given to state residents. Admission factors counted most heavily include GPA, MCAT, motivation and personality as evaluated by interview, and extracurricular activities. *Correspondence to:* Office of Admissions.

MINORITY STUDENTS: Comprise 9% of the first-year class; most of these students receive aid. Tutorial assistance is arranged through the Office of Student Affairs for students of disadvantaged backgrounds and who express an interest in securing such help. The application fee may be waived. *For additional information:* Director of Special Programs. Application for aid should be made upon student's acceptance of offer of admission.

---

*member AMCAS

University of Maryland*

School of Medicine
655 West Baltimore Street
Baltimore, MD 21201-1559
Tel: (410) 706-7478
http://som1.umaryland.edu/index.html

MCAT: required

GPA: 3.63

FOUNDED: 1808; *publicly controlled.*

ENROLLMENT: 60 men, 78 women (first-year).

TUITION & FEES: Resident, $13,129; Nonresident, $25,145.

APPLICATIONS: Should be submitted between June 1 and November 1; the application fee is $50. Notification begins October 15; response must be received within 3 weeks; no deposit needed to hold place in class. Early Decision plan is available. Preference given to state residents. Admission criteria weighted most heavily include GPA, MCAT, letters of recommendation, and interview. *Correspondence to:* Committee on Admissions, Room 1-005.

MINORITY STUDENTS: Comprise 14% of the first-year class. The application fee may be waived. *For additional information:* Dr. Robert L. Harrell, Jr., Assistant Dean of Student Affairs. Applications for aid are provided upon acceptance.

---

*member AMCAS

University of Massachusetts*
Medical School
55 Lake Avenue, North
Worcester, MA 01655
Tel: (508) 856-2323
http://www.umassmed.edu/

MCAT: required

GPA: 3.6 science

FOUNDED: 1962, admitted first class in 1970; *publicly controlled.*

ENROLLMENT: 45 men, 55 women (first-year).

TUITION & FEES: Resident, $10,347; Nonresident, not applicable.

APPLICATIONS: Should be submitted between June 1 and November 1; application fee is $75. Notification begins October 15; response must be received within 2 weeks; a deposit is needed to hold place in class. Early Decision plan is available. Currently, only residents of Massachusetts are considered for admission. Admissions decisions are based on the MCAT, GPA, letters of recommendation, character, maturity, and motivation. *Correspondence to:* Associate Dean of Admissions.

MINORITY STUDENTS: Comprise 5% of first-year students. Financial assistance is available; approximately 75% of all students receive aid. *For additional information:* Office of Minority and Community Academic Programs. Application for aid should be made after acceptance.

University of Medicine and Dentistry of New Jersey*

New Jersey Medical School
185 South Orange Avenue
Newark, NJ 07103-2714
Tel: (973) 972-4631
http://www.umdnj.edu/njmsweb

MCAT: required

GPA: 3.5

FOUNDED: 1954, acquired by state in 1965; *publicly controlled*

ENROLLMENT: 91 men, 79 women (first-year).

TUITION & FEES: Resident, $16,952; Nonresident, $25,119.

APPLICATIONS: Should be submitted between June 1 and December 1; application fee is $75. Notification begins October 15; response must be received within 2 weeks; a deposit is needed to hold place in class. Early Decision plan is available for state residents only, to whom preference is given. Admission factors weighted most heavily include GPA, MCAT, motivation, determination, recommendations, and extracurricular activities. *Correspondence to:* Director of Admissions.

MINORITY STUDENTS: Comprise 16% of the first-year class; most of these students receive aid. The Medical School sponsors a special summer program for minority and disadvantaged students. *For additional information:* Assistant Dean for Minority Affairs. Application for aid should be made upon acceptance.

---

*member AMCAS

University of Medicine and Dentistry of New Jersey*

Robert Wood Johnson Medical School
675 Hoes Lane
Piscataway, NJ 08854-5635
Tel: (732) 235-4576
http://www2.umdnj.edu/admweb/

MCAT: required

GPA: 3.57

FOUNDED: 1966 as a 2-year medical school, introduced clinical program for one half of each class in 1970; in 1974 the school graduated its first class of MDs; formerly known as Rutgers Medical School; *publicly controlled.*

ENROLLMENT: 78 men, 65 women (first-year).

TUITION & FEES: Resident, $17,424; Nonresident, $26,491.

APPLICATIONS: Should be submitted between June 1 and December 1; application fee is $75. Notification begins October 15; response must be received within 2 weeks; a deposit is needed to hold place in class. Early Decision plan is available. Preference is given to state residents. Selection factors include academic achievement, MCAT scores, faculty recommendation, and the personal interview. *Correspondence to:* Office of Admissions.

MINORITY STUDENTS: Comprise 17% of the first-year class. The Medical School sponsors a prematriculation summer program for accepted minority and disadvantaged students. *For additional information:* Assistant Dean for Special Academic Programs. Financial aid materials are available upon acceptance.

---

*member AMCAS

University of Miami*
School of Medicine
PO Box 016159
Miami, FL 33101
Tel: (305) 243-6791
http://www.miami.edu/UMH/CDA

MCAT: required

GPA: 3.67

FOUNDED: 1952; *private.* A special program enables a person with a PhD degree in science or mathematics to earn an MD degree in 2 years.

ENROLLMENT: 64 men, 79 women (first-year).

TUITION & FEES: Resident, $25,790; Nonresident, $35,790.

APPLICATIONS: Should be submitted between June 15 and December 1; the application fee is $50. Notification begins October 15; response must be received within 3 weeks; a deposit is required to hold place in class. Preference is given to state residents. Admission factors counted most heavily include GPA, MCAT, faculty evaluations, motivation, and the personal interview. *Correspondence to:* Office of Admissions.

MINORITY STUDENTS: Comprise 9% of the first-year students; a majority of these students receive aid. A Committee on Minority Affairs is involved in recruitment and assistance to minority students. Tutorial programs are available. *For additional information:* Associate Dean for Minority Affairs.

*member AMCAS

University of Michigan*
Medical School
1301 East Catherine Street
Ann Arbor, MI 48109-0611
Tel: (734) 764-6317
http://www.med.umich.edu/medschool

MCAT: required

GPA: 3.6

FOUNDED: 1850; *publicly controlled.* Combined 7-year program leading to the baccalaureate and MD degrees offered.

ENROLLMENT: 87 men, 57 women (first-year).

TUITION & FEES: Resident, $17,840; Nonresident, $27,400.

APPLICATIONS: Should be submitted between June 1 and November 15; the application fee is $50. Notification begins December 1; response deadline is flexible; a deposit is needed to hold place in class. Early Decision plan is available. Preference is given to state residents. Selection factors include academic achievement, MCAT scores, and personal qualifications as judged from the personal interview, letters of recommendation, and extracurricular activities. *Correspondence to:* Admissions Committee.

MINORITY STUDENTS: Comprise 10% of the first-year class; most of these students receive aid. A prematriculation summer program is available. *For additional information:* Assistant Dean for Student and Minority Affairs. Applications for aid should be made upon acceptance.

---

*member AMCAS

University of Minnesota—Duluth*
School of Medicine
10 University Drive
Duluth, MN 55812
Tel: (218) 726-8511
www.d.umn.edu/medweb/admissions

MCAT: required

GPA: 3.55

FOUNDED: 1972; *publicly controlled* 2-year basic medical and clinical sciences school. Upon completion of the 2-year program at Duluth, students transfer to the degree-granting program at the University of Minnesota at Minneapolis.

ENROLLMENT: 22 men, 30 women (first-year).

TUITION & FEES: Resident, $18,621; Nonresident, $33,481.

APPLICATIONS: Should be submitted between June 1 and November 1; there is no application fee. Notification begins October 15; response must be received within 2 weeks; no deposit is needed to hold place in class. Early Decision plan is available. Strong preference is given to residents of Minnesota. Residents of Manitoba, Canada, and certain northern counties of Wisconsin may also be considered. Admission factors counted most heavily include GPA, MCAT, and potential to practice primary care in rural areas or small towns. *Correspondence to:* Office of Admissions, Room 107.

MINORITY STUDENTS: Comprise 12% of the first-year class. Resident tuition may be granted to minority nonresidents. The school sponsors a special program that offers preparation for health professions to American Indians. *For additional information:* Director, Center of American Indian and Minority Health. Application deadline for aid varies according to specific program applied to.

----

*member AMCAS

University of Minnesota*

Medical School—Minneapolis
420 Delaware Street, SE
Minneapolis, MN 55455-0310
Tel: (612) 624-1122
http://www.med.umn.edu/

MCAT: required

GPA: 3.58

FOUNDED: 1888; *publicly supported.* The flexible program permits completion
of the 4-year curriculum in 3 years.

ENROLLMENT: 91 men, 74 women (first-year).

TUITION & FEES: Resident, $17,193; Nonresident, $31,025.

APPLICATIONS: Should be submitted between June 1 and November 15; the
application fee is $50. Notification begins November 15; response must
be received within 2 weeks; no deposit is required to reserve a place in
class. Early Decision plan is available. Preference is given to state residents.
Admissions decisions are based on the MCAT, GPA, and personal interview
as well as the honesty, dedication, and motivation of the applicant.
Correspondence to: Office of Admissions and Student Affairs.

MINORITY STUDENTS: Comprise 2% of first-year students. Financial aid is
available; resident tuition may be granted to minority nonresidents. *For
additional information:* Assistant to the Dean for Student Affairs. Application for aid should be made after notification of acceptance.

---

*member AMCAS

University of Mississippi*

School of Medicine
2500 North State Street
Jackson, MS 39216-4505
Tel: (601) 984-5010
http://www.umsmed.edu/

MCAT: required

GPA: 3.6

FOUNDED: 1903 as a 2-year school, introduced 4-year program in 1955; *publicly controlled.*

ENROLLMENT: 58 men, 42 women (first-year).

TUITION & FEES: Resident, $6,988; Nonresident, $13,498.

APPLICATIONS: Should be submitted between June 1 and November 1; there is no application fee. Notification begins October 15; response must be received within 15 days; a deposit is needed to hold place in class. Early Decision plan is available for Mississippi residents only. Preference given to state residents. Admission factors weighted most heavily include GPA, MCAT, motivation, and the personal interview. *Correspondence to:* Chairman, Admissions Committee.

MINORITY STUDENTS: Comprise 16% of the first-year class. The Office of Minority Student Affairs assists with recruitment. *For additional information:* Director of Minority Affairs. There is no deadline for financial aid applications.

---

*member AMCAS

University of Missouri—Columbia*
School of Medicine
One Hospital Drive
Columbia, MO 65212
Tel: (573) 882-2923
muhealth.org~medicine

MCAT: required

GPA: 3.7

FOUNDED: 1841 as a 2-year school, introduced 4-year program in 1955; *publicly controlled.*

ENROLLMENT: 50 men, 46 women (first-year).

TUITION & FEES: Resident, $5,189; Nonresident, $14,641.

APPLICATIONS: Should be submitted between June 1 and November 1; there is no application fee. Notification begins December 15; response must be received within 2 weeks; a deposit is needed to reserve place in class. Early Decision plan is available. Preference is given to state residents. Admission criteria include academic performance, MCAT results, and personal qualifications as evaluated from letters of recommendation, the personal interview, and the formal application. *Correspondence to:* Office of Admissions, MA202 Medical Sciences Building.

MINORITY STUDENTS: Comprise 10% of the first-year class; most of these students receive aid. The School of Medicine sponsors flexible curriculum alternatives and summer enrichment programs for students of disadvantaged backgrounds. *For additional information:* Assistant Dean for Minority Affairs.

---

*member AMCAS

University of Missouri—Kansas City
School of Medicine
2411 Holmes
Kansas City, MO 64110-2499
Tel: (816) 235-1870
http://research.med.umkc.edu/selection.html

MCAT: not required   **ACT:** required

GPA: not available

FOUNDED: 1971; *publicly controlled.* The School of Medicine sponsors only a combined 6-year program, in cooperation with the College of Arts and Sciences, leading to the baccalaureate and MD degrees.

ENROLLMENT: 45 men, 75 women (first-year).

TUITION & FEES: Resident, $19,323; Nonresident, $38,995.

APPLICATIONS: Should be submitted between August 1 and November 15; the application fee is $25. Notification begins April 1; response must be received by May 1; a deposit is needed to hold place in class. Residency in Missouri is of prime consideration. Admissions requirements include demonstrated ability to perform on a college level based on a combination of high school rank and scores on a standardized college aptitude test. Personal qualities such as leadership, stamina, reliability, motivation for medicine, and range of interests are also considered. *Correspondence to:* Admissions Office.

MINORITY STUDENTS: Comprise 12% of first-year students. Aid is available to medical students. *For additional information:* Director, Office of Minority Affairs. Application for aid should be made by March 15.

University of Nebraska*

College of Medicine
600 South 42nd Street
986585 Nebraska Medical Center
Omaha, NE 68198-6585
Tel: (402) 559-2259
unmc.edu/

MCAT: required

GPA: 3.7

FOUNDED: 1880; *publicly controlled.*

ENROLLMENT: 68 men, 52 women (first-year).

TUITION & FEES: Resident, $13,827; Nonresident, $25,568.

APPLICATIONS: Should be submitted between June 1 and November 15; the application fee is $25. Notification begins January 3; response must be received within 2 weeks; a deposit is needed to hold place in class. Strong preference is given to state residents. Admission criteria include scholastic record, MCAT scores, letters of recommendation, and the personal interview. *Correspondence to:* Office of the Dean—Admissions, Room 5021, Wittson Hall.

MINORITY STUDENTS: Comprise 12% of first-year students; a majority of these students receive aid. Academic assistance is made available to students who require such help. *For additional information:* Director Multicultural Affairs.

---

*member AMCAS

University of Nevada*†
School of Medicine
Mail Stop 357
Reno, NV 89557-0046
Tel: (775) 784-6063
http://www.unr.edu/unr/med.html

MCAT: required

GPA: 3.6

FOUNDED: 1969 as 2-year basic science school, in 1977 expanded to a 4-year program granting the MD degree; *publicly controlled.*

ENROLLMENT: 28 men, 18 women (first-year).

TUITION & FEES: Resident, $9,612; Nonresident, $23,421.

APPLICATIONS: Should be submitted between June 1 and November 1; the application fee is $45. Notification begins January 15; response must be received within 2 weeks; no deposit needed to hold place in class. Early Decision plan is available. Strong preference is given to state residents. The remaining places are filled with first preference to residents of WICHE states without medical schools (Alaska, Montana, and Wyoming), followed by candidates from other WICHE states. Admission factors include GPA, MCAT scores, college attended, letters of recommendation, and health care experience. *Correspondence to:* Office of Admissions.

MINORITY STUDENTS: Comprise 7% of the first-year class. The application fee may be waived. *For additional information:* Director of Recruitment. Application for aid should be made after acceptance, prior to May 1.

---

*member AMCAS
†member WICHE

University of New Mexico*†

School of Medicine
Albuquerque, NM 87173-5166
Tel: (505) 277-4766
http://hsc.unm.edu/som/admiss

MCAT: required

GPA: 3.52

FOUNDED: 1961; *publicly controlled.*

ENROLLMENT: 34 men, 39 women (first-year).

TUITION & FEES: Resident, $8,411; Nonresident, $21,714.

APPLICATIONS: Should be submitted between June 1 and November 15; the application fee is $25. Notification begins March 15; response must be received within 4 weeks; no deposit needed to secure position in class. Early Decision plan is available; nonresidents must apply through EDP. Preference is given to state residents and residents of western states without medical schools (Alaska, Montana, and Wyoming). Admission factors include academic performance, MCAT scores, letters of recommendation, and the personal interview. *Correspondence to:* Office of Admissions, Room 107, Basic Medical Sciences Building.

MINORITY STUDENTS: Comprise 40% of first-year students; most of these students receive aid. The School of Medicine sponsors a special Summer Basic Science Course for minority students of disadvantaged backgrounds, in addition to its recruitment program for such students. *For additional information:* Office of Cultural and Ethnic Programs.

---

*member AMCAS
†member WICHE

University of North Carolina at Chapel Hill*

School of Medicine
Chapel Hill, NC 27599-7000
http://www.med.unc.edu/

MCAT: required

GPA: not available

FOUNDED: 1879, became 4-year school 1952; *publicly controlled.*

ENROLLMENT: 81 men, 79 women (first-year).

TUITION & FEES: Resident, $3,597; Nonresident, $24,489.

APPLICATIONS: Should be submitted between June 1 and November 15; the application fee is $60. Notification begins October 15; response must be received by school within 3 weeks; a deposit is needed to hold place in class. Early Decision plan is available. Preference is given to state residents. The percentage of women enrolled usually reflects trends in the distribution of the applicant pool. Selection factors include academic achievement, personal qualifications, and potential for medicine. *Correspondence to:* Admissions Office, CB#7000 MacNider Hall.

MINORITY STUDENTS: Comprise 19% of the first-year class; most of these students receive aid. The School of Medicine sponsors an elective Summer Medical Sciences Program for minority and disadvantaged students. The Admissions Committee includes both minority students and faculty. *For additional information:* Dr. Marion Phillips, Associate Dean.

---

*member AMCAS

University of North Dakota[†]

School of Medicine
501 Columbia Road, Box 9037
Grand Forks, ND 58202-9037
Tel: (701) 777-4221
http://www.med.und.nodak.edu/

MCAT: required

GPA: 3.54

FOUNDED: 1905 as a 2-year basic science school; 1981 introduced a full 4-year program; *publicly controlled.*

ENROLLMENT: 27 men, 29 women (first-year).

TUITION & FEES: Resident, $11,477; Nonresident, $29,771.

APPLICATIONS: Should be submitted between July 1 and November 1; the application fee is $35. Notification begins December 15; response should be received by school within 4 weeks; a deposit is needed to hold place in class. Strong preference given to state residents; any remaining places will be filled with preference to residents of neighboring western states without medical schools (Alaska, Montana, and Wyoming). Admission criteria include academic record, MCAT results, letters of recommendation, and the personal interview. *Correspondence to:* Secretary, Committee on Admissions.

MINORITY STUDENTS: Comprise 16% of the first year class; 100% of these students receive aid. The School of Medicine sponsors a special recruitment program, INMED, to encourage applications from Native American Indians; approximately 5 places in the entering class are reserved for students accepted under this program. *For additional information:* Director, INMED Program. Application for aid should be made upon acceptance.

[†]member WICHE

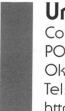

University of Oklahoma*
College of Medicine
PO Box 26901
Oklahoma City, OK 73190
Tel: (405) 271-2331
http://www.medicine.uohsc.edu

MCAT: required

GPA: 3.59

FOUNDED: 1910; *publicly controlled.*

ENROLLMENT: 93 men, 57 women (first-year).

TUITION & FEES: Resident, $10,188; Nonresident, $23,606.

APPLICATIONS: Should be submitted between June 1 and October 15; the application fee is $50. Notification begins December 1; response must be received by school within 2 weeks; a deposit is needed to hold place in class. Preference is given to state residents. Admissions decisions based on the MCAT, GPA, recommendations, and personal interview. *Correspondence to:* Admissions.

MINORITY STUDENTS: Comprise 26% of first-year students. A majority of these students receive aid. Financial aid is available; students may apply upon acceptance. *For additional information:* Office of Recruitment and Multicultural Affairs.

---

*member AMCAS

University of Pennsylvania*

School of Medicine
Suite 100, Stemmler Hall
36th and Hamilton Walk
Philadelphia, PA 19104
Tel: (215) 898-8001
http://www.med.upenn.edu/admiss

MCAT: required

GPA: 3.75

FOUNDED: 1765; *private.*

ENROLLMENT: 84 men, 59 women (first-year).

TUITION & FEES: Resident, $29,965; Nonresident, $29,965.

APPLICATIONS: Should be submitted between June 1 and November 1; the application fee is $55. Notification begins in February; response must be received by school within 2 weeks; a deposit is needed to hold place in class. Admission criteria include performance in academic courses, record of extracurricular activities and community service, MCAT scores, and character as judged by the Committee on Admissions. *Correspondence to:* Director of Admissions, Suite 100, Medical Education Building.

MINORITY STUDENTS: Comprise 16% of the first-year class; most of these students receive aid. *For additional information:* Director, Minority Affairs. Application for aid may be submitted upon acceptance.

---

*member AMCAS

University of Pittsburgh*
School of Medicine
Pittsburgh, PA 15261
Tel: (412) 648-9891
http://www.dean-med.pitt.edu/

MCAT: required

GPA: 3.7

FOUNDED: 1886; *state-related.*

ENROLLMENT: 70 men, 76 women (first-year).

TUITION & FEES: Resident, $21,877; Nonresident, $29,355.

APPLICATIONS: Should be submitted between June 1 and November 1; the application fee is $60. Notification begins October 15; response must be received within 2 weeks; a deposit is needed to hold place in class. Early Decision plan is available. Some preference is given to state residents. Selection factors include scholastic achievement, MCAT results, letters of recommendation, extracurricular activities, and the personal interview. *Correspondence to:* Office of Admissions, Scaife Hall.

MINORITY STUDENTS: Comprise about 12% of first-year students. Most of these students receive aid. *For additional information:* Director, Minority Programs. Applications for aid may be submitted by accepted students.

University of Puerto Rico*

School of Medicine
PO Box 365067
San Juan, PR 00963-5067
http://www.upr.edu

MCAT: required

GPA: 3.5

FOUNDED: 1950; *publicly controlled.*

ENROLLMENT: 60 men, 60 women (first-year).

TUITION & FEES: not available.

APPLICATIONS: Should be submitted between June 1 and December 15; the application fee is $15. Notification begins December 15; response must be received by school within 15 days; a deposit is needed to hold place in class. Preference is given to residents. Admission criteria counted most heavily include GPA, MCAT, recommendations, personal interview, and extracurricular activities. Application for aid may be made with application for admission or after acceptance. *Correspondence to:* Central Admissions Office.

University of Rochester
School of Medicine and Dentistry
601 Elmwood Avenue
Rochester, NY 14642-8601
Tel: (716) 275-4542
http://www.urmc.rochester.edu/

MCAT: required

GPA: 3.61

FOUNDED: 1920; *private.*

ENROLLMENT: 54 men, 46 women (first-year).

TUITION & FEES: Resident, $28,468; Nonresident, $28,468.

APPLICATIONS: Should be submitted between June 15 and October 15; the application fee is $75. Notification begins December 15; the response must be received within 2 weeks; no deposit needed to hold place in class. Admission factors weighted most heavily include GPA, with specific emphasis on performance in the natural sciences. Candidates are also expected to provide evidence of a varied background, intellectual curiosity, and demonstrated commitment. *Correspondence to:* Director of Admissions.

MINORITY STUDENTS: Comprise 9% of the first-year class; most of these students receive aid. Tutorial assistance and remedial work are provided for all students who exhibit special academic needs. *For additional information:* Associate Dean for Ethnic and Multicultural Affairs. Application for aid can be made either at the time of application or upon acceptance.

University of South Alabama*

College of Medicine
2015 Medical Sciences Bldg.
Mobile, AL 36688-0002
Tel: (334) 460-7176
http://www.southmed.usouthal.edu/

MCAT: required

GPA: 3.6

FOUNDED: 1969, accepted first class in 1973; *publicly controlled.*

ENROLLMENT: 39 men, 26 women (first-year).

TUITION & FEES: Resident, $8,975; Nonresident, $15,975.

APPLICATIONS: Should be submitted between June 1 and November 15; the application fee is $50. Notification begins October 15; response must be received within 2 weeks; a deposit is needed to hold place in class. Early Decision plan is available for Alabama residents only. Preference given to state residents. Admission factors counted most heavily include GPA, MCAT, premedical advisory committee recommendations, and personal interview. *Correspondence to:* Office of Admissions.

MINORITY STUDENTS: Comprise 12% of first-year students. The application fee may be waived. *For additional information:* Assistant Dean for Special Programs. Application for aid should be made upon acceptance.

*member AMCAS

University of South Carolina*
School of Medicine
Columbia, SC 29208
Tel: (803) 733-3325
http://www.med.sc.edu

MCAT: required

GPA: 3.58

FOUNDED: 1974, first class admitted 1977; *publicly controlled.*

ENROLLMENT: 46 men, 28 women (first-year).

TUITION & FEES: Resident, $8,617; Nonresident, $24,881.

APPLICATIONS: Should be submitted between June 1 and December 1; the application fee is $45. Notification begins October 15; response must be received within 2 weeks; a deposit is needed to hold place in class. Early Decision plan is available. Preference is given to state residents. Selection factors include academic and personal qualifications. *Correspondence to:* Associate Dean for Student Programs.

MINORITY STUDENTS: Comprise 16% of the first-year class. *For additional information:* Associate Dean for Student Programs.

---

*member AMCAS

University of South Dakota*

School of Medicine
414 East Clark Street
Vermillion, SD 57069
Tel: (605) 677-6886
http://www.usd.edu/med/som

MCAT: required

GPA: 3.58

FOUNDED: 1907 as 2-year school, became 4-year school in 1974; *publicly controlled.*

ENROLLMENT: 30 men, 21 women (first-year).

TUITION & FEES: Resident, $12,316; Nonresident, $26,345.

APPLICATIONS: Should be submitted between June 1 and November 15; the application fee is $15. Notification begins December 23; response must be received by school within 2 weeks; a deposit is needed to hold place in class. Strong preference is given to state residents. Applicants are selected on the basis of academic achievement as indicated on all scholastic records, MCAT, curiosity, study habits, learning ability, and fitness for the study of medicine as perceived by their instructors and estimates of character, motivation, and intellect as observed during the personal interview. Application for aid is made after fall classes begin. *Correspondence to:* Office of Student Affairs, Room 105.

MINORITY STUDENTS: Comprise 4% of the first-year class. *For additional information:* Minority Affairs Officer.

---

*member AMCAS

University of Southern California*†
Keck School of Medicine
1975 Zonal Avenue
Los Angeles, CA 90033
Tel: (323) 442-2552
http://www.usc.edu/schools/medicine/html

MCAT: required

GPA: 3.52

FOUNDED: 1885, *private.*

ENROLLMENT: 83 men, 69 women (first-year).

TUITION & FEES: Resident, $33,374; Nonresident, $33,374.

APPLICATIONS: Should be submitted between June 1 and November 1; the application fee is $70. Notification begins January 1; response must be received within 2 weeks; a deposit is needed to hold place in class. Early Decision plan is available. Admission factors weighted most heavily include GPA, MCAT results, extracurricular activities, the personal statement, letters of recommendation, and the interview. *Correspondence to:* Office of Admissions.

MINORITY STUDENTS: Comprise 16% of the first-year class. The application fee may be waived. The School of Medicine sponsors a Summer Workshop for minority and disadvantaged students, including both academic and hospital orientation programs. Tutorial assistance is available during the academic year. *For additional information:* Althea Alexander, Assistant Dean, Minority Affairs. Application for aid should be made upon acceptance.

----

*member AMCAS
†member WICHE

University of South Florida*

College of Medicine
12901 Bruce B. Downs Boulevard
Tampa, FL 33612-4799
Tel: (813) 974-2229
http://www.med.usf.edu

MCAT: required

GPA: 3.8

FOUNDED: 1965, accepted first class in 1971; *publicly controlled.*

ENROLLMENT: 51 men, 45 women (first-year).

TUITION & FEES: Resident, $10,941; Nonresident, $29,475.

APPLICATIONS: Should be submitted between June 1 and December 1; the application fee is $20. Notifications begin October 15; response must be received within 2 weeks; no deposit is necessary to hold a place in class. Early Decision plan is available for Florida residents only. Strong preference given to state residents. Admissions criteria include the MCAT, GPA, letters of recommendation, personal interviews, character, and motivation. *Correspondence to:* Admissions Office, Box 3.

MINORITY STUDENTS: Comprise 8% of the first-year class; some financial assistance is available. *For additional information:* Coordinator for Minority Affairs.

---

*member AMCAS

University of Tennessee, Memphis*
College of Medicine
790 Madison Avenue, Suite 119
Memphis, TN 38163
Tel: (901) 448-5560
http://www.utmem.edu/medicine

MCAT: required

GPA: 3.5

FOUNDED: 1851; merged with University of Tennessee in 1911; *publicly controlled.*

ENROLLMENT: 110 men, 60 women (first-year).

TUITION & FEES: Resident, $10,966; Nonresident, $22,402.

APPLICATIONS: Should be submitted between June 1 and November 15; the application fee is $50. Notification begins October 15; response must be received within 2 weeks; a deposit is needed to hold place in class. Strong preference is given to state residents. Admission factors counted most heavily include GPA, MCAT, course load and content, extracurricular activities, work experience, personal interview, recommendations, and evaluations. *Correspondence to:* Director of Admissions.

MINORITY STUDENTS: Comprise 23% of the first-year class. *For additional information:* Assistant Dean for Student Affairs. Application for aid should be submitted after acceptance.

---

*member AMCAS

University of Texas

Southwestern Medical Center at Dallas
Southwestern Medical School
5323 Harry Hines Boulevard
Dallas, TX 75235-9096
http://www.swmed.edu/

MCAT: required

GPA: 3.76

FOUNDED: 1943, acquired by state 1949; *publicly controlled.*

ENROLLMENT: 126 men, 77 women (first-year).

TUITION & FEES: Resident, $7,346; Nonresident, $20,446.

APPLICATIONS: Should be submitted between May 1 and October 15; the application fee is $55. Notification begins January 15; response must be received within 2 weeks; no deposit needed to hold place in class. Preference is given to state residents. Admission factors weighted most heavily include GPA, MCAT, the personal interview, and preprofessional advisory committee recommendations. All applications are processed by the University of Texas System Medical and Dental Application Center, Suite 620, 702 Colorado, Austin, TX 78701. *Correspondence to:* Office of the Registrar.

MINORITY STUDENTS: Comprise 41% of the first-year class. Tutorial assistants are available for those who require additional academic help. *For additional information:* Assistant Dean for Minority Student Affairs.

University of Texas
Medical School at Galveston
Galveston, TX 77555
Tel: (409) 772-3517
http://www.utmb.edu

MCAT: required

GPA: 3.59

FOUNDED: 1881; *publicly controlled.* The School of Medicine offers a 3-year program leading to the MD degree in addition to the 4-year curriculum.

ENROLLMENT: 119 men, 81 women (first-year).

TUITION & FEES: Resident, $7,015; Nonresident, $20,115

APPLICATIONS: Should be submitted between April 15 and October 15; the application fee is $90. Notification begins January 15; response must be received by school within 2 weeks; no deposit needed to hold place in class. Preference is given to state residents. Admission factors counted most heavily include GPA, MCAT, letters of recommendation, and the personal interview. All applications are processed by the University of Texas System Medical and Dental Application Center, Suite 620, 702 Colorado, Austin, TX 78701. *Correspondence to:* Office of Admissions, Ashbel Smith Building, G-210.

MINORITY STUDENTS: Comprise 33% of the first-year class; most of these students receive aid. The School of Medicine sponsors a Summer Orientation program and an ongoing tutorial program for minority and disadvantaged students. A Minority Student Office provides special training and counseling programs. *For additional information:* Associate Dean for Student Affairs. Application for aid should be made after acceptance.

University of Texas
Medical School at Houston
PO Box 20708
Houston, TX 77225
Tel: (713) 500-5116
http://www.med.uth.tmc.edu

MCAT: required

GPA: 3.4

FOUNDED: 1969; *publicly controlled.*

ENROLLMENT: 129 men, 86 women (first-year).

TUITION & FEES: Resident, $6,800; Nonresident, $19,900.

APPLICATIONS: Should be submitted between May 15 and October 1; the application fee is $55. Notification begins January 15; response must be received by school within 2 weeks, no deposit needed to hold place in class. Preference is given to state residents. Selection factors include GPA, MCAT results, premedical advisory committee recommendations, personal interviews, as well as evidence of leadership and potential for medicine. All applications are processed by the University of Texas System Medical and Dental Application Center, Suite 620, 702 Colorado, Austin, TX 78701. The application fee ranges from $45 up ($80 up for nonresidents), depending on number of schools applied to in the University of Texas System. *Correspondence to:* Office of Admissions, Room G-024.

MINORITY STUDENTS: Comprise 14% of the first-year class. *For additional information:* Associate Dean for Educational Programs.

University of Texas

Medical School at San Antonio
7703 Floyd Curl Drive
San Antonio, TX 78284-7701
Tel: (210) 567-2665
http://www.uthscsa.edu/som/som_main.htm

MCAT: required

GPA: 3.46

FOUNDED: 1959, first class matriculated in 1966; *publicly controlled.*

ENROLLMENT: 112 men, 88 women (first-year).

TUITION & FEES: Resident, $7,220; Nonresident, $20,320.

APPLICATIONS: Should be submitted between April 15 and October 15; the application fee is $45. Notification begins January 15; response should be received within 2 weeks; no deposit needed to hold place in class. Preference is given to state residents. Admission criteria include academic background, MCAT scores, recommendations from premedical adviser, achievements in areas other than academics, maturity, and motivation. All applications are processed by the University of Texas System Medical and Dental Application Center, Suite 620, 702 Colorado, Austin, TX 78701. *Correspondence to:* Registrar.

MINORITY STUDENTS: Comprise 15% of first-year students; most of these students receive aid. There are affirmative action programs for the women and minority applicants, students, and staff of the Health Science Center. *For additional information:* Associate Dean for Student Affairs.

University of Utah*†

School of Medicine
50 North Medical Drive
Salt Lake City, UT 84132
Tel: (801) 581-7498
http://www.med.utah.edu/som

MCAT: required

GPA: 3.6

FOUNDED: 1905 as a 2-year school, introduced 4-year program in 1943; *publicly controlled.*

ENROLLMENT: 62 men, 40 women (first-year).

TUITION & FEES: Resident, $10,141; Nonresident, $18,741.

APPLICATIONS: Should be submitted between June 1 and October 15; the application fee is $60. Notification begins November 1; response must be received within 2 weeks; a deposit is needed to hold place in class. Early Decision plan is available; nonresidents must apply through EDP. Preference is given to state residents. Approximately one half of the out-of-state students are residents of western states without medical schools (Alaska, Montana, and Wyoming). Applicants are considered on the basis of scholarship, evaluation by premedical instructors, MCAT scores, personality, and motivation. *Correspondence to:* Director, Medical School Admissions.

MINORITY STUDENTS: Comprise 10% of the first-year class. The Admissions Committee has an active subcommittee on minority admissions recruiting qualified minority students. *For additional information:* Coordinator, Minority Affairs. The school notifies incoming freshmen when it is time to submit applications for aid.

---

*member AMCAS
†member WICHE

University of Vermont*
College of Medicine
Burlington, VT 05405-0068
Tel: (802) 656-2150
http://www.med.uvm.edu/

MCAT: required

GPA: 3.42

FOUNDED: 1822; *publicly controlled.*

ENROLLMENT: 41 men, 54 women (first-year).

TUITION & FEES: Resident, $20,373; Nonresident, $34,673.

APPLICATIONS: Should be received between June 1 and November 1; the application fee is $80. Notification begins in December; response must be received within 2 weeks; a deposit is required to hold place in class. Preference is given to residents of Vermont and Maine. Admission criteria include GPA, MCAT, the personal interview, and letters of evaluation from faculty. *Correspondence to:* Admissions Office, C-225, Given Building.

MINORITY STUDENTS: Comprise 21% of the first-year class. *For additional information:* Associate Dean for Admissions. Application for aid should be made after acceptance.

---

*member AMCAS

University of Virginia*

School of Medicine
Box 235
Charlottesville, VA 22908
Tel: (804) 924-5571
http://www.med.virginia.edu

MCAT: required

GPA: 3.67

FOUNDED: 1824; *publicly controlled.*

ENROLLMENT: 71 men, 68 women (first-year).

TUITION & FEES: Resident, $13,154; Nonresident, $25,135.

APPLICATIONS: Must be received between June 1 and November 1; the application fee is $60. Notification begins October 15; response must be received within 3 weeks; no deposit required to hold place in class. Preference is given to state residents. Admission factors weighted most heavily include the MCAT, GPA, recommendations, interview, and personal qualities. *Correspondence to:* Director of Admissions.

MINORITY STUDENTS: Comprise 7% of the first-year class. There are various scholarships and loans available to students. The application fee may be waived. *For additional information:* Associate Dean.

---

*member AMCAS

University of Washington*
School of Medicine
Seattle, WA 98195-6340
Tel: (206) 543-7212
http://www.washington.edu/medical/som/

MCAT: required

GPA: 3.58

FOUNDED: 1945; *publicly controlled.* In 1969 the School of Medicine introduced the WAMI program, a decentralized curriculum in which students may take part of their elective phase (third and fourth years) at community clinical units away from the University.

ENROLLMENT: 74 men, 101 women (first-year).

TUITION & FEES: Resident, $9,210; Nonresident, $23,256.

APPLICATIONS: Should be submitted between June 1 and January 15; the application fee is $35. Notification begins November 1; response must be received within 2 weeks; a deposit is needed to hold place in class. Preference is given to residents of Washington and western states without medical schools (particularly Alaska, Montana, and Idaho). Candidates are considered comparatively on the basis of academic performance, medical aptitude, motivation, maturity, and demonstrated humanitarian qualities. *Correspondence to:* Admissions Office, Health Sciences Center A-300.

MINORITY STUDENTS: Comprise 7% of the first-year class. *For additional information:* Director, Minority Affairs Program. Applications for aid should be made after acceptance.

*member AMCAS

University of Wisconsin*
Medical School
1300 University Avenue
Madison, WI 53706
Tel: (608) 263-4925
http://www.medsch.wisc.edu/index.html

MCAT: required

GPA: 3.6

FOUNDED: 1907 as a 2-year school, introduced 4-year program in 1924; *publicly controlled.*

ENROLLMENT: 79 men, 64 women (first-year).

TUITION & FEES: Resident, $15,512; Nonresident, $22,826.

APPLICATIONS: Should be submitted between June 1 and October 15; the application fee is $45. Notification begins November 1; response must be received within 2 weeks; no deposit needed to hold place in class. Early Decision plan is available for Wisconsin residents only. Preference is given to state residents. Admission factors include academic performance, MCAT results, and personal qualifications as judged from interviews and letters of recommendation. *Correspondence to:* Admissions Committee, Medical Sciences Center.

MINORITY STUDENTS: Comprise 7% of first-year students; most of these students receive aid. *For additional information:* Assistant Dean, Minority Affairs. Applications for aid should be made upon acceptance.

----

*member AMCAS

Vanderbilt University*
School of Medicine
21st Avenue South and Garland Avenue
Nashville, TN 37232
Tel: (615) 322-2145
http://www.mc.vanderbilt.edu/medschool/

MCAT: required

GPA: 3.73

FOUNDED: 1873; *private.*

ENROLLMENT: 60 men, 43 women (first-year).

TUITION & FEES: Resident, $26,610; Nonresident, $26,610.

APPLICATIONS: Should be submitted between June 1 and October 15; the application fee is $50. Notification begins October 15; response must be received by school within 2 weeks; no deposit needed to hold place in class. Early Decision plan is available. Admission factors weighted most heavily include GPA, MCAT, recommendations, and evidence of motivation. *Correspondence to:* Office of Admissions, 109 Light Hall.

MINORITY STUDENTS: Comprise 6% of the first-year class. The application fee may be waived. The School of Medicine seeks to enroll a diversified entering class and encourages application from women and members of ethnic minority groups currently underrepresented in medicine. *For additional information:* Director, Office of Minority Student Affairs. Application for aid should be made by June 1.

---

*member AMCAS

Virginia Commonwealth University School of Medicine*

School of Medicine
PO Box 980565
Richmond, VA 23298-0565
Tel: (804) 828-9629
http://www.vcu.edu

MCAT: required

GPA: 3.49

FOUNDED: 1838; *publicly controlled.* The School of Medicine offers the option to earn the MD degree in three years.

ENROLLMENT: 98 men, 74 women (first-year).

TUITION & FEES: Resident, $12,876; Nonresident, $29,182.

APPLICATIONS: Should be submitted between June 1 and November 15; the application fee is $75. Notification begins October 15; response must be received within 2 weeks; a deposit is needed to hold place in class. Early Decision plan is available. Preference given to state residents. Admission factors counted most heavily include GPA, MCAT, personal characteristics, premedical evaluations, and interviews. *Correspondence to:* Admissions.

MINORITY STUDENTS: Comprise 5% of the first-year class; most of these students receive aid. *For additional information:* Medical School Admissions. Application for aid should be made upon acceptance.

---

*member AMCAS

Wake Forest University School of Medicine*

Medical Center Boulevard
Winston-Salem, NC 27157-1090
Tel: (336) 716-4264
http://www.wfubmc.edu

MCAT: required

GPA: 3.48

FOUNDED: 1902 as 2-year school, became 4-year school in 1941; *private.* A Parallel Curriculum is problem- rather than discipline-based and emphasizes critical thinking and clinical reasoning; not all students participate.

ENROLLMENT: 63 men, 45 women (first-year).

TUITION & FEES: Resident, $27,500; Nonresident, $27,500.

APPLICATIONS: Should be submitted between June 1 and November 1; the application fee is $55. Notification begins November 1; response must be received by school within 2 weeks; a deposit is needed to hold place in class. Admissions decisions are based on the MCAT, GPA, letters of recommendation, interview, and personal characteristics. *Correspondence to:* Office of Medical School Admissions.

MINORITY STUDENTS: Comprise 12% of first-year students. A summer program is available to entering minority students. *For additional information:* Director of Minority Affairs.

---

*member AMCAS

Washington University*

School of Medicine
660 South Euclid Avenue
St. Louis, MO 63110
Tel: (314) 362-6857
http://www.medicine.wustl.edu/

MCAT: required

GPA: 3.82

FOUNDED: 1899; *private.*

ENROLLMENT: 59 men, 62 women (first-year).

TUITION & FEES: Resident, $31,700; Nonresident, $31,700.

APPLICATIONS: Should be submitted between June 1 and November 15; the application fee is $50. Notifications begins October 15; response must be received within 2 weeks; a deposit is needed to hold place in class. Admissions decisions are based on the MCAT, GPA, extracurricular activities, personal interview, motivation, character, and attitude. *Correspondence to:* Committee on Admissions.

MINORITY STUDENTS: Comprise 12% of first-year students. *For additional information:* Minority Admissions. Application for aid may be filed upon acceptance.

Wayne State University*

School of Medicine
540 East Canfield
Detroit, MI 48201
Tel: (313) 577-1466
med.wayne.edu/

MCAT: required

GPA: not available

FOUNDED: 1868; *publicly controlled.*

ENROLLMENT: 139 men, 115 women (first-year).

TUITION & FEES: Resident, $12,560; Nonresident, $24,307.

APPLICATIONS: Should be submitted between June 1 and December 15; the application fee is $30. Notification begins October 15; response must be received within 3 weeks; a deposit is required to hold place in class. Early Decision plan is available. Wayne State gives preference to state residents. Admission criteria include academic record, MCAT scores, interview, recommendations, and personal character. *Correspondence to:* Director of Admissions.

MINORITY STUDENTS: Comprise 11% of first-year students; most of these students receive aid. *For additional information:* Student Affairs. Application for aid should be made after acceptance.

---

*member AMCAS

Weill Medical College of Cornell University*

445 East 69th Street
New York, NY 10021
Tel: (212) 746-1067
http://www.med.cornell.edu

MCAT: required

GPA: 3.62

FOUNDED: 1898; *private.*

ENROLLMENT: 46 men, 55 women (first-year).

TUITION & FEES: Resident, $27,640; Nonresident, $27,640.

APPLICATIONS: Should be submitted between June 1 and October 15; the application fee is $75. Notification begins October 15; response must be received within 2 weeks; a deposit is needed to reserve place in class. Early Decision plan is available. Admission factors include academic records, letters of evaluation, personal qualifications, extracurricular activities, and the personal interview. *Correspondence to:* Office of Admissions

MINORITY STUDENTS: Comprise 18% of the first-year class. The application fee may be waived. The Medical College sponsors a summer fellowship program for about 20 minority-group premedical students who have completed their junior year. *For additional information:* Associate Dean, Equal Opportunity Programs. Application for aid should be made upon acceptance.

---

*member AMCAS

West Virginia University*
School of Medicine
1170 Health Sciences North
PO Box 9815
Morgantown, WV 26506-9815
Tel: (304) 293-3521
hsc.wvu.edu

MCAT: required

GPA: 3.68

FOUNDED: 1902 as a 2-year school, introduced 4-year program in 1961; *publicly controlled.*

ENROLLMENT: 50 men, 38 women (first-year).

TUITION & FEES: Resident, $9,324; Nonresident, $23,262.

APPLICATIONS: Should be submitted between June 1 and November 15; the application fee is $45. Notification begins October 15; response must be received within 2 weeks; a deposit is needed to hold place in class. Early Decision plan is available for West Virginia residents only. Preference is given to state residents. Admission factors counted most heavily include GPA, MCAT, and personal qualifications exhibited through the interview and recommendations. *Correspondence to:* Assistant Director of Admissions and Records.

MINORITY STUDENTS: Comprise 2% of the first-year class. *For additional information:* Associate Dean for Student Affairs.

----

*member AMCAS

Wright State University*

School of Medicine
PO Box 1751
Dayton, OH 45401
Tel: (937) 775-2934
http://www.med.wright.edu/

MCAT: required

GPA: 3.46

FOUNDED: 1973; *publicly controlled.*

ENROLLMENT: 40 men, 50 women (first-year).

TUITION & FEES: Resident, $10,842; Nonresident, $15,348.

APPLICATIONS: Should be submitted between June 1 and November 15; the application fee is $30. Notification begins October 15; response must be received within 3 weeks; no deposit needed to hold place in class. Early Decision plan is available. Preference is given to Ohio residents. *Correspondence to:* Office of Student Affairs/Admissions.

MINORITY STUDENTS: Comprise 15% of the first-year class. Financial aid is available. *For additional information:* Director of Recruitment.

---

*member AMCAS

Yale University

School of Medicine
367 Cedar Street
New Haven, CT 06510
Tel: (203) 785-2643
http://www.info.med.Yale.edu/medadmit

MCAT: required

GPA: 3.71

FOUNDED: 1810; *private.*

ENROLLMENT: 58 men, 47 women (first-year).

TUITION & FEES: Resident, $29,400; Nonresident, $29,400.

APPLICATIONS: Should be submitted between June 1 and October 15; the application fee is $60. Notification begins March 15; response must be received within 3 weeks; a deposit is necessary to hold place in class. Early Decision plan is available. Admission decisions are based on the MCAT, GPA, recommendations of instructors, integrity, common sense, scientific skill, stability, and dedication. *Correspondence to:* Office of Admissions.

MINORITY STUDENTS: Comprise 11% of the first-year class. Numerous fellowships, scholarships, and loans are obtainable. *For additional information:* Assistant Dean for Multicultural Affairs. Application for aid should be made upon acceptance.

APPENDIX III
Survival Bibliography

In my second book, *You Can Get into Medical School: Letters from Premeds,* I ended with a bibliography of books, periodicals, and articles that I found indispensable. They covered such major topics as statistics on applicants, medical school admission policies, undergraduate preparation for medicine, the MCAT, minority admissions, older applicants, and financial aid, as well as some less common areas, such as the premed syndrome, the student with disabilities, and the approaching physician glut. I implored students to keep a file of relevant premedical literature, having collected over seventy magazine, journal, and newspaper articles myself.

I remember how I obtained my information: through frequenting bookstores and libraries. Because I live in the country, articles had to be ordered through the library's interloan service and took one to two months to arrive. Books only took a week or two. If I had specific questions, I had either to write letters or try to track people down by telephone. The process was extremely laborious.

How things have changed over the years! I did all my research for this revision at home on my PC through the Internet and e-mail. What follows is a listing of Web sites that are useful jumping-off places for you in amassing information. If you know of other home pages with health professions links, clue me in!

ChronoNet
http://chrononet.hypermart.net/medschool

Simply the best premed Web site that I have found to date. In fact, I liked it so much that when its constructor, Greg Chronowski, a third-year medical student at Jefferson Medical College in Philadelphia, found that his costs for maintaining the site were mounting and asked if anyone was interested in a sponsorship, I immediately took him up on it. As a result, the Mendocino Foundation now helps to keep ChronoNet out there in cyberspace. The site is a treasure trove of information and includes a search engine, biographies of famous doctors, useful premedical links, and some personal information about Greg. Most useful, however, are the forums for premeds and Greg's own advice about getting into medical school. I include it here just to show you what great information can be found on the Net:

"In the fall of 1993 I had just completed two years of a postbaccalaureate premedical program at Columbia University in New York City with the hope of getting into medical school. I sat down with my adviser in order to evaluate my record and to determine what schools I should apply to. She perused my credentials, placed them on the desk, and calmly said, 'I don't think that this is going to happen for you. My advice is that you choose another career and get on with your life.'

"It is now 1996, I am presently a third-year medical student at Jefferson Medical College in Philadelphia, I'm doing well academically, and, ironically, I served as an admissions coordinator for the Admissions Committee here at Jefferson. I offer the above anecdote as an example of how cheap advice really is and how easy it is to doubt yourself and be led astray through the maze that is the medical school admissions process. With that said, it's still my opinion that most advice should be taken with a grain of salt, including mine.

"The admissions process for medical applicants has become increasingly competitive within the last few years. Contrary to what many believe, I feel that this is probably due to the perception of many college students that medicine is a sure thing in an increasingly bleak job market, and probably not a result of a miraculous upwelling of altruism in the youth of today. Nevertheless, medicine is a calling and you will be *very* unhappy as a physician, especially in the present uncertain climate, unless you have a fundamental love of what the profession entails.

"With regard to the mechanics of applying, unfortunately grades and MCATs do matter. A very rough estimate is 9s on the MCAT with a science GPA of around 3.3. I realize that many readers are groaning already, 'Does that mean it's hopeless if I don't make that cut?' The answer is probably no, but here's my opinion of what you need to consider if you decide to continue.

"First of all, it's imperative that you take a long, hard look at yourself and assess whether or not you feel that you're capable of making it through the academic and emotional rigors of medical school. In reality, if you've never liked school or studying you're not going to miraculously become a scholar once accepted. If after some hard reflection you decide you're both capable and motivated, you should begin the application process. However, keep the following in mind.

"You need to *prove* that you can maintain at least around a 3.3 GPA in the sciences; however to be fair, 3.3 is the low end of the cutoff. However, don't despair. Bottom line, medical school admissions is not just about numbers it's about your ability to make a good physician, and that concept transcends grades. However, this may mean going back to school and taking some core upper-level science courses such as physiology, biochemistry, and histology. A structured postbaccalaureate program may not be necessary, but extra work is mandatory. There is nothing more self-defeating than reapplying year after year without showing the admissions committee that you can maintain a minimum level of scholarship. Let's be frank—you won't get in by just wishing it so. With that in mind, I earned a C in one of my physics courses during my postbac. This isn't a fatal grade; however, a 2.7 GPA is unfortunately not competitive in the present climate.

"I would also not recommend applying until you feel that you've improved your academic record significantly. Sending out an uncompetitive application can cost a lot of money, time, and heartache. It may be advisable to wait for a year or two; it's better to send one strong application than to potentially compromise your record by sending a mediocre application. In addition, it often helps to put some distance between a lackluster undergraduate record and your present one.

"My biggest piece of advice, and one I did not live by, is *to have a contingency plan for if you don't get in*. Medical applicants are unique in that for some odd reason, many of us tie our whole sense of self-worth to whether or not we become physicians. This is unhealthy and potentially devastating. I certainly don't want to discourage anyone from trying, but there *are* worse things in life than not becoming a doctor (I know—that's easy for me to say). Professions such as physical therapist and physician's assistant can be very rewarding and provide just as much patient contact as medicine. In addition, the lifestyle of these professions is excellent, although the monetary compensation may not be as high. However, if you factor in the high cost of loans for medical education, this becomes far less of an issue.

"OK. Let's assume that you've gone back to school, gotten decent grades (3.4 and above), and done well on the MCATs (9s and 10s). Basically, you're in the running, but frankly, literally thousands of applicants just like you are out there. Now it's time to do something that will distinguish you from the pack. Winning a Nobel Prize in biochemistry isn't necessary, but research and volunteer work can help. The ultimate goal in research is to coauthor an abstract or paper that is published or presented at a national meeting. I realize that it sounds trivial, but for some dubious reason, many medical schools look more favorably at an applicant who has his or her name on a mediocre abstract far more than someone who just worked in a lab. Volunteer work can also make a difference, but it should be something you believe in rather than just something to put on your application. Furthermore, shadowing a physician is a good way to learn more about what being a physician entails, however, most medical schools do not rate the experience nearly as highly as meaningful volunteer work. I often recommend hospice as a very high-yield experience. It provides valuable insight into the psychosocial aspects of medicine as well as allows students to speak to dying patients one-on-one.

"Another unsavory fact of life in medical school admissions is that connections are extremely valuable. Thus, it's time to get your own PR machine rolling. Try to get letters of recommendation from physicians you know who are somehow connected to the schools to which you are applying. If you don't have these connections, try hard to develop them. This is very difficult. I know that I felt pretty pushy asking to meet with people I didn't really know to ask for a letter, but students need to be proactive in this regard. Prepare a packet consisting of your resume and perhaps some essays regarding medically relevant topics. Even if the individual is unfamiliar with you, this shows that you're serious, and it also provides substance for the letter.

"Next, you need to sell yourself. Stay in touch with the admissions offices of the schools you are applying to. Be polite and sincere with the office staff. Trust me—if you're rude and terse, it can hurt you. As a physician, you will be interacting with many different individuals, and it's imperative that you always behave with respect toward everyone from the lab techs to your attending. Write letters to the dean or the committee telling them what you've been up to (you *have* been doing things, right?). I have yet to hear of someone who was rejected because they stayed in touch with a school by calling and writing frequently. I know that many schools track such interest calls; they can only help. If you're in that area, stop by the admissions office and introduce yourself. Always make sure that your application is complete. The burden to do so is on you, *not* the admissions office. If something has been misplaced or lost, don't get mad—overnight mail the document ASAP.

"On the same note, a key factor is gaining acceptance to a medical school is to distinguish yourself as a person as opposed to just a file. That means that you need to speak with or actually visit with someone directly involved with making a decision on your application. This takes finesse in order not to seem pushy or make a nuisance or yourself. However, if done right, it can make the difference between acceptance or rejection; I know that it did in my case. Sell yourself—what do you have to lose?

"Moreover, take some time with your personal statement. At all costs, avoid taking the why-I-want-to-be-a-doctor approach. Committees read thousand of letters of that type. Rather, think of an interesting anecdote or quotation to start your essay with and base your essay around that theme. If you choose a good one, it makes your essay memorable, which is what counts. Without saying, syntax and spelling must be flawless. For God's sake, don't handwrite the thing—type it. And of course, get your application in *at the very earliest time possible,* even if your MCATs or transcripts aren't ready yet. This is probably one of the most important things you can do to assure your acceptance to medical school. It's also probably one of the most common mistakes made by unsuccessful applicants.

"The interview. Be prepared! Some schools have an easygoing style whereas other have interviewers who grill applicants. Read up on managed care, know what HMOs and PPOs are, and know what *capitation* means. Be prepared with explanations (not excuses) regarding the weak points in your application. Come up with questions that *you* have regarding the school. Don't hem and haw if you don't know the answer to a question; simply tell your interviewer 'I don't know.' This is often a trick played on you by interviewers. What's important is how you handle the question, not your answer. Wear a suit and leave flashy accessories and jewelry behind. At many schools, the student interview is the most important part of the application. If you have a student interview, don't trivialize it by slipping into a colloquial or casual tone. Don't appear uptight, but students are often tougher on applicants than attendings are. Always send a thank-you letter to your interviewer. Again it might not help, but it can't hurt.

"Now, once you've been through this whole mind-numbing process, it may happen that you don't get in your first time around (I didn't). If so, it's time for another round of reevaluation and soul-searching regarding reapplication. Did you get interviews and were wait-listed? If so, these are the schools that you need to target when you reapply. Strongly consider applying Early Decision to the school you feel you were most competitive at. Call the schools that rejected or wait-listed you. They may have valuable feedback regarding your weak points (have you noticed the stay-in-touch theme?). Some schools may even cut a deal with you such as promising you admission if you fulfill certain criteria, i.e., A's in your next two science courses. Whatever you do, don't reapply unless you have in some way improved your application. In closing, I recommend reapplication, however, there comes a point when things may become futile. A rough estimate is that if after three years of unsuccessful application you're still not in, it may in fact be time to move on (God, I *hate* that term).

"Let me close with two quotations. The first is by Norman Cousins and pertains to the doctor-patient relationship. However, I think that it has relevance to medical school admissions as well.

"'The human body experiences a powerful gravitational pull in the direction of hope. That is why the patient's hopes are the physician's secret weapon. They are the hidden ingredients in any prescription.'

"The second quote is from my late grandfather. It accurately sums up my opinion of medical school admissions.

"'If they don't let you through the door, climb in through the window!'"

Stephen Georges Health Professions Page
http://www.amherst.edu/~sageorge/health.html

This is Amherst College's page, with links to information sources for premedical students, personal accounts of students' experiences, questions and advice, summer opportunities, MCAT preparation services, information about health professions careers other than medicine, med school application info, postbac programs, and listings of premedical student organizations. This is an excellent place to start your search.

Brad's Premed Resource Center
http://geocities.com/CollegePark/Union/8194/premed.html

Here you will find links to general information, advice, MCAT prep, schools, interviews, and other home pages. I don't know who Brad is, but he has links I haven't seen anywhere else, such as a medical school interview feedback page and places where you can have questions answered.

The Interactive Medical Student Lounge
http://www.studentdoctor.net/

A top 5 percent Web site, this home page includes links on how to apply to medical schools, general medical sites and medically related home pages, medical school lists, residencies, and the USMAL. Of particular interest are bulletin board messages with forums for premeds and medical students and a volunteer list of medical students at home and abroad whom you can e-mail with questions about their schools.

Erick's Guide to Medical School Admissions
http://lonestar.texas.net/santos/MedGuide.html

Essentially the author's own story and opinions about the facets of medical school admissions and education, but many worthwhile links to other premedical sites and other personal accounts of getting into medical school.

MedWeb Educational Resources
http://www.medwebplus.com

A comprehensive listing of all things medical, including detailed information on most medical specialties, electronic publications, guides, and sites. There are valuable links to the National Library of Medicine and the American Association of Medical Colleges.

Other Important Sites:

The American Association of Medical Colleges (AAMC)
http://www.aamc.org

The *first* place to start surfing the net, the AAMC controls medical education in this country. Their home page has a student and applicant section.

This is dogma, and the AAMC Guidebook is the bible from which it comes. One can peruse and download for hours at this Web site. This information is the official line and the place to learn the rules. There are sections for admissions (including the American Medical College Application Service, or AMCAS), applicant information, data on financial aid and minority programs, and on the MCAT. All U.S. and Canadian medical schools are listed and hyperlinked to their home pages.

☐ Premed
http://premed.edu/imsl/

An extremely worthwhile site sponsored by Hunter College that, among other things, has a section on application essays and a listing of national premed associations. In addition, there are links to over thirty national premed organizations. An interactive premed lounge is under construction.

☐ National Association of Advisors for the Health Professions
(NAAHP)
http://www.naahp.org/amit/homepage.html

This site has listings of publications the association has for sale to premeds—these may be ordered online—and a hyperlink to the National Prehealth Student Association.

☐ Stanley Kaplan MCAT page
http://www.Kaplan.com

Although Kaplan is a commercial operation and is trying to sell you their course and study materials, there is some useful information here about the structure and scoring of the MCAT with test dates and registration information. There is also a message board and student links that are quite good.

☐ Princeton Review
http://www.review.com

Another proprietary service, Princeton Review's Web site offers useful information about medical schools that do not accept out-of-state residents, the few medical schools that do not participate in AMCAS, and those that do not require the MCAT. The MCAT information is rudimentary, but there is a free MCAT available for downloading.

The following is a useful listing of other health professions Web sites:

American Association of Colleges of Osteopathic Medicine
(AACOM)
http://www.aacom.org

American Association of Dental Schools (AADS)
http://www.aads.jhu.edu

American Association of Naturopathic Physicians (AANP)
http://aanp.net/

American Medical Association (AMA)
http://www.ama-assn.org

American Podiatric Medical Association (APMA)
http://www.apma.org/

General Nursing Resources
http://www.yahoo.com/Health/Nursing/

The Nursing Network
http://www.nursingnetwork.com/

Any of the search engines on the Internet (Infoseek, Alta Vista, Excite) are great places to start looking for premedical links. In fact, that's where I found all of mine. Many individual college premed programs and services will come up there as well as more general sources. Spend the time surfin' the Net and you'll be surprised how much data you will find.

I do not mean to imply that there is no useful knowledge other than that gleaned from cyberspace. To the contrary, your premedical library should include the current AAMC *Medical School Admissions Requirements, the MCAT Student Manual,* and MCAT Practice Tests, also put out by the AAMC. Barron's also publishes *How to Prepare for MCAT—Medical College Admission Test* and *Guide to Medical & Dental Schools.* James L. Flower's book, *A Complete Preparation for the New MCAT,* published by Betz, is helpful, as are the quarterly issues of *The Advisor* and *Between the Issues,* put out by the NAAHP, and, of course, my other book, *You Can Get into Medical School: Letters from Premeds.*

Write to the AAMC at 2450 N Street NW, Washington, DC, 20037, the NAAHP at POB 5017, Station A, Champaign, IL 61820. My book is available for $9.95 postpaid c/o the Mendocino Foundation, POB 1377, Mendocino, CA 95460, e-mail: mfhe@mcn.org, Web site: www.mcn.org/b/mfhe.

Good luck in your quest to become a physician!

Index to U.S.
Medical Schools

Albany Medical College, NY, 139

Albert Einstein College of Medicine of Yeshiva University, NY, 140

Baylor College of Medicine, TX, 141

Boston University, MA, 142

Bowman Gray (Wake Forest University) School of Medicine, NC, 257

Brown University, RI, 143

Case Western Reserve University, OH, 144

Chicago Medical School, The (Finch University of Health Sciences), IL, 153

City University of New York, The, (Mount Sinai School of Medicine), NY, 176

Columbia University, NY, 145

Cornell University (Weill Medical College), NY, 260

Creighton University, NE, 146

Dartmouth Medical School, NH, 147

Downstate Medical Center (State University of New York), 189

Duke University, NC, 148

East Carolina University, NC, 149

Eastern Virginia Medical School, VA, 150

East Tennessee State University (James H. Quillen College of Medicine), TN, 151

Emory University, GA, 152

Finch University of Health Sciences (The Chicago Medical School), IL, 153

F. Edward Hébert School of Medicine (Uniformed Services University of the Health Sciences), MD, 198

Georgetown University, DC, 154

George Washington University, The, DC, 155

Hahnemann University, PA, See MCP Hahnemann School of Medicine of Allegheny University of the Health Sciences.

Harvard Medical School, MA, 156

Health Science Center at Syracuse College of Medicine (State University of New York), NY, 190

Howard University, DC, 157

Indiana University, IN, 158

James H. Quillen College of Medicine (East Tennessee State University), TN, 151

Jefferson Medical College of Thomas Jefferson University, PA, 159

John A. Burns School of Medicine (University of Hawaii), HI, 213

Johns Hopkins University, The, MD, 160

Loma Linda University, CA, 161

Louisiana State University (School of Medicine in New Orleans), LA, 162

Louisiana State University (School of Medicine in Shreveport), LA, 163

Loyola University of Chicago (Stritch School of Medicine), IL, 164

Marshall University, WV, 165

Mayo Medical School, MN, 166

MCP Hahnemann School of Medicine of Allegheny University of the Health Sciences, PA, 167

Medical College of Georgia, GA, 168

Medical College of Ohio, OH, 169

Medical College of Pennsylvania (MCP Hahnemann School of Medicine of Allegheny University of the Health Sciences), PA, 167

Medical College of Wisconsin, WI, 170

Medical School at Galveston (University of Texas), TX, 247

Medical School at Houston (University of Texas), TX, 248

Medical School at San Antonio (University of Texas), TX, 249

Medical University of South Carolina, SC, 171

Meharry Medical College, TN, 172

Mercer University, GA, 173

Michigan State University, MI, 174

Morehouse School of Medicine, GA, 175

Mount Sinai School of Medicine of the City University of New York, NY, 176

New Jersey Medical School (University of Medicine and Dentistry of New Jersey), NJ, 221

New York Medical College, NY, 177

New York University, NY, 178

Northeastern Ohio Universities, OH, 179

Northwestern University, IL, 180

Ohio State University, OH, 181

Oregon Health Sciences University, OR, 182

Pennsylvania State University, PA, 183

Ponce School of Medicine, PR, 184

Pritzker School of Medicine (University of Chicago), IL, 208

Robert Wood Johnson Medical School (University of Medicine and Dentistry of New Jersey), NJ, 222

Rush Medical College of Rush University, IL, 185

Saint Louis University, MO, 186

School of Medicine (Virginia Commonwealth University), VA, 256

School of Medicine and Biomedical Sciences (State University of New York at Buffalo), NY, 191

School of Medicine in New Orleans (Louisiana State University), LA, 162

School of Medicine in Shreveport (Louisiana State University), LA, 163

Southern Illinois University, IL, 187

Southwestern Medical Center at Dallas (University of Texas), TX, 246

Stanford University, CA, 188

State University of New York (Downstate Medical Center), NY, 191

State University of New York (Health Science Center at Syracuse College of Medicine), NY, 190

State University of New York at Buffalo (School of Medicine and Biomedical Sciences), 191

State University of New York at Stony Brook, NY, 192

Stritch School of Medicine (Loyola University of Chicago), IL, 164

Temple University, PA, 193

Texas A&M University, TX, 194

Texas Tech University, TX, 195

Thomas Jefferson University (Jefferson Medical College), PA, 159

Tufts University, MA, 196

Tulane University, LA, 197

Uniformed Services University of the Health Sciences (F. Edward Hébert School of Medicine), MD, 198

Universidad Central del Caribe, PR, 199

University of Alabama, AL, 200

University of Arizona, AZ, 201

University of Arkansas, AR, 202

University of California, Davis, CA, 203

University of California, Irvine, CA, 204

University of California, Los Angeles, CA, 205

University of California, San Diego, CA, 206

University of California, San Francisco, CA, 207

University of Chicago (Pritzker School of Medicine), IL, 208

University of Cincinnati, OH, 209
University of Colorado, CO, 210
University of Connecticut, CT, 211
University of Florida, FL, 212
University of Hawaii (John A. Burns School of Medicine), HI, 213
University of Illinois, IL, 214
University of Iowa, IA, 215
University of Kansas, KS, 216
University of Kentucky, KY, 217
University of Louisville, KY, 218
University of Maryland, MD, 219
University of Massachusetts, MA, 220
University of Medicine and Dentistry of New Jersey (New Jersey Medical School), NJ, 221
University of Medicine and Dentistry of New Jersey (Robert Wood Johnson Medical School), NJ, 222
University of Miami, FL, 223
University of Michigan, MI, 224
University of Minnesota—Duluth, MN, 225
University of Minnesota Medical School—Minneapolis, MN, 226
University of Mississippi, MS, 227
University of Missouri—Columbia, MO, 228
University of Missouri—Kansas City, MO, 229
University of Nebraska, NE, 230
University of Nevada, NV, 231
University of New Mexico, NM, 232
University of North Carolina at Chapel Hill, NC, 233
University of North Dakota, ND, 234
University of Oklahoma, OK, 235
University of Pennsylvania, PA, 236
University of Pittsburgh, PA, 237
University of Puerto Rico, PR, 238
University of Rochester, NY, 239
University of South Alabama, AL, 240
University of South Carolina, SC, 241
University of South Dakota, SD, 242
University of Southern California, CA, 243
University of South Florida, FL, 244

University of Tennessee, Memphis, TN, 245
University of Texas (Southwestern Medical Center at Dallas), TX, 246
University of Texas (Medical School at Galveston), TX, 247
University of Texas (Medical School at Houston), TX, 248
University of Texas (Medical School at San Antonio), TX, 249
University of Utah, UT, 250
University of Vermont, VT, 251
University of Virginia, VA, 252
University of Washington, WA, 253
University of Wisconsin, WI, 254
Vanderbilt University, TN, 255
Virginia Commonwealth University (School of Medicine), VA, 256
Wake Forest University School of Medicine (Bowman Gray), NC, 257
Washington University, MO, 258
Wayne State University, MI, 259
Weill Medical College of Cornell University, NY, 260
West Virginia University, WV, 261
Wright State University, OH, 262
Yale University, CT, 263

Notes

Notes

Notes

Notes

Notes

Notes

Notes

Notes

Notes

Notes

Notes